ALASKA...Comin' 'Atcha

by
Larry Kaniut

Anchorage, Alaska

Paper Talk
4800 Natrona
Anchorage, AK 99516
Email: kaniut@alaska.net
Web site: www.kaniut.com

Printed in the USA

ISBN 978-1955728225 (paperback)
     978-1955728232 (ebook)

DISCLAIMER

Since the bulk of this anthology's tales are from Alaska, I thought the title was appropriate.

For any mistakes herein, I apologize.

Larry

Table of Contents

INTRODUCTION

My writing is due to my efforts to interest a publisher in a collection of Alaskan stories...From 1967 to 1973 I tried unsuccessfully to encourage publishers to produce an anthology of Alaskan adventures. I assumed an editor could whip up a book and my English department would authorize purchase of a classroom set. Then I could incorporate high adventure for my literature of the North students at A. J. Dimond High School in Anchorage, Alaska.

There were only a few high interest books to speak of so I persisted in using my manual typewriter, onion skin and carbon papers to pound out a 14-page outline with some vignettes. I kept a copy for my next rendition, whenever the spirit moved me, a few times a year. No cigar.

I received some wonderfully worded rejection letters that included nice letter heads on publisher stationery and my return address all nicely typed. (Going into the late 1990's the rejection standard evolved into a form letter with boxes and check marks)

After our Alaska Department of Fish and Game friend Al Johnson was mauled in Denali National Park September 11, 1973, while on a photo mission, he said he was going to write a bear book. Following several years of failed effort to acquire a publisher for an adventure anthology, I received confirmation from Byron Fish in 1974 that Alaska Northwest Publishing Company thought I could "do a bear book." I immediately contacted Al and told him "you plan a bear book; they want a bear book; when it's done, let me know and I'll buy a copy."

Al informed me he'd changed his mind (he gave me a slip of paper with two men's names on it—Lloyd Pennington and Bill Brody [?], who might have stories). I contacted the publisher suggesting I'd give it a shot but not to hold their breath.

In order to begin my formal research, I visited *Alaska Magazine's* local office January 1975. I scanned every bear related piece I found back to 1935 but the person in charge of the magazines so intensely protected the bound volumes that I wondered if I'd have to leave my birth certificate and a sample of my firstborn's blood. By March I had completed that research by copying and pasting anything related into nineteen Manila folders ranging from false charges to fatalities.

I wearied of bear stories...wanted to see no others forever.

With nary a copy of the manuscript, I mailed a fourteen and a half pound box to Jim Rearden of Homer, Alaska, editor for *Alaska Magazine*. He later arrived at our home with the original red-lined manuscript, said it was the best bear research he'd ever seen and wished he were doing the book. Pumped me up and left.

The manuscript and I were within a few steps of the fireplace when my wife intervened. I told her I'd assured the contributors their story would be in the book and in their words...not part of it. She asked if it wouldn't be better to have some of their story than none. She had a great point.

In December 2021 Chuck Weschler of *Sporting Classics* contacted me, offered to pay me for a few stories for his anthology of adventure and I told him I'd send a few. Upon reflecting over the matter, I decided I had enough stories to provide my own anthology of adventure. So, I let him know I'd be working on my own book.

Coming full circle since 1973 we've completed nineteen books and decided that perhaps this book is the one I sought early on...a few amazing stories compiled into one book. Most stories occurred in Alaska. We selected a few from our books. Unbeknownst to me—until now—it appears I've created our own adventure anthology. But I no longer need a classroom set. Hmmmmm. (Retrieve me to seventy three...I've got the book; I'm ready for thee.)

Introduction to Alaska's "Charm"

"Call me danger. Call me death. Call me rugged terrain, hypothermia, or severe turbulence. Call me anything you want. But know this. I seek to kill. To maim. To destroy. I stalk the careless. I lay in wait for the unprepared. I look for the ignorant. I waylay the unsuspecting. I devour the weak. I pursue the complacent. And I embody death. I go by many names and I'm clothed in many forms. Some of these are avalanche, ice, drowning, midair collision, crevasse, freezing, steep terrain, grizzly. The bottom line is this…if I find you, death follows in my footsteps because…I inhabit the Land of Death."

Source: *Danger Stalks the Land*

Too Little, Too Late

"I can't get out. I don't want to stay here in this water. I don't want to drown."

The GI struggled in the waist-deep muck of upper Cook Inlet not many miles north of Anchorage, Alaska. He ventured to near the mudflats while duck hunting with friends and now expended energy in a desperate effort to free him from the glue-like glacial silt that held him tightly in its grasp. He knew that the tide was due to change; if he failed, the inlet's cold, glacial waters would cover him within a few hours.

A short time later an airboat roared to the GI's aid. Three rescuers helped him break down his shotgun to use as a "straw" should the tide come in sooner than they could extricate him. Their efforts were futile.

The GI panicked and begged them to shoot him so that he would not suffer death from drowning. They refused and left him in the mud as the gray-brown waters washed over his head, another victim claimed through carelessness.

That's the story the newcomer heard in 1966. He was a gun ho outdoor kid fresh from Oregon. Buoyed by visions of adventure, he gobbled up anything he could about the Last Frontier. I know because I was that kid.

After thirty-two years' embellishment it's time to chronicle the facts. In November 1988, I drove to Palmer, Alaska, to interview one of the key players in that tragic story. Lynn Puddicombe warmly welcomed me into his home and told me about his experience.

It is a sad story that serves as a warning to prospective hunters. Steer clear of the forbidden banks of the inlet; practice caution before entering that land of death.

For decades hunters have frequented the flats on Knik Arm northeast of Anchorage. A common bond connects those water fowlers—get up early, savor the hot coffee, down some food, put on the hip waders, head for the blind, bag some birds and go home. September 7, 1961, started out as such a day. However, it ended much differently.

A father and his sons enjoyed the day, hunting geese from their Coffee Point cabin near the hay flats. Forty-four-year-old Merle "Doc" Puddicombe enjoyed the outing with his teenage sons Larry, Lynn, and Joe. Because there is often little water to run and an airboat has a shallow draft, the men were using the family airboat. It was a dry-run Banks Maxwell drive, fourteen-foot wood-and-fiberglass hull, with a sixty-five-horse Continental power plant.

In the midst of the hunt they heard an airplane, looked up, and saw it coming in just over the blind. The men figured it was one of the many pilots whom they knew and didn't think much of it. The pilot swung around, opened his door, and hollered at the men. Something about "stuck in the mud." They couldn't understand it. He made another pass. He shut down power and came in at idle. He pointed down the inlet and shouted, "Man stuck in the mud!"

Doc and the two older boys burst into action.

The low tide required some effort to work the boat free and into the water. By the time they freed the boat, the tide had started coming in. A foot bore tide was racing up the inlet, and Doc shouted over the roar of the engine, "It doesn't look good, but I still think we can save him."

The hunter was standing dead center in Wasilla Creek on the lower end of Palmer Slough, 150 to 250 yards from either shore. He was surrounded by mudflats.

They couldn't tell how deep the water was but assumed it was ankle-to-knee-deep. They pulled up to him and Doc stuck a pole in. Larry and Lynn jumped out of the boat, landing in ankle-deep water. The hunter was mired crotch deep in muck, water lapping at his waist. The rescuers knew then that it was pretty bad.

The mud is soft when the tide is out. When the tide comes in and moving water hits the mud, it hardens up like cement. As long as a person keeps moving, there is no danger of getting stuck.

Larry and Lynn thought their stoutness was an advantage. Larry was twenty-one-years old, six feet and180 pounds; Lynn was seventeen, six feet three and approaching 200 pounds.

They learned the trapped hunter was Sp5 Roger J. Cashin, a thirty-three-year-old soldier stationed at Fort Richardson in Anchorage. He had been hunting with three fellow soldiers. At first they laughed at him because he was stuck. They were sitting on the shore thinking it was pretty funny.

Once they saw the water coming in and realized the seriousness of the situation, they went into action. One took off to phone the Rescue Coordination Center at Elmendorf Air Force Base in Anchorage. He had to go all the way across the hay flats at least one and a half miles.

His two friends shouted encouragement from the bank but were afraid to venture out into the mud. A large quantity of driftwood covered the beach. If they'd known what they were doing, they could have built a trail to him and gotten him out.

Doc gave Cashin's two friends a gas can and told them to build a signal fie on the bank. One of them lit a match and dropped it onto brush, then poured gas onto the flame! Although it blew him up the bank, at least they got a fire going.

Cashin had been stuck long enough to fire all his ammunition. He had used the three-shot signal to attract attention. Hunters in the area didn't hear his shots, and even if they had, it's not likely that they would have paid any attention because evenly spaced shotgun reports are common.

Freeing Cashin would have been easier if he's been wearing hip boots. His choice of footgear would be a major factor in his chances of rescue. Unfortunately he wore regular army boots that lace up about halfway to the knee. Veteran hunters fear wearing ankle-tight hip waders that can't be removed.

Initially the rescuers tried to free Cashin with the boat. Doc revved the airboat's engine while Cashin held on, but the boat pulled straight up. Next they used the boat's lift for leverage. Cashin held on to the side of the boat while Doc fired the motor a couple of times, but that also failed.

Then Larry and Lynn hung on to him, hoping to get some leverage from inside the boat to pull him out. That effort met with failure also.

Their tools were limited, consisting of a machete and two pry bars. The rescuers tried to scoot the mud from around his legs.

There was no way to break the suction on him. They slid the machete down his leg hoping to get hold of the laces and cut them. He was stuck too deep to allow the machete to reach his laces.

Larry and Lynn took turns using the machete and keeping the boat close while Doc manned the boat. The tide increased in volume.

Recalling other experiences motivated the rescuers to work frantically. They recalled past hunting situations where they'd shot ducks that fell into the soft mud. The birds beat their wings and disappeared into the muck. They'd seen several moose stuck in the same area. Although moose appear strong enough to get out of anything, they couldn't escape the inlet goo.

Doc had always told his sons, "Never go out in that mud. If a moose can't get out of there, you should think about what you're going to do."

Time flashed by as the men worked feverishly. The teenagers were near convulsions from the paralyzing ice-cold, glacial water. Because the water was getting deeper, they abandoned digging.

They tried to get leverage by running an oar through Cashin's belt and over the gunwale then lifting up, trying to pry him loose.

It was hopeless but they refused to give up.

Larry and Lynn put an oar across their shoulders and Cashin held on to it. They tried to lift him out. It didn't work.

Doc stayed in the boat. He reminded the boys to keep moving, sometimes yelling at them. He'd shut down the engine. The boys kept one arm on the boat whenever they could. They kept working, trying to keep from sinking.

Larry got hung up in the mud a couple of times and Lynn pulled him loose. They kept their hip boots on, moving enough to pop them out of the mud if they started sinking.

Cashin had a tough time standing. He'd been there so long that he must have been numb.

Next the boys bent down and put one of Cashin's arms over each of their shoulders. They bowed their necks underneath his shoulder in his armpits and tried to stand up. They could see it hurt him too badly. Their efforts were futile.

They exhausted every idea they had. There was nothing more they could do.

The water rose higher and higher. Before long the water was approaching Cashin's chest as the boys bent over him in knee-deep water.

When the Puddicombes hunted the flats, they always knew the exact size of the tides. That day they expected a small tide. Soon the water started running out.

Lynn told Larry, "This guy's gonna make it." Doc watched the tide and the boys held Cashin up.

They were overjoyed for a second as the water started receding. But all of a sudden the wind shifted, and they felt a strong wind in their faces. That's common on the mudflats. The wind picked up hard and came across the inlet. When the wind does that, it takes the tide.

The tides on upper Cook Inlet are run by the wind. Where a normal twenty-five-foot tide stops without a wind, the wind piles the water up another five or six feet, resulting in a thirty-foot tide! The wind can also bring the tide in an hour earlier, tricky things.

By then water was underneath Cashin's chin. The rescuers were desperate. They took apart a shotgun and told Roger, "If the tide comes over your head, pinch your nose and breathe through the barrel." But he never used the shotgun for breathing. He didn't want any part of it. It seemed he didn't think he could survive anyway.

Meanwhile a big Hercules flew up and down the river. The military was looking for Roger. When the emergency message finally reached Elmendorf, somehow the location of the stuck hunter was given as the Knik River. Two planes and two helicopters were searching the wrong area—they were flying over the Knik River instead of the duck flats!

With the incoming tide, pandemonium reigned. The ice-cold water kept surging into the area. There was a lot of noise and commotion.

One pilot flew over the Knik trying to motion the military to come over to the duck-flat side. Another pilot flew down the inlet and found Roy Knapp. Roy arrived, parked his boat nearby, and built a huge fire.

About that time another pilot in his new Super Cub flew over. He attempted to land in the grassy, shallow water near the scene and flipped his plane over.

Roger was still alive. Doc was worried Cashin might panic and grab one of the boys. But Roger wasn't panicked.

Roger remained calm. He never got tripped up. He never panicked. He never cried. He didn't scream and ask to be shot. The boys were amazed at his reserve. He looked at Lynn and said, "I don't want to stay here. I don't want to stay in this water."

Lynn replied, "Well, I hope you don't have to either."

When it became apparent that the Puddicombe's couldn't help him, Roger took his wallet out and said, "Give that to my wife. Please tell her I love her."

Reluctantly the men realized there was nothing they could do.

When the tide went over his nose, Roger tipped his head way back.

Lynn held the back of his neck. Roger didn't yell; he didn't scream. He just went limp. He died before the water went over his nose. Maybe it was shock. The boys held Roger for a minute. They noticed his hair floating at the surface. No bubbles came up. One minute he was breathing with them; the next minute he was gone.

Doc told his boys the soldier knew there wasn't anything they could do. In spite of their failure, the rescuers felt good because they had done the best they could.

The rescuers did so much in so short a time, it seemed as though they had all day to save Roger. But when it was all said and done, they'd worked with Cashin no more than thirty minutes...possibly as little as fifteen.

Since Lynn had been in the water the longest and was on the verge of hypothermia, a pilot flew him to Palmer. He was met by his mother and younger brother Craig.

On the next shallow tide, officials set out to recover Cashin's body. They put ropes around him and tried to pull him out. They thought they would put a belt around him and take pressure up in the helicopter, however, the nylon trope broke when the helicopter attempted to hoist his body from the mud.

Doc Puddicombe received a letter from the U.S. Army, Alaska, a few days after the incident, commending him and his sons for their very determined effort to rescue Sp5 Roger J. Cashin.

Larry Kaniut

EPILOGUE

It didn't have to happen. It was a senseless death. Had Roger Cashin's hunting buddies responded early on instead of taking the situation as a joke, Cashin would be alive. Doc Puddicombe was disturbed about that until the day he died.

People said the Puddicombe's could have saved Cashin. Each skeptic had his reasons. People said, "Why didn't you remove his legs with a chain saw?" If the army was there with a doctor, the Puddicombe's could probably have removed his legs and pulled him out. (How many people could survive having their legs cut off? Would a doctor ever let someone do that? Probably not. Most people hunting geese do not carry a shovel or a chain saw!)

Under the circumstances the military couldn't have done any more than the Puddicombe's had done, even if they had arrived immediately. Their equipment as inadequate. The only thing that will get someone out of the mud is high pressure water, and that process wasn't in use at that time.

Now rescue groups are equipped with portable compressors to deal with the problem. Helicopters can set down even if the water is deep or hover above the water.

The fire department and rescue units flush them out. The jet pump effectively blows away the muck.

Roger Cashin didn't die in vain. His death saved a lot of lives through the years. A lot of people woke up to the dangers that mudflat country presents.

It was much worse before the 1964 earthquake. The cut banks were thirty feet high. Bore tides with six-foot heads sloshed up the slough. They rumbled into the hunting area sounding like a train in you your living room. Locals joked about it: "The train's coming."

When it roared in, big slabs of mud fell from those mud banks and smacked the water. All night or all day long it sounded like cannon fire echoing up the slough.

Now water comes in and fills the whole area, even on a small tide. A thirty-three-foot tide will sneak up on you and steal your boat. It's quiet because there are no banks anymore—just tapered, shallow shoulders. (Many people who hunt the mouth of the Little Susitna don't realize that its conditions are similar to upper Knik Arm's...under the right conditions a twenty-eight-foot tide will fill the area in ten minutes, completely covering the numerous tide guts.)

During the terrible ordeal and up to the very end Roger Cashin's attitude was remarkable. A rescuer stated, "It was a privilege to have known him. I wish we could have saved him."

For Roger Cashin to die, everything had to happen perfectly. And it did.

Source: *Danger Stalks the Land*

Larry Kaniut

Wilderness Nightmare

Some writers assigned my bear stories as "bear chew" books and accused me of making zillions of dollars...but they were unaware that I agreed to write about bears because those publishers asked me to do so. Some noted that the books had vicious covers, not knowing that the author has very little to say about the finished product. Some thought the stories were mythological or tall tales, failing to realize that the stories were written just as the contributor told them—no embellishment nor stretchin' the goal posts.

One lady asked me if I embellished the stories. I responded, "Let's see. A grizzly's running through the woods on three legs—a foreleg wrapped around your body and with your head in its mouth. How do you embellish that?" And that story follows.

When Al Thompson delivered his written story to our home and I saw him, I figured he had not been mauled by a bear. But when he removed his Alaska state trooper beaver cap and I saw the scars on his head, I realized, "Yep. He's been mauled." The sad part of the story, besides the mauling, is that he handed me his wife's version in an envelope marked Pleasantville, New York...her original story. A few years later an editor from *Reader's Digest* came North to acquire stories. I referred him to Al and Joyce, he visited them then wrote the story in the July 1979 issue of *Reader's Digest*. Not nearly as exciting as Joyce's story...which they had rejected. Her verbatim story follows

His head was huge and round, and he looked like gray driftwood in the moonlight. He towered above us momentarily as we lay in our Visqueen covered lean-to, then he roared down upon us, trying to tear me from my sleeping bag. A scream passed from my lips, which was never heard above the rage of the huge brown bear. I knew it would be a sudden death, with his strong claws ripping through my flesh; or perhaps those powerful jaws would break my neck first. I could see no way of coming out of this alive and was sure I was going to die.

Dying was the farthest thing from my mind in September 1972, when my husband Al Thompson and I planned our backpacking trip for trophy moose into the Kenai National Moose Range on Alaska's famed Kenai Peninsula, an area mostly closed to aircraft or tracked vehicles. We planned to catch the last 10 days of moose season, which closed the end of September. Al was archery hunting; but if time ran out and he failed to get one, I would shoot one with my rifle. We only wanted to take one moose and had arranged for horses to pack out the meat should we succeed.

The night before leaving, we gathered our gear together into one spot, double checking and eliminating any items we could get along without. Al was taking this 65-pound bow and glass arrows tipped with razor sharp, black diamond delta heads. He would carry his .44 magnum revolver, and I would take my .30-06 rifle. We finished by stuffing our gear into two very full packs.

The next morning a friend dropped us off at a horse trail where we would start our hike, thus eliminating our leaving our truck along the road for 10 days.

We adjusted our packs and started down the trail on a typically beautiful Alaskan fall day—the leaves were golden, it was warm and sunny, and the smell of Alaskan autumn filled the air.

Eight and a half bone-weary hours later we reached the area where we wanted to camp. Every muscle in my body ached and my feet were sore. As it was almost dark, we made a hurried camp, fixed something to eat and turned in for the night.

The next day we developed our camp into a very comfortable one. We built a leanto out of logs and clear plastic, placing boughs on the ground for a mattress and covering them with a plastic floor. The front of the leanto had a plastic flap to close out the cold night air. Al built a makeshift table from a piece of wood we found. We gathered an abundant supply of firewood and picked up paper and litter left behind by others.

That day we saw small bulls which Al passed up. We marveled at the ancient ritual of rutting moose during mating season—the bulls come down from above timberline, paw a 20-to 30-inch area and urinate in it to attract feminine company.

On our third day we started out at daybreak and spotted two bulls with 60-inch-spread antlers calling to challenge each other, but Al was unable to get close enough to either for a shot with his bow. We walked about eight miles. The day had been sunny and warm, but the warmth disappeared with the setting sun. After eating our evening meal and cleaning up camp, we sat enjoying the magical quality of our campfire. The moon rose full and bright and bathed our camp in moonlight. The campfire glowed, and the only sound was the crackling of the fire. I placed more logs on the flames, put on a pair of long underwear and crawled into my sleeping bag.

Before crawling into his bag, Al located matches, a light, placed his .44 magnum on a piece of yellow paper towel for easier spotting and laid my .30-06 by his side with the safety off and a shell in the chamber. Unlike me, he left his sleeping bag partially unzipped for quick access to a weapon. The combination of a warm sleeping bag, a tired body, and the crackling of the fire soon had me drifting off to sleep.

I was awakened about 4:00 A.M. by Al's whispering into my ear. He had sensed something and whispered to me not to move as something might be out there in camp. I listened, straining to hear a sound which might locate an animal. As I kept watching into the moonlight night, I saw a silhouette of a brown bear move alongside of me.

Al did not see the bear from his position. The animal was only inches from me, with just the plastic between us, and it didn't make a sound. It seemed to be moving away, when all of a sudden the bear was on top of me. He plunged through the top of our leanto with a bellowing roar. This was Al's first sight of the bear.

Al grabbed the rifle; but with the impact of the bear, the rifle flew from his grip. For a fraction of a second the bear appeared confused as the logs broke and the plastic tore. He stood on his hind legs, towering over us. He was enormous, like a huge, gray driftwood log.

There was no time for Al to locate the .44 revolver. He knew the only way to save me was to immediately distract the bear from me to him. He also reasoned that if he turned his head in search of the revolver, the bear might instinctively go for his neck, thus killing both of us. As the bear dropped to all fours, Al grabbed its head with his left hand and slugged him with his right. The bear grabbed Al's left forearm in his jaws and by standing up, pulled Al out of his sleeping bag, tossing him through the air.

He landed at the foot of the leanto. Like a flash the animal was over him. The claws ripped through Al's right side, almost penetrating the lung, and pinned Al to his chest. His teeth raked along Al's skull and managed to grip the scalp. The bear picked Al up with its mouth and one foreleg and ran on three legs.

With Al dangling by his scalp, the bear stood straight up shaking his head violently as a cat with a mouse. Al's feet never touched the ground. The bear ran a distance of approximately 25 yards, and a large portion of scalp tore loose from Al's head causing the bear to momentarily lose his grip.

While all this was taking place, I rose, realizing the heavy weight of the animal and the horrible noise was gone. Al's sleeping bag was lying beside mine, empty. I had not seen Al's struggle with the beast because my head was covered, and I was baffled as to where he and the bear had gone.

I stood up in my sleeping bag, pulled it down and stepped out of it. Searching for a weapon, I saw the .44 revolver lying on the yellow piece of paper towel. The rifle was not in sight. Where was Al? Where was the bear? Even though it was not total darkness, I could not see any movement or forms nor hear any sound. I had a strong feeling of danger and of the bear charging me at any moment.

My first impulse was to run, to get away from the area. My common sense told me my best chance was to stay in this clearing and in camp as the bear would overtake me, and heading to an area of denser cover would only tend to give him a more secure feeling. My next thought was to stick the revolver in my waistband and try to climb a tree. Unlike black bears, brown bears do not climb trees unless they pull themselves up by using the limbs.

I was dressed completely in white, including socks, which must have made me very visible as I moved in the moonlight. The trees were large with no limbs low enough for me to reach. Dismissing any chance of escape, I cried, "God, please help us," and braced myself, holding the revolver in both hands. I may not kill a charging bear before he got me, but I would not give up my life without a fight.

As Al was being carried by the bear, he thought, "What a hell of a way to die." Then he thought of me, faced with the shock of my having a dead husband, miles from anywhere or anyone, and having to hike out of there alone. He became angry, and a strong will to fight for survival overcame him.

A brown bear is capable of dragging off a full-grown moose. His strong legs and claws can move boulders and huge hunks of earth. A blow from his paws can break the neck of a moose or another bear. No man could come close to matching his strength. Al Realized his only chance was to convince the bear he was dead.

When the scalp tore off and the bear momentarily lost his grip, Al fell onto a hump of moss. He grasped the hump with his right arm, holding his face and stomach down to keep from being ripped open, took a deep breath and held perfectly still. The bear cuffed at him, leaving horrible claw marks all along his side and shoulders. He bit into Al's back twice, while standing over him, looking for a sign of life. There was none. Al's playing dead displayed remarkable self-discipline, as the pain was excruciating.

Then I heard the bear. He was moving away from me,

heading toward cover in the direction of the little lake in the area. As I stood listening, trying to locate him, I heard Al call to me. He was running toward me. Moving closer to him, I could see his knit shirt was torn and he was covered with blood. "I'm hurt bad, but I'm going to live," he said. In the next breath he ordered, "Find the rifle, quick!"

"Where do you think it is?" I asked.

"Look at the end of the leanto; it may have landed there," he replied. As he wiped the blood from his eyes, he held the revolver while I searched for the rifle. I had to feel around for it in the darkness. I found it and also a shirt for him to hold on his head, as blood was pouring down over his eyes.

Our minds were working fast, lining out immediate things to do. A fire! Got to get a big fire going! Thanks to the dry wood, kindling and paper we had collected on our cleanup this was quickly accomplished. In a few seconds the flames were high.

Al slumped on the sleeping bag. He was cold and started to shake. The temperature was about 25 degrees. He must have lost a great deal of blood and was possibly starting to go into shock. Got to get him warm and look at his wounds. I pulled our sleeping bags close to the fire for him.

We started to check his wounds. He had been badly mauled. I looked for spurting blood which would indicate bleeding from an artery. His legs were uninjured. He had a large hole in his side under his right arm from the bear's paw. This required a large compress which we had included in our first-aid kit.

I had sewn large game bags from unbleached muslin for this hunt. The material was new and clean. I tore the bags into long strips for use for bandages.

Al's head was very bloody—half of the skin on his forehead was missing, from the bottom half of his left eyebrow extending back into his hair. Due to all the blood and poor light, I did not notice part of the scalp was gone. I thought it had been torn back and was still attached.

I wrapped his head around and around several times with

bandages which were quickly soaked with blood. His left arm was badly chewed, and the pain was very severe. He instructed me to take my knife and cut off the shredded piece of flesh that was hanging from the largest wound. There appeared to be a great deal of muscle and nerve damage.

All I could do was squeeze a tube of first-aid cream on the wounds as far as it would go and wrap up his arm. I had placed some strong tea in the fire and gave it to him to drink, along with some aspirins. During the process of bandaging, it was necessary to watch and listen for any sign of the bear's return.

We still had three hours to wait for daylight. The night air was causing the water to freeze in our plastic water jug. Up until now I hadn't noticed the cold even though I had no shoes on. I found my shoes and clothes and quickly pulled them on. This was the longest three hours in my life. I talked loudly, often repeating myself just to be making noise. Al lay resting and drinking strong tea. I circled the fire, listening for any noise in the brush and watched for any moving shadows. It took a large share of the wood we had gathered to keep the fire bright until daylight.

As daylight approached, I moved more freely around camp but never without my rifle. We discussed our plans for the trip out. It was still too dark to start down the trail. I prepared a pack to carry which contained a space blanket, matches, candy bars, canteen of juice and a sleeping bag which I would pack just prior to leaving. We wanted to get as far away from this camp as Al was able to walk in case the bear returned. If I had to leave him and go ahead for help, he would stay warm in the sleeping bag until I could return with a helicopter.

I got Al into his socks, shoes and wool trousers and made a sling for his arm. We put a piece of foam rubber against his neck and secured a nylon rope from his sling over his back to his belt to keep the weight of his arm from pulling the sling against his neck.

I gathered most of our possessions and threw them into the lean-to for what protection it would offer, as it was still half intact. We left enough disarray to alert any passing pilot that something was wrong.

I stuffed the sleeping bag into the pack and helped Al to his feet. The hours of lying and the loss of blood made him dizzy for a moment. The possibility of having to stay alone while I went for help formed in his mind but vanished when his head cleared. He wrote a note on the back of one of our maps indicating the time, date, that we had been attacked by a brown bear, needed a doctor and were trying to walk out.

At 6:50 A.M. we started down the trail. Al carried his .44 revolver in his right hand, and I followed with the pack and my rifle. The brush was thick in places, and we stayed close together preparing for another bear confrontation. A short way from camp we saw fresh brown bear manure in the trail. Since we had not seen any such sign on our way in or while hunting, we had good reason to believe the brownie that attacked us had passed through here sometime during the early morning.

Al set a fast pace, and my walk was hurried to keep up with him. After covering a few miles, Al put his revolver into his holster and I put my rifle on my shoulder. He kept up the same pace even up the hills. I was forced to rest a few seconds on the steeper hills.

It was a beautiful, clear, sunny day, and as the ground thawed, it became slippery. After about 10 miles I found myself getting behind. It was miraculous the way Al was covering ground. He had lost several pints of blood, was in a great deal of pain, his head rested on his shoulder (as a result of being hit on the side of his head); and yet, he was still going strong. We passed up several good clearings where a helicopter could easily land, but he didn't want to stop. With God's help and Al's determination it appeared he was going to walk all the way out.

As we neared the road I became concerned that I might have to leave Al and hike several miles into Soldotna. Al reached the road ahead of me and was resting when a lady we know drove up and saw Al beside the road. She was on her way to Soldotna, and as I arrived, Al was asking her to notify the troopers to send an ambulance and call the hospital.

We had hiked out two hours quicker than we had hiked in. Al was totally exhausted and in great pain—face, hands and bandages covered with dried blood. Ten minutes later we heard a siren. In another 10 minutes state troopers and the ambulance arrived. Al explained it had been an unprovoked brown bear attack. They carefully lifted him into the ambulance, and I crawled in back with him. As we hurried over the gravel road, one of the troopers held up Al's wounded arm.

The Soldotna hospital had been open only for about a year, and we were thankful for it. Since this was Sunday, there was one doctor on call. She had been alerted and was waiting in the emergency room. While undoing the bandages, she noticed the missing piece of scalp. After seeing the extent of wounds and noting the amount of work ahead, she instructed the nurse to try again to locate the surgeon who was fishing. Another doctor arrived and asked if we had any idea where the scalp was. Al told me where it would most likely be in relation to our leanto.

Al went into surgery while I returned with some troopers to our camp via helicopter. The miles that had taken us hours to cover were behind us in minutes. I stood by the lean-to suggesting the most likely place to start looking, and soon one of the troopers spotted a great deal of blood. He followed the blood trail, found the scalp, put it into a clean plastic bag covered with a special solution, and we departed while the remaining troopers stayed to investigate the scene and look for the bear.

On coming through the emergency door, I noticed a pair of hip boots—they must have found the surgeon. The doctors worked on Al for hours—cleaning, cutting away dead flesh, stitching some of the wounds and leaving others to drain (for later stitching). The piece of scalp was cleaned and stitched in place. It was about 11:00 P.M. before I saw Al in the recovery room. He was in critical condition. He had been given a shot to make him sleep.

Our friend Mary insisted on staying with me, and I went home about 12:00 A.M.; but I could not sleep. When I closed my eyes, I was haunted by the memory of the bear and the bellowing roar, as I was for many nights to follow.

I spent the next day with Al whose face and left arm were swollen. He had been given four pints of blood and large doses of drugs to counteract infection so common in animal wounds. He would receive two more pints of blood later. He was so weak it took two nurses and me to help him stand by the bed. He said, "How'd I ever walk that far when I can't even stand up by myself?"

I saw no change in Al during the next two days. He looked so pale and swollen. On the drive home that evening tears began to fill my eyes. I felt so helpless.

The next day I walked into his room and saw a change. Color was showing in his cheeks, and he looked better. He would have a long struggle ahead of him, but he was going to make it.

During our ordeal many good friends and local people volunteered their services. Some donated blood, and others sat with me. Troopers and wardens became commonplace as they stopped by to check on Al, who is a game warden.

The media picked up the attack story and distorted the facts. Several days later I heard a report that the guilty black bear had been destroyed. Other false reports indicated we had camped next to a moose kill or Al had wounded a bear with an arrow (a broken arrow in his quiver had dried blood on it from the previous year's moose kill). I was angry with this misinformation and concerned about the possibility of another hunter being mauled by the same bear before moose season ended.

Another hunter was attacked a few weeks later in the same area. He scared the bear away, but it stalked him and charged a second time. The hunter was able to wound the animal, and it left him. He was not seriously injured though his wounds were similar to Al's as only the right canine tooth punctured he flesh. If it was the same bear, it showed no normal fear of human scent.

Al wanted to destroy the bear and returned to the woods for two days with other officers, but his commissioner heard of it and wisely instructed Al to stay home. Despite intensive searches, the bear was never found. Al feels the bear may have died from its wounds during the winter.

During the next year, Al underwent two more surgeries for skin grafting on his head and forehead. The scalp never took. Through several months and hours of painful exercising, he has regained most of the use of his left hand and arm and continues with his profession as a warden

I keep telling myself the chance of the same thing happening again is too remote to consider, but when I camp out, I find it takes longer to fall asleep, and I find myself listening intently for any unwelcomed sound. I also believe my love for the wilderness, climbing mountains, walking along game trails, looking out over miles of beautiful country will be strong enough to overshadow the nightmare that was for real. And I thank God for giving us a second chance.

Source: *Alaska Bear Tales*

Generated Stories

At a book signing with my son-in-law Brad Risch, a guy told us he had hauled *Alaska Bear Tales* on a sheep hunt. I was stunned as sheep hunters usually pack only what is necessary for their stay in the mountains. He said his partner snored the first night. After their supper the second night, the hunter read from his copy of *Alaska Bear Tales* to his co-hunter...and that the companion did NOT snore any more. I told Brad that we needed to start collecting stories our books have generated so that we could showcase them.

BRAD RISCH

The year was 1983, I was 13 and an avid reader. I loved to read science fiction and ate westerns as snacks between the sci fi titles I found. Then, I came across *Alaska Bear Tales* at the grocery store. This was my first real true-life nonfiction book that I had read. I purchased the brown eyes that looked at me from the cover and took it home. It was then put into the lineup that was on my nightstand table; western, sci fi, *Alaska Bear Tales*, western. Little did I know that this book not only would change my reading habits but its content made me much more aware in the coming years while camping and hiking. Its author would surprisingly come into my life unexpectedly, blessing me with not only friendship, life mentorship, accepting me into his family and truly blessing me as my father-in-law.

When I start to read I may not be the fastest reader but I am a thorough reader and as I read the pages of *Alaska Bear Tales*, the movie of the stories started to play. To say that these pages playing before my eyes made a big hairy impression is to say the least. For three days I would get up for school and live life as normal but at 9pm it was bedtime and lights out! So as not to disturb my parents that so dutifully patrolled for light emanations from the crack of my bedroom door, I, a flashlight, *and Alaska Bear Tales* crawled under my thick comforter. *I* read *Alaska Bear Tales* in three nights, getting very little sleep. When finished, it went right back into the rotation; western, Alaska Bear Tales, science fiction. I read *Alaska Bear Tales* two times that month.

I have been very fortunate and honored to go on several interviews with Larry. To hear the contributors in their own words the Alaskan adventure, plane crash survived or mauling they endured and prevailed from. It is absolutely amazing to me the strength of the human spirit that is displayed between Larry Kaniut's written pages.

WILLIAM CHAPPELL

July 8, 2001

Dear Larry,

Sorry for the delay, but the computer thing just isn't so simple for those of us still living in caves (culverts, underpasses, and/ or abandoned cars).

You don't know how great it was to meet you at Wal-Mart in Wasilla (06-14-01). Our conversation caused me to think back to 1984 when I was preparing to attend my 20th high school reunion (Savannah High School) in Anaheim, California. I had wanted to prepare a couple of packages from Alaska to be given as door prizes. I had purchased two boxes of Wildberry candy and two very nicely, hand-painted tree fungi, both bearing a scene of a cabin in mountain wilderness. Yet I wanted something else as well, one more thing (rustic spice) for each of the packages. As I walked past the Book Cache, my eyes lit upon your *Alaska Bear Tales*, and I knew, there it was! At that moment, your first book was all the rage up here, and I bought three of them...two to give and one to read.

After having the two bundles gift-wrapped, I was off, not being able to investigate your bear tales just then.

Later, at the reunion, the presents were very well received, and both winners hunted me up to thank me.

One beautiful lady from Laguna Beach, California, who remembered me, but I couldn't place her (I felt like a beet), asked of me, "Can a person still live this simple kind of life in Alaska?" I thought for a second, and then responded, "Yes, as much as anywhere."

The other recipient, an old rediscovered buddy, grimaced a bit and then said, "I've been reading about the simple life," then held up your book and grinned, stating, "Simple, maybe, but, oh, what a grizzly neighborhood!"

We all had a good laugh and I couldn't help but feel there were at least two more coming up to look around.

Truly,

William S. (Chaparral) Chappell

KIM BLANAS

This morning August 22, 2001, I visited Dr. Robin Robbins at Advance Chiropractic in Anchorage for an adjustment. After my meeting, Kim Blanas, office receptionist, told me that they had recently taken their pooch, a microscopic member of the canine community, to their vet. There they encountered a huge yellow lab tipping the scales at 120 pounds. The dog's name was Kaniut. Kim's husband Peter, a former student of mine, asked the lab's owners how they came to name their dog Kaniut to which they replied, "We named it after the guy who writes the bear books."

I told my wife I've fulfilled my life's goals—I have a dog named for me.

MARK TAYLOR

While selling our first self-published book *Bear Tales for the Ages* at the Great Alaska Sportsman's Show in April 2001, a man approached and said, "I'd like to shake your hand." I was somewhat surprised and wondered why. He responded that "you are one of the reasons that I moved to Alaska. I read *Alaska Bear Tales* and decided to move here from Kansas…and I read Michener's *Alaska*." Marc agreed to write for this section… neither of us realizing that within two years he'd ask me to write an intro to his own book *Hunting Hard…in Alaska*.

From June 8, 2003 email from Marc: What you read in this book may change your life forever.

Back in 1993 I picked up a paperback book called *"Alaska Bear Tales."* I don't remember specifically why I bought it, but I remember that I was drawn to the romantic notion that there was a state that produced stories about encounters with bears that were worthy of an author documenting them. Of course, that book was written by a man whose name I could not pronounce, but it sounded like an "Alaskan" name, so that made it all the better.

As a reader, I was drawn into that place called Alaska, so I actively sought to read more about the so-called "Last Frontier". Being a hunter, I began to dream of someday venturing to the state where bears roam wild and can be experienced in their natural environment. Of course, nearly everyone has glimpsed a bear as it paces back and forth in the confines of a zoo, but I wanted to view a bear that had never seen steel bars and gawking spectators; one that might decide to stalk a hunter under the right (wrong) conditions. I was not attracted by the danger; I was attracted by the untamed wilderness that produces such beasts.

One thing I know for certain – If you truly want something bad enough, you will find a way to make it happen, so I was fortunate enough to accompany some good friends on a caribou hunt in the Alaska interior. And yes, I watched a huge grizzly bear as it "stalked" our meat bags on the fourth day of the hunt.

The experience was so overwhelming that I then made a way to move my family and I to Alaska.

Although the largest state, Alaska is the least populated, so it wasn't long before I bumped into the man whose book lit the tinder in this now blazing inferno. I learned to pronounce his name, although I misspell it every once in a while, and not quite a year later he and I shared the meat of my first bull moose.

Nothing is free in this world, especially moose meat. Therefore, much later, Larry Kaniut got to help me publish a book about my hunting experiences since moving to Alaska.

Think about it – After reading a book, much like the one you hold in your hand, I was able to create a new life for myself in a land that once only existed in my dreams; and of course in the book that you hold.

Read on. Dream on. Then turn those dreams into your reality!

ERIC BADGER

I was in the M Bar D fetching 2 bales of Timothy hay, 3 Don's complete horse grain and an apple picker for Pam's horse Prince today (Nov. 29, 2005). Joined conversation with Scott and a guy from Alaska Marine Lines. We talked a bit then the guy left with a wave to Scott who had to answer the phone. The guy shook my hand and said "Eric Badger."

I said, "Larry Kaniut." Didn't know if the Kaniut was necessary but I thought polite.

Eric nearly did a back flip returning from his departure toward the door and stated in a question, "The writer?"

"Yes."

"Oh, I've read all your books. Well, maybe not all...but the bear books. I've been reading one about the hardships and dangers people face."

"*Danger Stalks the Land*?"

"Yes."

AVRIL

My wife Pam and I attended a meeting with Kay Stevens of Thompson-Shore of Michigan at the Windbreak Restaurant in Wasilla where we met Avril Johannes. Avril shared her story with us and I asked her to email it to me…which follows.

Larry.

Is this what you had in mind?

Used to seeing Larry Kaniut books in local stores in Alaska where I live, I was delighted to find his book, "*More Alaska Bear Tales*," while vacationing in a tiny village in Mexico.

This was the second time I'd come across one of his books while far from home. Earlier I found one while staying at a remote jungle resort in Belize.

Congratulations, Larry. Your books are obviously internationally read.

Avril Johannes   3/30/2003

An avid reader, I always look for books while on vacation. In Mexico, I scrounged through the books available to visitors and found your book. In Belize a friend asked me if I knew who you were. I told her I had bought all your books for my son-in-law and that you had signed them, so, yes, I was familiar with you and all your books.

JEFF DAVIS

Bears were on my mind when I first arrived in Alaska in 1983. So much so that the first book I bought in Alaska was Larry's recently released *"Alaska Bear Tales."*

I knew about bears. My first year out of high school, I worked at a National Park. This was back in the days of open garbage dumps. My free time was quite often spent watching and photographing the freeloaders. The park service even appointed me unofficial guide to a Canadian researcher who was interested in our local population. Years later, Dr. Herrera and I laughed about that summer of '69 when we realized we'd met so long ago.

After a couple of close calls which turned out to be bluff charges, and one more serious adventure that luckily ended up with no more damage than a large bear-head dent in the side of my car, I came away from that summer with a healthy respect for anything with hair, teeth and claws.

Despite my ursine experiences, Larry's first bear book was an eye-opener as I nervously read through it that first spring, waiting on warmer weather, salmon runs and hunting season.

Over the next 19 summers, I had reason to reflect on the experiences chronicled in the book. Every spring I faithfully pulled the book off my book shelf and reread it, knowing how important it would be to keep those unfortunate incidents fresh in mind every time I left Anchorage. (And today – even for those of you in Anchorage!) Often over the years, I'd crawl out of a tent on a distant stream and find huge, deep, clawed impressions in the mud around my tent. I saw many bears on distant hillsides. A couple even inadvertently wandered into rifle range so that I have two nice wall-rugs.

The book became a classic. More adventures followed in succeeding years. The definition of "a Real Alaskan" changed from something to do with the Yukon River, grizzly bears, etc, to having your own chapter in one of Larry's books. I have mixed emotions about not reaching that exalted status. Probably best to leave well enough alone. And hope for another collection of bear stories from Larry Kaniut, Alaska's best known spinner of bear tales!

Jeff Davis, Oregon City, May 2010
Author: *Return To Toonaklut* (Safaripress)
Fifty-Five Years in the Alaskan Bush (iUniverse)
Northern Lights, Frozen Nights (iUniverse)

KANIUT REFERRED TO KANIUT

In the search for more good bear stories for *Some Bears Kill*, I stopped by B Detachment State Troopers on Tudor in Anchorage. I had hoped to find the folder that Capt. Robert Penman had in the mid-1970's when I interviewed him and saw the story of Mc Edwards and Roberts on Burma Road. The person I spoke with at the Troopers said their bear stuff had been turned over to ADFG. That person suggested that I call ADFG, offering me the use of their phone.

When I reached ADFG, I told them that I was attempting to locate the folder which the Troopers previously had. The person said that the Troopers—not ADFG— had the folder. I asked if the person had any other suggestions to which she replied, "You could contact Larry Kaniut; he's written several books about bears in Alaska."

Not having the heart to tell her she was speaking to him, I thanked her.

Source: *What's Bruin?*

Death Wouldn't Wait

The local newspaper carries a great deal of tragic news during a year's time. But one of the saddest stories I ever read involved a newlywed couple recently moved to the Last Frontier, I couldn't help wondering a number of things as I went over their plight.

You're mired in mud to one knee in the tide flats and unable to free yourself. You see the malevolent waters of the incoming tide flooding toward you. Your newlywed spouse stands nearby. What thoughts course through your mind? What is your spouse thinking? What are rescuers arriving at the scene thinking? What about parents, siblings or other family members when learning your plight? What goes through the mind of the person holding you up to stave off your drowning...or his suffering the same dilemma. What about those onlookers onshore? Or the one responsible for bringing and starting the lifesaving equipment? This whole scenario is not pleasant to consider...but it is reality.

Jay and Adeana Dickison eagerly anticipated their outing, one that offered them the opportunity to explore their new state and possibly to provide them with some extra money. Early that Friday morning, July 15, 1988, the newlyweds unloaded their silver pickup truck at the head of Turnagain Arm some forty miles southeast of Anchorage. Jay was twenty-five, Adeana was eighteen.

Nothing but excitement filled their minds. The newcomers, recently arrived from Dayton, Nevada, had lived the past month in Eagle River, a bedroom community a dozen air miles northeast of Anchorage.

Although only 5 A.M. it had been daylight several hours in those northern climes. It was an incredibly terrific summer day.

They off-loaded their Honda, four-wheel, all-terrain vehicle and hooked up the trailer. Once the trailer was loaded with their gold-dredging equipment, they stared off toward the creek.

Clumps of wild rye grass welcomed the young couple as they motored west over the hard, sandy soil. Their destination only a few miles beyond, was easily accessible, within a thirty-minute drive on their puttering machine. Seattle Creek sliced seaward through timber-choked mountains. Seattle Creek was a popular area for placer mining only four miles from the New Seward Highway.

They were unaware that the terrain they crossed is one of the most treacherous pieces of real estate in the entire state of Alaska, an area whose concrete-like surface belies its Jell-O-like characteristics depending upon the tide or locale. Numerous glacier-fed streams dump fine glacial silt into Turnagain Arm. This silt settles when the tide goes out, allowing relatively safe passage as it is firm in most areas. However, when the tide turns and starts in, the silt softens.

A person standing in one spot while moving his body like a dip netter can get stuck in the mud. The movement, along with the person's weight, pushes his feet down into the mud. Pressure builds as the feet sink until there is no pulling him free.

The Dickison's jaunt onto the flats would not be the first… but would remain one of the most widely read about and tragic tales of stark terror and tragedy to surface in Alaska.

Jay and Adeana reached an empty channel and dropped over the shoulder of the tide gut. In moments they were mired in the soft underbelly of the channel. With Jay attempting to drive the four-wheeler out of the goop, Adeana pushed on the machine.

People would find it inconceivable that a person could sink in mud up to the ankle or even the knee and not be able to escape. But on the mudflats surrounding Anchorage, it happens all too often.

Although Jay was trying to help dig it out, Adeana's right leg remained firmly stuck in the muck. Jay tried for three hours with no success. At length, and knowing that the returning tide would fill the channel, he reassured Adeana that he was going for help.

Just before 8 A.M. he ran the half mile to the highway and asked a couple of Minnesotans to help. One departed immediately for the Tidewater Café at Portage, half dozen miles en route to Anchorage; the other returned with him to the machine and Adeana.

Alaska state trooper Mike Opalka related later, "I got the call about seven fifty-two. I called the fire department and told them to get on down there. I walked on ahead to see what kind of situation we had." (1)

Opalka arrived and saw Jay and one of the tourists trying to dislodge Adeana from the mud. While the men tugged at Adeana's limbs and torso, a few men pulled on a rope that had been tied around her body. But there was no dislodging the woman.

Sucking the heat from their bodies, the water's thirty-eight degree temperature sapped everyone's strength. And Adeana had been there for over three hours. Imagine her thoughts and fears. Her agony.

River-like, the brown-gray water roared into the channel, rapidly covering everything in sight. By the time Opalka reached Adeana, the murky, frigid water had risen to her chest. He said, "I talked to her. Told her everything was going to be all right, we were going to get her out of there." (1)

By this time the firemen arrived with their water-pressure porta-pump that was designed to force water through a pipe and out the various holes along its length, reducing or offsetting the pressure so that a person could be freed.

When Opalka saw the firemen coming with their equipment, he left Adeana only long enough to run a hundred yards across the flats to help them haul the pump and fire hose to her.

By the time he reached her again, water was covering her head. The water was too swift and too high for the equipment to be used successfully.

Knowing it was a dire emergency, Opalka grabbed a piece of hose from the mining equipment and handed it to her, hoping the frightened woman could use it as a breathing tube while the firemen tried to start their pump to free her.

With his hands beneath her armpits, Trooper Opalka held on to Adeana. As she screamed in panic, the water rose over her head.

Someone on the bank said, "She's under." Fireman Mike Polzin got to the stone-faced Opalka, who said, "She's been under awhile." Polzin dived down and grabbed a leg. It was Opalka's. Mike came to the surface and went under again but Adeana's leg was cemented in.

Hope dwindled with the rising tide and Adeana lost the tube.

Mike Opalka lost his strength.

Mike Polzkin said, "I couldn't believe Mike's stamina out there. My hands turned white. I could barely get a rope around her. I pulled on her with all my might. Mother Nature had her." (1)

Later Opalka said, "I was holding on to her as she drowned. I'm hanging on to her and I had to let go. I had no feeling in my arms. I just had to let go. She was alive, conscious. There was nothing that we could do." (1)

Jay Dickison stood helplessly by.

For twenty minutes after the water covered Adeana, the men continued trying to free her. At length and with water around their necks, they were forced to leave her behind and haul themselves up the rope to the beach. Her lifeline became theirs.

The men left the water cold, exhausted, frustrated and with pockets full of heavy silt that claims so many people's lives in glacial waters.

The rescuers stood by helplessly as the mud of the arm held Adaena fast and the roaring incoming tide covered her like a liquid shroud. Nothing more could be done for her except to grieve.

Thirty–three feet of water poured into the area, forcing all to leave for their safety.

A backup emergency team that included divers arrived from Anchorage an hour later. Tragically, it was too late.

Had the firemen and troopers been contacted sooner, they could have rescued Adeana, and none of the papers or the news media would have had a story. No stories are the best stories.

The tide ebbed, and six hours later the channel was all but dry. The firemen accepted their gruesome task of hauling their equipment onto the flats and releasing Adeana's trapped leg and thus her body.

Having wondered what it would be like to have someone die in your arms when there is virtually nothing you can do about it, I wanted to hear trooper Mike Opalka's version of the tragedy. After several days of telephone tag I met him. When he opened the door and welcomed me into his home, I realized immediately that Mike is a man's man—at least six feet four inches and 280 pounds with military style, graying hair. He told me he'd been in law enforcement thirty-five years since his MP days in Vietnam prior to working for the Denver Police department and in Alaska. I asked him to share his thought and he does here.

It was a nice day. I remember vividly because I have a routine. I get up between five-thirty and six-thirty, go out, get the paper, drink a cup of coffee before I get ready to go to work.

I had a forwarding device so whenever a phone call came in for the State Troopers, it would automatically redial the dispatch in Anchorage. It had a speaker on it, so I could hear the conversation back and forth.

I'd just started reading the paper and I heard the guy say, "My wife's stuck in the mudflats," and he gave the location. I got into a pair of coveralls. Then I had the dispatcher call the fire department here in Girdwood for a mudflat rescue. I headed south to see what was goin' on.

I left here and was headed toward Ingram Creek, about a fifteen, twenty minute drive. I expedited, but I didn't go crazy. I got there, saw a car and saw what was going on.

It was about a quarter of a mile at least from my vehicle to the girl. You had to walk down a trail and over a bank. There was no way she was visible from the road, and besides that she was down in the gully.

When I first made contact with the lady, she was scared spitless, but there was nothing critical. I was convinced we were going to get her out. Nobody's gonna drown; I'm not going to let anybody die in my arms.

I went down there and talked to her, held her hand, calmed her down. I assessed the situation. By that time the fire department had arrived back up on the road. So I ran back up to the road and grabbed a shovel and waited for them. I don't know what in the world I was going to do with a shovel because it was worthless.

You don't dig that stuff and, besides that, water was rushing in. That's like trying to go out into the middle of Eagle River to dig in that sand. You just don't dig in it, period. Even if there's no water around. You just don't dig that mud.

We started back down and they were bringing a porta-pump, a device to pump water in to relieve the suction.

By the time I got back down, the tide had started to come in. It was in the gut, a fifteen-foot-wide and six-foot high channel. It was a significant current, and it was rising fast. That's when I started getting worried.

I stuck the shovel in the water right beside me and grabbed her under the arms and started liftin' on her to see if I could jerk her out. By this time a couple of other firemen had come down without the pump and gotten in the water with me. We were workin' on her to get her out.

It was apparent things were not going to go well, and she was starting to scream. We were trying to calm her down and get her out of the water. All we could do was tug on her.

It finally got to the point where I couldn't hold her up because she was underwater and that water's so cold I had no control whatsoever of my arms and my hands. It's a shock that renders you helpless. I'd been in the water fifteen to twenty minutes. I couldn't do anything or grasp anything.

One of the firemen had tied a rope around her. Mike Polzin was in the water with me. We thought if the force of the water was able to her out, we wouldn't lose the body. I think she was already dead then but we weren't willing to admit it.

After I got everybody else out, I started to get out of the water. I said, "I'm coming out." I had to put the rope underneath my arm between my elbow and body and kind of inch myself along, then they helped me to get out.

Thinking about the danger never entered my mind. None of us thought of that at the time. I was convinced that we were gonna effect a rescue and go away fat, dumb, and happy.

The husband was there and everybody was kind of numb to the situation. The fire department started loading up to leave, and I said, "No, guys, we've got to get a dive team down here, we've got to wait because when the tide goes out, we need to have a body recovery, we're still going to need you."

So they hung around and I got the dive team from the Anchorage fire department to come down in case I needed them, too. Between the time we came out of the water and time the tide started goin' out, hordes of people started showing up.

There were helicopters. I was on the handheld radio screaming to my dispatcher, "I need a helicopter!" If you need something urgent, my standard procedure is to call my dispatcher, they call the Anchorage tower, and if there's a helicopter in the area, they'll see if they can divert that guy to come down;

Our helicopter takes an hour to get going if he's not in the air, or the 210th Air Rescue at Kulis takes an hour and a half with a crew.

One helicopter was operating that morning so they diverted it to come down. I don't know which company, EAR or Alaska Helicopters or Temsco. By the time he got down there, it was over with.

A helicopter would have done no good, none at all. I was going to tie a rope on her and have the helicopter pull her out. Well, the helicopter wouldn't have pulled her out.

On the way down I passed a military bus from Fort Richardson going to Seward for recreation. It was about up here to Girdwood when I passed. Later I thought, "If I could get somebody up at the road, I'd have somebody flag that bus down and have all those guys come down here and help." But that didn't' work out. We just didn't have the time. That's all there was to it.

If there had been enough time, we could have saved her. She'd gotten both feet stuck from pushing on the ATV. Her husband had started his gold prospecting suction dredge and sucked up the mud from one foot. He started on the other one, but the dredge quit. Finally when he realized it wasn't working, tide's starting in, he went for help. At that point if a bunch of people had been right there, it would have turned out all right.

But we had no time.

It took a long time for it to set in. I couldn't believe it actually happened...that somebody actually died in my arms and I couldn't get them out. But after the tide went back out... another six hours, we got the body out. When all the hype was over, the news media was gone, all the hardware was gone, the helicopters, the buses and the press, the people and the investigators, all that was over with...I was in the car returning to Girdwood, yes, I cried...for her, for the situation, for myself. I was not happy with it. It was not something I expected to go that way, and then I had time to think about it. I didn't go to pieces on it. I didn't go sobbing, but it was a situation where I broke down and cried.

Afterward there was a critical-stress debriefing done. The chaplain came down and talked with a few people. I don't know what the fire department did in detail with their people, but I know they did some follow-up. I don't remember exactly what the procedure was.

At that time it was just starting to become a situation that the organization recognized had to be dealt with. They recognized that maybe people weren't coping too well, but they pretty much let the person come forward and ask for assistance. If somebody needed help, wanted to talk with them, they would provide something.

It's been more refined since then. Now it's almost a mandatory thing with a psychologist, it's written into the policy that you will go through this, et cetera, et cetera.

I don't think you ever get over it: people deal with it in their own ways just like I deal with it. In this line of work and the training that comes with this job, you either deal with it and cope with it and develop an attitude that "I feel sorry for these people, but I'm glad that it didn't happen to me," or you can't do the job. If in each and every situation where these deaths come about or these tragic situations arise and you're not able to deal with it, if you internalize it and take it home with you, your life will go to hell in a handbag real fast. You'll end up getting divorced, you'll have mental breakdowns and stuff, or you better quit the job. One of the two. That's all there is to it...you probably become cold to it, and that doesn't sound like the proper word, but, yes, you become cold to it and you suppress it. Otherwise you can't do the job.

With all the traffic-related deaths...the worst ones, of course, are kids and children, infants and stuff.

Source: *Danger Stalks the Land*

Disobedient Guy

Anger filled him. It was not a foreign emotion because he had been angry many times. But he was angry now.

He sulked on the eastern edge of the city…whining that his benefactor had done exactly as he'd expected him to do. He sat beneath a shaded shelter he'd completed. Whining.

He said he'd rather be dead than alive. The vine grew quickly and spread broad leaves, providing enough shade to keep him happy…momentarily.

Overnight a worm ate through the plant's stem, removing the shade. And the next day was excruciatingly hot coupled with a scorching east wind. The intense heat beat down upon the man's head. He grew faint, wishing to die, believing that death was better than life.

Maybe after you've read the rest of his story, you will consider the man's attitude.

Although given a simple task, he feared the results and fled to the coastal town of Joppa. It's funny that Jonah feared the assignment more than he feared God.

The Lord distinctly told Jonah to travel to Nineveh to tell the people that God planned to destroy the villagers whose "wickedness rises before me" and "smells to the highest heaven." (Jonah 1:2)

Rather than obey the Lord, Jonah took passage on a boat to Tarshish and "hid" from the Lord in the dark hold.

But the Lord had other plans. He created a tremendous wind over the sea, resulting in a storm that threatened the boat and sailors' safety—the implication being that the boat would end up on the bottom of the sea.

Sailors frantically prayed to their gods and jettisoned their cargo in an effort to keep the boat afloat. Meanwhile Jonah slept below.

When the captain went below and found Jonah sleeping, he admonished him to get up and cry out to his god for mercy and safety.

The sailors drew straws to determine the man whose fault it was that they were fighting for their lives. When Jonah drew the short straw, the sailors asked him his name, occupation, nationality and home country. They asked what he had done to imperil them.

While the wind and sea raged and built in tempo, Jonah confessed that he was a Jew who was running from Jehovah, the creator of the earth and sea.

Shouting with anger, the frightened sailors shouted to Jonah, wondering what they should do to stop the storm.

He admitted the terrible storm was the result of his decision to run from God. "Throw me into the sea and it will become calm again."

They rowed harder to overcome the storm's wind and battering waves. But the storm held the upper hand. They shouted a prayer to Jonah's god, "Don't make us die for this man's sin and don't hold us responsible for his death. It is not our fault. You have sent this storm upon him for your own good reasons." Then they grabbed Jonah and tossed him into the angry sea.

And the storm stopped.

The sailors stood in awe, so amazed that they sacrificed to God and confessed that they'd serve Him.

If you think the calming of the sea was something, wait till you read more about Jonah...as he floundered in the water.

Jonah realized his mistake, that he would never see God's holy temple. Jonah sank into the wild, walloping waves. He admitted his error and that because of it, he had rejected God.

Waters closed over him. Seaweed wrapped around his head. He went down to the mountains rising from the ocean floor. He was locked out of life and a prisoner in the land of death.

Unbeknownst to Jonah, God had prepared a gigantic fish for him. The fish swallowed Jonah. Imagine what must a have been Jonah's thoughts. Not for a little while…but for three days.

When Jonah had lost all hope, he thought about the Lord and told his God, "I will never worship anyone but You…You have snatched me from the yawning jaws of death!" (Jonah 2:6) He admitted "my deliverance comes from the Lord alone."

Then God ordered the fish to spit Jonah onto the beach. And it did.

This time when God told Jonah to go deliver the message to Nineveh, Jonah complied. On his first day in Nineveh Jonah preached that in forty days the city would be destroyed. When the king, his nobles and citizens heard Jonah's words, the king declared that everyone—including animals—should eat nor drink nothing…and perhaps God would spare them. And the king told them to cry out mightily to God. The citizens fasted. And prayed. And put on sack cloth. And sat in ashes.

God saw the efforts of the citizens and spared the city.

But Jonah became angry. He admitted God's grace and told the Lord that he knew God would cancel his plans to destroy Nineveh. That's when he resorted to sulking and told God he'd rather be dead.

God asked Jonah if it was right for him to be angry because the plant died. He told Jonah that he felt sorry for himself when the shade was destroyed and that he had done nothing to put it there. And God reminded Jonah that 120,000 people in utter darkness were spared.

Did I mention the sailors aboard the boat? And Jonah?

Doesn't it appear that Jonah's anger resembles ours when we don't get our way? Doesn't Jonah's attitude reflect our own when we don't get our way? Was Jonah justified in his anger?

Was his running away from the assignment the right thing to do?

Source: *Snatched from Death*

...and check out a modern day diver...

Whale and Diver

'Everything went dark': humpback whale swallows and spits out diver

The Cape Cod fisherman estimates he was in the beast's mouth for 30 seconds; experts say the encounter was a fluke.

Associated Press, Sat 12 Jun 2021

A commercial lobster diver who got caught in the mouth of a humpback whale off the coast of Cape Cod on Friday morning said he thought he was going to die.

Michael Packard, 56, of Wellfleet, told WBZ-TV after he was released from Cape Cod hospital that he was about 45ft (14 meters) deep in the waters off Provincetown when "all of a sudden I felt this huge bump, and everything went dark".

He thought he had been attacked by a shark, common in area waters, but then realized he could not feel any teeth and he wasn't in any pain.

"Then I realized, oh my God, I'm in a whale's mouth ... and he's trying to swallow me," he said. "And I thought to myself OK, this is it – I'm finally – I'm gonna die." His thoughts went to his wife and children.

He estimates he was in the whale's mouth for about 30 seconds, but continued to breathe because he still had his breathing apparatus in.

Then the whale surfaced, shook its head, and spat him out. He was rescued by his crewmate in the surface boat.

His sister, Cynthia Packard, originally told the *Cape Cod Times* that her brother broke a leg, but he said later that his legs are just bruised.

Charles "Stormy" Mayo, a senior scientist and whale expert at the Center for Coastal Studies in Provincetown, told the newspaper that such human-whale encounters are rare.

Humpbacks are not aggressive and Mayo thinks it was an accidental encounter while the whale was feeding on fish, likely sand lance.

Bear Attack

Most bear mauling victims believe their attack lasted twenty to thirty seconds from start to finish—quicker than you can open the refrigerator, remove a quart of milk, reach down a glass from the cupboard, fill it with milk and return the container to the fridge.

Because the majority of people have no clue as to the speed, agility, ferocity and power of an attacking bear, I wanted to give the reader an idea of what happens when man meets bear. I've reviewed dozens of mauling victims' stories and created a simulated grizzly bear situation below, attempting to break down the attack by the second.

Let's say that you're in bear country with a partner. It's 10:00 AM on a clear, sunny mid-August morning. Neither of you carries a firearm, however you have a canister of pepper spray in a hip holster. And, of course, you're wearing bear bells…that is, they are tied to your pack, tinkling a melodic tune as you travel the trail.

You're in the lead by ten yards, thumping along the well-worn path through the timber and talking with your companion when suddenly you hear a sound. You look up and spot three bears, a mother grizzly and two cubs. They're thirty yards ahead and walking the path your way. Your eyes and the sow's lock. Suddenly you're at ground zero and the second hand is ticking. The meltdown begins:

10:00.1   An earth shaking roar fills the air. She's coming. You stiffen in shock, disbelief and denial…"it's not a bear…it's a dog." You have just enough time to be in denial, reach for your spray and shout "bear!"

You see a wall of brown-beige fur in a full attack, paws barely touching the earth as she claws her way toward you.

Her ground-eating gallop covers the space between you in a blur...6, maybe 7 jumps...at a rate of 40 miles an hour...or 30 yards in 1.6 to 1.8 seconds.

00.25   You're unable to un-holster the spray. Making no effort to slow down, the 350-pound sow slams into you like a runaway VW, ramming into you at mid-thigh to waist level with her chest and sending you flying...the force so great it feels like your guts might come out your mouth.

00.35   You land ten feet away on your stomach in the grass and vegetation.

Almost before you hit the ground, she's on top of you, biting. You try to convince yourself that this isn't happening. And even if it were, it's not happening to me! You don't know it now, but your upper thighs will bruise and you'll feel the pain of mashed muscles for days.

You shout to your buddy, "Help! Get her offa me!" You wonder if you'll survive. You wonder if she'll go after your partner. Then what?

00.4   While holding you down with her right front paw, she bites your left leg, lower teeth penetrating the calf, her top canines ripping your pants, breaking the skin, scraping across the shin bone and leaving twin parallel groves. You hear her teeth rip cloth and flesh. The lower canines leave two puncture wounds 2-inches apart and 2 ½-inches deep.

Your buddy is looking frantically for a weapon. Trees. All he sees is trees! Then he spots a football-sized rock protruding from the ground at his feet. He drops to his knees and starts prying and digging at it.

00.5   She bites your left thigh three times in rapid succession, like semi-automatic pistol fire—chomp, chomp, chomp, leaving four puncture wounds each time.

00.6   Her right paw reaches under you and lifts you off the ground, her 3-inch dagger-like claws, ripping open your clothing and your right side and back. She leaves you a souvenir of 5 claw marks 2-inches apart, 4-inches long nearly half an inch deep. You hope that your pack will protect most of your back. Instantly she clamps onto the back of your neck with her canines.

00.7-10   She bites up and down your neck rapidly from the top of your shoulders to the base of your skull.

Your partner can't free the rock but keeps trying. It's his only weapon. He's baffled and fearful, unclear why she hasn't come for him too.

She opens her jaws as wide as she can and bites onto your head. The pressure's so great that you think your eye balls will pop out. You see a bright light in your head. Her lower canines find purchase in the skin above your right ear as her top teeth rake over the skull from mid-left ear to the right-top side of your head, ripping off the top half of your left ear and scraping loose that portion of your scalp.

You wonder if she's going to crush your skull. It sounds like she's grinding one 40-pound boulder across another.

Then she bites your face and her upper canines enter your left cheek, one just below the eye bone, the other beside your right nostril; her lower canines enter the soft tissue beneath your jaw on either side of your chin. She closes her jaws and your facial bones break. She releases her grip without pulling your face off and turns her attention to the top of your head.

She tries to bite the skull again, three times in all. But she can't get your head into her mouth to crush your skull.

You've heard that a bear's breath reeks if they've been feeding on carrion—a cached moose or an elk kill. But her breath smells almost sweet. Maybe she's been eating grass and berries.

00:10-12 She looks around for her cubs. They are standing twenty yards away, gazing at their mother, a look of bewilderment on their first year faces.

00.13-16   She returns to your neck. Bites once, looks away then bites your lower back. Then she grabs your upper right thigh in her teeth and lifts you off the ground and shakes you before dropping you. She swats at your torso then goes for your right leg.

00.17   Your companion has freed the rock and rises, 13 yards away. But just as he starts to step forward, the sow looks around again to assess the location and the condition of her cubs. They've started to move away, glancing back over their shoulders. Your partner freezes in fear, hopeful that she'll follow after her cubs.

00.18-19   She bites your right leg at mid-thigh leaving 4 puncture wounds over 2-inches deep then bites the right calf. Again her lower canines puncture the calf muscle but the upper ones slide across the shin bone.

00.20   Content that you're no longer a threat and aware that her cubs are confused, perhaps frightened, she spins away from you, catches a glimpse of your friend from her peripheral vision, chooses not to harm him and sprints after her cubs.

Now what? How severe is the damage? How far from medical help are you? Can you walk? Have you a cell phone, radio, Emergency Locator Transmitter, Personal Locator Beacon or a SPOT GPS? What have you in the way of First Aid supplies?

Are you bleeding heavily? Spurting blood?

Source: *SAFE with Bears*

Glacial Tragedy

I re-wrote the following from two news accounts and information from a former student who was a para-jumper.

Who would have thought he would not use the return flight ticket? What would it be like to lose a teenager? Who would have guessed that when you said goodbye to your son, that you'd never see him again? What would it be like to slide into a glacial crevasse while fetching water? To what extent would rescuers search for a missing teen? What are the risks of dangling beneath a helicopter on a cable? And descending beneath the surface of a glacier, between its icy walls? Fumbling your way along while searching for that missing teenager?

It was July in Alaska. To be more specific, July 13, 1999. Matanuska Glacier. A twenty-seven mile river of ice birthed in the Chugach Mountains. Eighty miles east of Anchorage. What was to be an outdoor adventure became much more than that. So much more.

A nightmare. For all concerned.

Tom Nazzaro, a high school senior from New Jersey, participated in the National Outdoor Leadership School. Tom was a good kid. He participated in cross country and lacrosse, was a well liked altar boy and a Boy Scout.

He and students from all across America had spent twenty-six days of a month long experience—climbing numerous peaks and hiking on the glacier. Tom and ten students set up camp on a flat stretch three miles up the glacier, without instructors. They had earned the right to test themselves. Around 6 PM Tom left camp to fetch water in order to cook dinner.

He did not return.

While searching for him, his campmates discovered a partial

pail of water near a glacial drainage hole. A couple of students hiked back to inform the instructors. Students and teachers searched the area before calling for help with a hand-held aviation radio Monday morning around 6 AM.

The Alaska Air National Guard showed up with a helicopter. Master Sgt. Carl Brooks, one of four para-rescue men helped with the search. While hovering, they lowered Tech Sgt. Eric Taylor into the hole. He descended one hundred feet in twenty minutes. The walls of the glacier narrowed to four feet in width. Even though Taylor wore a dry suit and neoprene gloves, his hands were nearly numb. He saw no sign of Nazzaro. He requested being brought up.

A 200-foot-long fiber-optic cable equipped with a video camera was lowered into the crevasse later that day. Alaska State Trooper spokesman Tim Desapin said, "It is almost certain that the young man fell into that hole. The hole is of undetermined depth...at 250 feet, all the camera could see was swirling water and ice. There is no way to go any deeper into the hole. At this time, we have no plans of resuming the search."

Trooper Sgt. Rae Arno, one of two officers who flew to the glacier said, "It just goes down for forever. You can see him thinking, 'I'm never going to fill these pots with this trickle.'" A constant stream of ice-cold water poured into the six by eight foot moulin, about 50 feet away. Arno noted, "It's like the way snow hangs off the eaves of a roof. It comes down, then it rounds away and drops away. By the time you see it, it's too late. There's no hope of a rescue right now."

Perhaps Tom crossed the sloping ice without seeing the hole which was tucked against the base of the ice wall. A tragic loss of a young man seeking to enhance his outdoor skills.

Sources:

Visiting teen disappears, likely fell in glacier hole, S.J. KOMARNITSKY, *Anchorage Daily News*, July 13, 1999

Harsh land takes away beloved son, Bob Tis, Staff Writer,

Seacoastonline, July 14, 1999, updated Dec. 15, 2010 Para-jumper, Eric Taylor. His grandfather Ken Taylor Sr. was one of three airmen who got off the ground on Pearl Harbor in 1941.

Mauling Victims and Doctors

I've wondered about the types of injuries a man normally incurs in a bear mauling. I also wanted to know 1) the amount of injuries a man could receive and still live and 2) the first aid and medical attention he would need to survive. I pursued the subject while researching the mauling of Dick Jensen. Dick was treated by a cannery doctor in Naknek after his bout with a sow, and later Jensen was attended by a team of five medical specialists, two of whom were Milo Fritz and Dr. Donald Addington. Both doctors agreed to comment on medical aspects of mauling victims.

I queried Dr. Addington about the types of injuries inflicted by a bear, the amount a person could withstand and the medical treatment he would need. Dr. Addington replied with the following letter:

3 July 1977

Dear Mr. Kaniut:

Re: Your letter of 21 April 1977

I read your letter with a great deal of interest and I will try to answer your questions. Basically, the type of wound sustained is usually a rip made by the bear claw, tearing into anything which happens to be in the way. The level of injury is dependent on what is hit. If it happens to be a vital organ, then the victim is in serious trouble. If the wound does not involve a vital organ the victim can usually get to medical help.

If the victim is mauled, i.e., where the bear actually "squeezes" the victim, in all likelihood he or she will never make the trip to the emergency medical facility. This type of crushing wound is the most severe, encompassing broken limbs and organs.

The emergency treatment is in reality no different from that of most other areas of emergencybmedical treatment, i.e., the ABC's of emergency care:

A. Airways—Secure and open airway;

B. Breathing—Make the person breathe. Either spontaneously or by mouth-to-mouth;

C. Cardiac—Keep the heart beating, by itself or by external cardiac massage;

D. Treatment—Care of the specific wounds.

In Mr. Jensen's case, the airway was extremely important in that he sustained a laceration of his trachea in addition to his other wounds.

In all honesty, I have treated only about three or four victims of bear attacks and then mostly of lacerations of varying degrees of seriousness. Some have been extensive. As to the initial reaction to a bear attack victim...surprise, since considering the amount of people foraging about in the wild there are really very few cases of attacks. Most of these occur when the victim places himself between the mother and her cub as you well know. I hope that this information will be of some help to you. If I can be of any further service, please don't hesitate to contact me.

Cordially,

Donald B. Addington, M.D.

...and from Dr. Milo Fritz...

I alerted the surgical crews; I said, 'Look, we've got a patient coming in with a badly injured eye; he's been mauled by a bear. He will have other injuries too.'

Having been mixed up with things like this before, the first thing I did was to alert the people I would possibly need to have on hand at the hospital, not after the patient got there and these people began their day's routine or scheduled chores, but right now.

I called up Don Addington, a plastic surgeon; John Smith, an orthopedic surgeon; Dr. Chei Mei Chao, an anesthesiologist; and Jack Smith, who's a younger chap in my line of work and whose training is more intensive and more recent than mine. I very anxiously wanted him to consult with me and took off for Anchorage International Airport in time to pick up Dick. The ambulance got there when I did, and meanwhile I'd also alerted the tower so I wouldn't get shot by the guards if I dared to go through the gates.

When we got to the hospital, we started an intravenous flow of sugar and salt solution right away. I immediately cut stitches on his throat (if the doctor had put in one more stitch, Dick would have died to suffocation). When I opened up the wound, the front half of his upper windpipe and the cricoid bone underneath his Adam's apple had been torn lose, all but just a little sliver of soft tissue holding it there. A neophyte might have cut that off and thrown it away; but I've been in this work a long time and save everything. If the tissue dies, it will be sloughed. If it lives as it did here, the airway or windpipe will heal."

When Smith came, I said, 'I'll assist you now.' He's younger. He's had more extensive experience and more recent training than I. The two of us patched up what was left of the important cricoid bone. Below the upper three tracheal rings, like signet rings, which makes the windpipe flexible, had been torn loose. "We put a tracheotomy tube through the fourth tracheal ring. We tied it around the patient's neck with ribbons to secure it. He breathed through that easily and his color improved. Every once in a while the anesthetist would say, "'Would you suction him out; a little blood has gotten down there.'

When he stabilized because he'd been so brave having had only a quarter-grain shot of morphine since four o'clock in the morning and this was maybe eight, nine or ten o'clock (when the airway was clear and the tracheotomy in place), we put him to sleep and then continued the repair work without hurting him.

Dr. Fritz told me this was his fourth bear mauling victim, the first being the mayor of Wrangell around 1940. Fritz had put him onto a steamer for Seattle but the mayor didn't make it. Fritz told me that there are organ banks today and he could have saved the mayor had he just given him a new lung.

Source: *Alaska Bear Tales*

Alaska Terminology

Bear insurance - A proven repellent for protecting mankind from bear kind...such as a bazooka, honey-scented hand grenade or slower partner.

Cheechako - Newcomer, greenhorn, rookie, amateur, neophyte.

High grader - Thief.

Iditarod - The route the mail carriers took evolved into a big time dog sled race.

Iliamna monster - Fabled big fish inhabiting Lake Iliamna... kinda like Nessie of Loch Ness.

Prudhoe Bay - When oil was discovered on Alaska's North Slope in 1968, the "rush" for liquid gold was on. Enter oil companies.

Mount Marathon - A bunch of nuts in tennis shoes and shorts show up in Seward on the Fourth of July and "run" up and down (3 miles and 3500 feet in elevation) a mountain to best the one hour round trip.

Spenard Divorce - Euphemistic phrase for murder. When the town known as Spenard was located some few miles southwest of Anchorage, Alaska, the act of exterminating your spouse in order to terminate your marriage was referred to as a Spenard divorce...somewhat common in Spenard, Alaska.

Turnagain Arm - Another mistaken route over the North Pole by Captain Cook wherein the process of turning around again became Turnagain.

Source: *Instant Sourdough*

Cool Headed Coogle

He immediately retreated, taking several steps backward while shouting a warning to the bears.

John Coogle navigated Ship Creek alone. His is one of the most incredible stories I ever heard regarding a close call between man and bear. The tale came my way in the early fall in the1980's. *The Anchorage Daily News* carried a story by Howard Weaver about Anchorageite John Coogle and some bears he had trouble with near Arctic Valley. The saga climaxed in a matter of moments after John's initial shot.

An echoing blast reverberated up the canyon, thundering off the timber-sided walls. Adrenalin pulsed through the lone hunter's veins, riveting his attention to the business at hand. Momentarily shaken by the gun's roar breaking the morning's solitude, his energy focused on his survival. Before the echo of his shot died away, he realized he was in trouble. He had just dropped one of two brown-grizzly bears. The other fled. Even as the canyon sounds returned to normal another pair of brown-grizzlies rose to face him.

A thousand thoughts flashed through his mind as one. How could he have known these four bears only moments before had been feeding on a moose carcass? He had surprised them and they chose to fight for their cache.

Even though the hunter, John Coogle, wasn't looking for a fight, he was confident in his shooting ability. He had spent countless hours afield in Florida hunting white tail deer with dogs which provided lots of fast action as the rocketing deer ricocheted through the timber.

Now here he was on an Alaska moose-hunt-turned-survival-outing. Earlier that morning he'd left the lights of Anchorage behind and driven in the pre-dawn darkness the few odd miles to the Arctic Valley ski area. John had eagerly anticipated a successful moose hunt. He left his rig and hit the trail toward Ship Creek.

It was August 20, the last day of moose season. In a few short weeks a kaleidoscopic landscape, Disney-fied in living colors, would capture the grandeur of Alaska in the fall. Jack Frost's autograph would grace the countryside. A yellow patchwork, from streamside cottonwoods on the valley floor and aspen groves higher on the crimson-fired hillside, would polka-dot this dale. Green-black tongues of evergreen would lick their way up the alder pocketed slopes. Alder leaves would shrivel in the cold and metamorphose from sticky green to crinkled brown. A blend of high bush cranberries and dying cottonwood vanes would fragrance the valley. Willow-bordered beaver ponds would layer with a skim of thin ice and Old Man Winter's white head and silver beard would be but a whisper away.

But at the moment John Coogle's mind was occupied with thoughts of moose meat on winter's table. He hastily thumped along the trail, his goal the public hunting ground which lay beyond the military reservation he was crossing. Early on the ghost-like dawn shrouded the woods and prevented him from discerning details, but as he neared his hunting area and the light became better and the details became clearer, he peeled a sharper eye for moose, knowing they inhabited the environs.

Rounding a corner, Coogle came face to face with two brown/grizzlies. He immediately retreated, taking several steps backward while shouting a warning to the bears and thinking, This is it!

His hunting experience tempered his action—he responded in a heartbeat. He shouldered his scoped Ruger model 77. It was chambered in .338 Winchester Magnum. His bolt action rifle held four rounds, one in the chamber and three in the magazine. The 250-gain Nosler bullets were designed to mushroom on impact for greatest effect.

When he'd initially encountered the two bears, his first shot had dispatched one while the other bear had run away. He had instinctively chambered a second round. But now he was faced with two additional bears. One stood up.

With two bears in his face and three bullets in his weapon John's rifle belched. His second bullet ripped into the standing animal's chest. The other bear instantly charged. John bolted a third shell home and hammered his shot into the beast's shoulder, turning it. But its mate was still coming. John found its head in his rifle scope and launched his final bullet. The bear was four steps distant when the Nosler took him through the skull and jellied its brain, dropping the final curtain on the party. John reloaded and dispatched the shoulder-shot animal.

Four bears...five bullets...three dead animals...one missing in action. Total time elapsed...twelve seconds. Now the shakes. John's knees turned to jelly. How many men have faced four alarmed brown-grizzlies (three of which charged), cradling a weapon filled with four bullets and survived the episode?

Quick thinking coupled with instant action (based on extensive experience) prevented serious consequences to John Coogle; and one must wonder about God's part in providing protection in this drama.

Source: *Some Bears Kill*

Larry Kaniut

Mountain Monarch

From Alaska's Interior tundra—high benches, blueberries and such—

to the Great Land's Southeastern Panhandle—devil's club, alders and brush...

from a six-inch-long, kitten-sized bear cub, stone blind and near hairless at birth, to a mountain monarch of thirty springs, the grizzly's the king of the earth.

*   *   *

He is born the first month of the season, with his twin their mother's giv'n birth. Together they live in their winter's den in the deep, dark bowels of the earth.

And in April or May at their den site on a slope facing to the north they emerge. Guaranteeing their debut, at thirty pounds each comes forth.

The cub's nourishment comes from his mother though she feeds on grass and some roots, skunk cabbage, blueberries and carrion, small rodents, slick salmon she loots.

His mother's warm love is protective, and all of his needs she supplies.

For two seasons long she's directive; her stern Code of Law she applies.

As the young cub matures to adulthood, he learns from the Law of the Zone.

Soon he wanders away from his mother to seek for a life of his own.

*   *   *

He meets her above a big river on the slopes where the winter winds boom; they spend several weeks together from May through the middle of June.

Their courting begins rather lightly and lengthens, the summer days see... down countless streambeds interwoven, on spruce covered side hills and scree.

Summer ends. Their mating is finished. She'll mate not again for three years.

But during mom's time without callers, her cubs will learn all about fear.

*   *   *

There's no beast upon earth that's more awesome. Old Ursus is greater by far in spite of the places one finds him, whether mountains or river bars.

He lumbers along in the morning mist upon a gray, gravel shore; he wades to the center of boiling froth, unscathed by its maddening roar.

His eyes are glued to its silvery host as he's watched in the years gone passed.

The distant, ear-splitting *nyeee* of chainsaws, tells him loggers are at their task.

Regardless of all, he is master here. He proudly surveys

everything—

from tundra to thicket throughout the Great Land, from his birth to death he's the king.

*　　　　*　　　　*

But then comes the day he faces his foe, and the doings of man are heard.

Ursus is wakened from slumber below by the drone of a distant bird.

He cocks an ear and looks into the sky as a Super Cub passes low.

From within its gut four eyes peer out; and their great bear they see below.

This aged veteran of many a brawl has never a battle lost—

should any opponent get in his way, he'll fight to the death at all costs.

He strolls across the green, grassy slope; Mother Nature has turned her back.

Two men hunker near a far alder patch, awaiting with rifles and pack.

A soft-point bullet mushrooms through his frame, and he feels the stabbing of pain.

The wind shifts then, springs up at his back—Monarch catches man's scent once again.

Rage bursts within his hammering chest; he charges to the echoing boom .

Undaunted by lead expanding in him, he presses the charge to his doom...as one shot is more than he can withstand; it shatters his massive bear spine.

A final explosion bursts in his face; his reign upon earth he resigns.

Yet part of the tale has already spread, how he grew from an infant small to the Mountain Monarch...His Majesty. His reign's just begun after all.

Source: *Some Bears Kill*

Liberty High School

September-October

Tragically the head on collision resulted in two fatalities. It wasn't pretty. It never is when the Grim Reaper makes his play on the highway. Hospital-bound for Liberty Heights, the lone survivor charged away amidst blue and red flashing lights and a screaming siren.

BDK always said a composition or speech should have a beginning, middle and ending. In this case I chose to begin at the end. You will discover the details of the beginning and middle as you read. And, of course, you'll discover more about BDK and the B.G.

We're the Liberty High Angels. Some fantasize about being America's team but we're not. We're like any high school—the good, the bad, the aborted. Change the era, change the locale, change the culture. We pretty much share the template of high schools everywhere, whether we're talkin' racin' the bay, the chariot, the Porsche...whether the cliques include stoners, Geeks, Dagos, preppies, parking lot crowd...whether you name those good and those lousy staff members...whether our parents are together or not and love us or not.

We share the teenage affliction called high school.

Source: *The B.G.*

Pam Fights Back

About a week before Valentine's Day 2006 Pam had a mini-adventure. She was walking down the hall by our bedroom when she spotted a cute, 4-legged shrew migrating from our old study to Ben's bedroom-new study. Needless to say she was not happy. She watched the critter slither over and around piles of paper and other objects mis-laid on the floor and she came up with a plan.

She figured it was just a matter of time before the cute little fuzz ball returned to her locale so she took off a boot with the intent of rendering the innocent little creature defuncto.

Before long, as Pam squatted with boot held hammer-like in right hand in a javelin thrower's position and watched, here comes the fuzz ball.

Whap!

Flat fuzz ball. No quiver. No nothing. Just a defuncto shrew.

She came to the kitchen to fetch her ever faithful husband, crooked her right index finger in a "follow me" motion and took me to see her trophy. Quite like the happy cat who's returning to the house with mouse in mouth.

Source: *Heavenly Rose*

Larry Kaniut

Fuel Starvation

Call me danger. Call me death. Call me fuel starvation, wind sheer, oil leak. Call me anything you want. But know this. I'm watching you. Waiting for you to mess up. You come into my space and I'm all over you.

I'm clothed in many forms: icing, ignorance, density altitude. Call me bad magnetos, rising terrain, unfiled flight plan.

The best way to avoid me is to know the game, practice the skills and anticipate the unexpected. For instance, you're outward bound, mid-channel at 1500 feet over Knik Arm with clearance when you notice oil on your left window. Can you reach Goose Bay? Want to try for Merrill? What's most important?

Source: *Alaska AirTales*

Twenty-two Hours

They heard it coming. Like a freight train rumbling out of the mountains and roaring across the tundra for miles, the wind galloped in waves. Each time it threatened to tumble them from their perch and into the deadly cold water below.

The two friends sat atop the airplane floats. Normally the float surfaces would be beneath the water, the plane above; however the plane lay below them, upside down on the bottom of the lake. Fortunately the water was not very deep and the floats thrust above the surface high enough for them to sit on the bottom of one.

Their only protection from the chilling air was the small, dismantled tent they had managed to save from the plane's interior. They kept it wrapped around them. But the wind ripped at this meager defense and it was all the pair could do to keep the tent fabric in place.

Night had fallen over the lake and the Alaska sunrise was still many hours away. Reuben Lyon and Dennis Long clutched each other as they clung to the pontoon of the overturned airplane. They were slowly freezing to death.

It was October. It was Alaska. It was cold!

They weren't exactly sure where they were; the pilot who had that information died when the Cessna 206 flipped and sank. Lawrence Wooten made it out of the cabin but never got to the surface. Now he lay submerged in the frigid waters near the lake bottom, 10 feet below the two men on the plane float.

The two survivors knew they were on a small lake somewhere close to Lake Iliamna, Alaska's largest body of fresh water, some 90 by 25 miles in size. The trio had left Anchorage to do some caribou hunting and had flown a couple of hours southwest.

At about 5 p.m. that day, Wooten had reduced power for a landing on the lake surface. Though there was a wind, it appeared steady and Wooten set the single engine Cessna down on the water.

Just then a gusty side wind hit the aircraft and flipped it.

As the 206 went over and began to sink, "It was like fast slow motion," recalled Lyon with that perception of time peculiar to accident victims. "Once it hit the water, it sank real fast and the water was real, real cold."

The plane's cabin was already full of water by the time Long and Lyon struggled through the door on the pilot's side—Lyon first. Beyond that, neither man remembers much about those moments. Neither remembers seeing pilot Wooten actually escape the plane.

But when the two got to the lake surface and clutched the upside-down floats, they realized Wooten wasn't with them. Climbing onto the floats, the men looked down and saw Wooten through the distortion of the lake water. He was clear of the plane but was submerged and apparently lifeless.

Soaked and thoroughly chilled in the 20- to 30- knot winds, the two men did not go after their companion. Their instincts wouldn't permit them to reenter the cold water—no matter how much they wanted to.

"After we saw the pilot, he was for the most part dead," Dennis Long remembered. "He was Reuben's friend for a long time, and (Reuben) kind of went crazy—he was yelling 'That's my friend down there, that's my friend down there!' and all I could do was yell back 'He's gone—he's gone.'"

"You think about this constantly, and its' hard to get it out of your mind," Long said. "But still you get the same answer: There's not much you can do risking anybody else to go back in this water, when from what we saw there was no sign of life."

Now, with the long night ahead of them, it was all the two men could do to save themselves. The temperature sank below freezing and kept on dropping. The wind showed no signs of slowing.

They were dressed in the lightest of clothes, and they were wet. Both men suffered minor injuries in the crash; that, combined with the painful cold, was inducing shock in both of them. Moreover, they had nothing to eat.

Most importantly of all, they had no life jackets, no raft and no means of getting safely to shore.

The men estimated shore to be somewhere between 75 and 125 yards away. They struggled with the decision whether or not to swim for it. But within minutes of the crash the cold had begun to eat their strength away. Lyon said, "Of course we were wet, and the wind was blowing on us, and we were losing our strength pretty fast. The way the water was and the wind blowing and what we had on...neither one of us knew how far it would be until we could touch bottom..."

The decision was made—neither could face the prospect of going into the water.

So the pair settled in for the night, with the knowledge that no one would report them missing. It was only Friday. Their families would not be looking for them since their arrival was not expected until after their weekend hunting trip.

Both officers with the Anchorage Police department, Long and Lyon used to work the graveyard shift at the courthouse together. The hours had been long and boring, and plenty of times they had fought to stay awake. That experience would prove invaluable as they struggled to survive.

"We knew that he had to stay awake all night long in order to stay on the float," Lyon said. "We knew that if we dozed off, we'd lose our balance and fall into the water—and it would be all over."

Lyon was raised in Stevens Village on the Yukon River, where his father was a Bush pilot. A memory came back to him now: Once, one of his father's companions had died after falling asleep in sub-zero weather.

"That's one thing you've got to do in cold weather, is stay awake," he said. "The key to the whole thing for us was to stay awake, because if you go to sleep, you'll never wake up again."

The two men caught each other dozing off time and again, but their sleepiness was the fatigue of hypothermia. They fought it back with conversation.

They discussed the options they would face in the morning; they talked about family and work; they wondered aloud whether the Cessna had an emergency locator transmitter and, if so, whether ELTs worked while submerged in water. They prayed—they prayed a lot.

Periodically, Lyon remembered the loss of his friend, whose body lay just a few feet below them in the darkness.

"Reuben kept on reverting during the night to saying, 'Larry…he's gone.'" Long recalled. "Hell, that was his friend. It was really agonizing."

It was so cold that the two men screamed in pain. They didn't have enough room to shift their hunched-up sidesaddle positions on the narrow underside of the float, and their legs began to cramp severely.

When dawn came, they didn't even notice. With their tent wrapped around them and Lyon's thin jacket pulled over their heads, they huddled together, not looking at the world outside their shelter. One of the few things the two men could do on that unnamed lake was tell time because Lyon had a watch. More than twelve hours had passed.

By then, Long had lost all sensation from the knees down. He believed they were frozen. One consolation was that his feet didn't hurt any more.

About 11:30 a.m., the worst that could happen did. Lyon lost his balance, slipped from the float and fell through a layer of new ice into the lake water. Long struggled to help him back up onto the pontoon.

The situation was deteriorating. Both men wanted desperately to think of some kind of flotation device they could make that would allow them to get to shore. But suffering advanced hypothermia, they could barely think at all.

The cold water merely solidified their decision to stay with the float and not attempt reaching shore. Lyon was deeply chilled and the incident reminded both of them that going into the water again would mean "instantaneous freezing," in Long's words.

The midday sun shone, but provided no warmth. They saw their deaths approaching. In nearly 24 hours they hadn't heard a single aircraft. They were entirely alone, and weakening. It was below freezing. The wind clawed at them relentlessly.

"We figured we had by the time nightfall came to live, that we'd be dead by morning because our condition was deteriorating that fast, not only physically but mentally," Long said. "The biggest thing was trying to keep our minds straight, not go bonkers..."

The day began to wane as the low southern sun started down, making longer shadows and casting a pallor of fall over the lake and nearby shore. The two men on the float prayed some more.

Time crawled.

Then, suddenly, Long threw off the jacket covering their heads. He reached into his shoulder holster, pulled out his .357 Magnum and started firing into the air.

He had heard the sound of an airplane. Ridiculous as it seems now, he was trying to attract the pilot's attention with the sound of pistol fire, an impossible hope as the engine noise within the cabin drowns out all other sounds besides intercom radio dialogue.

Lyon's watch indicated the time was 12:42 p.m.

When they caught sight of the plane, they waved Lyon's bright red jacket in the air. The plane changed course and came toward them, soon nodding its wings in acknowledgement.

As the aircraft disappeared into the distance, the two men realized their ordeal was not over.

"I told Reuben it would be an hour to an hour-and-a-half before they got a chopper to us," Long said. It turned out to be an hour and 40 minutes, the longest hour and 40 minutes either man had ever spent.

The chopper arrived at the lake, hovered over the pair of men for a few moments, then went to shore and landed. Inexplicably, it took off again and disappeared.

"This old boy here went a little ballistic, knowing a helicopter came that close and then left," Long said about himself. "I started to cry. I just couldn't handle that he got so close and left again. My mind was fried.

"We could hear someone yelling at us from shore, but we couldn't hear what they were saying—we didn't come out from under the tent.

"I think we were going pretty quick. We just kept on telling each other that we had to hold on a little bit longer."

Soon the helicopter returned and descended to within a few feet of the two stranded men. State trooper Curt Harris dressed in a survival suit, jumped into the lake, climbed up onto the float and muscled Long onto the chopper's skids. Long remembers the intense agony as his legs were unfolded for the first time in 22 hours.

The chopper shuttled him to shore, set him down and returned for Lyon. On shore, rescuers stripped Long's clothes off and put him in a sleeping bag.

By now, the two recall, there were airplanes "all over the place." The silent tundra had turned into a bustle of rescue activity. Long and Lyon believe that by the time all was said and done, about 150 people—mostly from the village of Iliamna—aided them in some way or another.

When their oral temperatures were taken in Iliamna, Lyon's was 94 degrees; Long's was 93. The two men were evacuated to Providence Hospital, where Lyon stayed for five days, and Long for eight.

Both men initially were listed in serious condition. They were treated for back injuries and severe hypothermia, while Long also suffered cold injury to his feet. They wouldn't be back on their police beats for several weeks.

In retrospect, the two men agree on one thing above all: If they had been carrying some survival gear on their persons, they would not have come so close to death.

Both say they won't get back in a floatplane without wearing carbon dioxide-type inflatable vests. In the event of a watery crash landing, survivors must have a way to get to shore.

Marine-type flares would have given them greater peace of mind, at least. Had they heard a plane in the middle of the night, they might have been able to attract its attention.

And food. Had Long and Lyon had some trail mix, candy bars or other high-calorie sustenance in their pockets, they would have been much better armed against the cold.

Extra clothing would have been helpful, too, they say, although both warn that if they had been wearing a lot of bulky clothes at the time of the crash they might never have escaped the aircraft at all.

State troopers at the scene are convinced that if the pair had tried to dive for Wooten, they would have perished as well. Yet their inability to rescue their friend haunts them.

Later, both men would emphasize that if they had had access to their gear, everything would have been different. But it was stored in the Cessna's pontoons, right beneath them but impossible to get to, blocked by a barrier of frighteningly cold water and doors that were held fast by screws.

"Some lessons have come out of Larry's death," Long said, "If a lesson can be learned that could help other people under similar circumstances or change the way people think, there'll be some good come out of it—and that's all I'm hoping."

After his release from the hospital, Lyon spoke of the pilot, his close friend for more than a decade, "People will always do whatever they can to help us not feel guilty about what happened, but that doesn't ease my mind any."

Long, consigned to a back brace and armchair during his convalescence, is trying to come up with a design for airplane floats that would have yielded up their contents in the Iliamna emergency.

The floats of Wooten's Cessna 206 had doors secured with four screws apiece. Long said. If they had been equipped with latches that release, the two men might have been able to recover some of their provisions without spending too much time in the water.

Long and Lyon are all too familiar with the floats on a Cessna 206. They spent 22 hours huddled on top of the underside of one.

"We're not talking about the top, where it's flat," he said. "We're talking about the bottom—it's about 12 inches wide."

"If you ever get a chance, take a look at the float of a 206—upside down."

Fortunately, these men were found before Alaska's cold swallowed them alive.

Rewritten account of Reuben Lyon and Dennis Long, "Survivors recount chilling 22-hour ordeal," by Joe Bridgman, *The Anchorage Times*, Sunday, November 4, 1984

Source: *Alaska Air Tales*

World War II Pilot

While listening to host Herb Shaindlin, from *The Talk Show*, KFQD radio, Anchorage, May 10, 2000, I heard the following story and paraphrased it.

A young man, wanting to follow the example of former American military men and excited about aviation, received the proper flying instruction, graduated at the top of his class, underwent the proper celebratory congratulations and was shipped off to the Pacific to do battle during World War II.

On his first day off the aircraft carrier he went aloft and engaged in harried dog fighting, shooting down six Japanese Zeros. He looked about and discovered another group of Zeros above his position. Eagerly he climbed to engage them in battle. To his complete satisfaction he succeeded in downing all nine of his combatants.

Realizing he was low on fuel, he hastily dropped in elevation in preparation to landing on the carrier. After touch down he proudly approached the commanding officer and asked, "How did I do on my first day, Captain?"

The officer looked at him with a smile on his face, bowed and replied, "Amellican, Pirot, you make one belly bad mistake."

Source: *Alaska Air Tales*

Larry Kaniut

Alaska Roots

By Patty Wagstaff

When people ask me where I learned to fly, I proudly tell them Alaska. Sure, every pilot dreams of flying in Alaska and maybe giving it all up for a month, a year, a lifetime to be an Alaskan bush pilot. There is a mystique and aura about Alaskan bush flying and I was lucky to have had the opportunity to take advantage of it from my very first lesson.

I was living in Dillingham where I met my ex-husband. On our first "date" he took me for a flight in his Cessna 185 on Edo floats and I'll never forget the feeling of the floats breaking free of the water at Lake Hood. I had been around aviation all of my life, but the airplanes my father flew were big. He let me sit in the cockpit as a kid and since then my natural inclination was to want to fly, to feel the yolk, to feel wings in the wind. I guess I'll never get enough of flying.

Flying in Alaska is different. Like some of the really good aerobatic pilots I know who started their airshow careers being crop dusters, I began my aerobatic career with low level bush flying.

I remember my first flight down Turnagain Arm, into the Chugach Mountains, through Whittier Pass into Prince William Sound, flying low enough over the water to be below the edge of a glacier.

Back in Dillingham, I chartered a small airplane to take me to a village on business. It was during spring breakup, the small dirt strip was muddy, and the young foolish pilot behind the wheel didn't use the full length of it. Sure enough we crashed off the end of the runway, and ended up upside down. The pilot, myself and the other passenger, while covered with mail, survived with a few bruises, but even I knew at the time he'd made a really dumb mistake. That was when I knew I had to get my license and that I could do better than that.

I begged one of the local Air Taxi operators, one of the few CFI's in town, to give me some dual instruction. I found an airplane to rent, a Cherokee 180, and after pleading with him a few more times, he relented and agreed to give me lessons when he had the time.

Dillingham only had one runway and there was always a cross-wind. Later on, when I started flying in Anchorage, I always turned the yolk all the way to one side when taking off much to the surprise of my instructors later in Anchorage who had to break me of this habit. For S-turns across a road, we used the curve of a river or a creek. For turns around a point, we used a moose; for emergency landings -- a river bed. We flew low enough so that I had to look outside and feel the airplane, not stare at the instruments to see if the ball was centered. I had to feel it in my butt.

I moved to Anchorage and, after soloing on my birthday at Birchwood, I finished my private license in a Beech Sport. I continued to fly the I85 and continued to pursue my ratings. In the days before Loran or GPS, I learned about weather flying, IFR, both instrument flying and "I follow Rivers." I learned about pre-heat and scraping the windscreen with a driver's license or credit card; and learned that just when you were finished with a two hour winter pre-flight the fog would roll in. When we went camping in Iliamna, I learned about mountain passes and saw the wreckage of airplanes that didn't make it. I learned slips and short field landings; and touch and gos in mud, dirt and gravel. I learned that the glare off an icy airstrip can blind you to oncoming traffic and I learned what it was like to land on a beach. When I started instructing, after the initial experience of working for a couple of flight schools at Merrill Field, I freelanced and taught people how to fly tail draggers. And, of course, I discovered that instructing is when you really start learning.

With the help of the Alaska Student Loan Program I finished my commercial, CFII, Seaplane and Multiengine ratings and part of my helicopter rating. After I soloed a Wilbur's Bell 47, I would fly it out behind Muldoon and used the skids to carve my initials in the snow. I landed at the base of the Chugach and looked at moose looking back at me.

We flew all over Alaska for business and pleasure. After I was handed the keys and told it was mine to fly whenever I wanted, I flew out to Dillingham to pick up a girlfriend for a flying adventure. On that trip I learned that it's real easy to get lost around the hills behind Togiak when the weather is coming down, and I got my instrument ticket wet when I had to turn around, climb and find my way back to Dillingham while picking up ice and outside of VOR range. The next day we took off again and headed for Bethel, up the Kuskokwim; over to the Yukon, Fairbanks and Denali.

I took my first aerobatic lesson over the BLM strip in Anchorage where we always used to practice, continued to instruct in tail draggers and bought my first aerobatic airplane, N1118E, a blue and red with starburst painted Super Decathlon and started giving aerobatic instruction in it.

Why didn't I stay and become a bush pilot? For sure, the challenge I needed was there. Flying in the bush, mountain flying, glacier flying, weather flying, the thrill and the beauty is all there. But we all find our element somehow, and I found mine in 3-D flight, doing aerobatics. For me, nothing could compare.

I flew the Decathalon down to the Lower 48 in late July one year to compete in my first aerobatic contest, I was pretty unprepared for what the contest had to offer, but I could fly the airplane by Alaska standards –- knowing and understanding weather; getting the most out of a climb by keeping the ball centered; how to slip and skid the airplane and to place it exactly where it needed to be placed.   I had learned to make quick decisions based on a challenging environment and most of all I learned to keep my eyes outside of the cockpit and feel whether the ball was centered by the seat of my pants, with my butt. I didn't win the contest, but I didn't come in last either!

So, when I say I'm proud to have learned to fly in Alaska, and to have spent the first five years of my aviation life exclusively there, it was more than just a romance with the magic of flying the bush. I had the best instructors who taught me what real flying is and how to keep my butt square in the seat and the ball in the center. I also learned the most important aviation lesson of all from the best of the best--and that is what the bush pilots taught me. The best pilots are the most humble pilots because they know they always have more to learn.

Source: *Alaska Air Tales*

Larry Kaniut

Sole Survivor

"We've had twenty-six crashes through the twenty-sixth of August with eighteen deaths—that's one plane crash a day for this month."

Every year many private aircraft fail to return from flights in Alaska. When I read about one such event and the young woman who spent the night aboard a crashed airplane only a few miles from Anchorage, I tried to imagine her desperation. Although I wanted her words to tell others of the agony and heartache she endured then and since, I was unsuccessful in obtaining a personal interview. I rewrote the story from the newspaper clippings.

Rythmic rattling reverberated off the canyon walls as the olive drab helicopter waddled up the valley. The crew knew there was no such thing as normal rescue mission—every launch to find or save someone brought something new, different or unexpected. They were near the 3,700-foot level and on the north side of a ridge near Eklutna Lake, twenty-eight miles northeast of Anchorage. Below them, on a ridge of the Chugach Mountains, lay the crumpled wreckage of a Cessna 172 aircraft.

As the MH-60 Pavehawk chopper neared the plane, one of the crewmen noted a face through the window and a hand waving. "We've got a live one!" he exclaimed into his headset mike. The pilot jockeyed the guppy-shaped bird into position for landing.

Inside the 172, Cari Britton felt overwhelming joy. They came to get me. I'm going to make it. Tears formed in her eyes and gradually trickled down her cheeks. Her long hours of fear and doubt were over. Waves of relief washed over her.

It was 9:45 a.m., Friday, August 23, 1991. For fourteen hours

Cari had lain alone in the twisted aluminum remains of the four-place aircraft. During the long night she had wondered if it would be her casket.

What would it be like finding yourself on a mountain ridge, the sole survivor of a plane crash? Your last memory is of watching sheep off your left wing. You must have crashed and blacked out. You can't move.

Robert Works, your friend who is visiting you and your boyfriend, sits beside you dead.

You repeatedly call for Lloyd, but there is no response.

Darkness comes a couple of hours later, bringing cooler temperatures. You're cold. Can't sleep. Must try to stay warm. You have no food or water. Worse than that, you have no companionship. You wonder if everyone else is dead. And worst of all, you think, What if Lloyd is dead? You're unable to do anything to help the others.

After a while you realize that Lloyd will never answer you again.

Are there any bears in the area? Will they smell blood and come to the plane?

You're familiar with flying. Yours is a flying family. Your parents have their pilot's licenses and have owned a small plane. You knew about forced landings. Even though you were ready to put your flying knowledge into practice, you were trapped.

It was clear and sunny at 7 p.m. the previous evening when you and three others left Merrill Field in Anchorage to look for Dall sheep. The long daylight hours were dwindling, but darkness was still two to three hours away. Plans were for a weekend hunt. A flight over the area would give the hunters an idea where the sheep were and hence where to establish base camp for their hunt. After that it would be a matter of time before a sheep-and-hunter rendezvous took place.

For the past year you and your boyfriend, Lloyd H. Jones, twenty-seven, have lived and worked in Anchorage. You were employed as a manage trainee for the National Bank of Alaska; he worked as an administrative assistant at United Parcel Service. You and Lloyd enjoyed being outdoors together and spent a good many weekends there.

Your friend and Lloyd's, Robert Works, twenty-six, of Casper, Wyoming, was a law student who had come to Anchorage to visit you two.

The pilot, Ronald Pritchard, twenty-two, of Anchorage, had his instructor's rating and his commercial pilot's license. The plane, owned by Joseph Wilbur, was operated by Flight Safety of Alaska, an Anchorage-based flight school. The aircraft's records indicated that it was well maintained.

During the night you agonized over physical pain and discomfort. However, that agony paled by comparison of the mental anguish, knowing your cabin mates were dead...and wondering if you would be joining them. And if so, how soon?

You wonder what life will be like without Lloyd. How you'll cope. Then you think of your family...what your loss will mean to them. You determine not to give up. You remember the motivation for this flight.

After leaving Merrill Field the Cessna flew over the low ridges of the Chugach Mountains, occupants looking below for white dots. As the plane approached a ridge top, the group watched sheep on the mountainside out their left windows. One moment they were airborne; the next moment, without warning, they were splattered against the ridge. Forty minutes after takeoff the Cessna 172 was down.

The Federal Aviation Administration requires aircraft to carry emergency locator transmitters. These transmitters are activated by a 4-g impact, which sends a signal to overhead satellites. The signal in turn is sent to various agencies. Sometime after midnight Thursday, the Civil Air Patrol in Anchorage picked up an ELT signal.

The 210th Air Rescue Squadron from Kulis Air National Guard Base at Anchorage International Airport responded to the emergency signal. The rescuers flew to the crash site and landed seventy-five yards above the crashed airplane.

Guard Tech. Sgts. Eric Sachs and Patrick Malone left the chopper and hiked downhill to the plane. They discovered Ron Pritchard's body beneath the fuselage. The men tore the plane's door off and found the other two men dead. Sachs and Malone spent an hour freeing Cari from the wreckage, stabilizing and transporting her to their helicopter.

The mercy flight departed immediately to Humana Hospital, Anchorage, where Cari was admitted. Her condition was diagnosed as critical but stable. She initially underwent four hours of surgery for leg injuries, a back injury (crushed vertebra), and internal injuries.

Her sister Lori Gross arrived from Lyman, Wyoming, to be with Cari, and in short order Cari was on her way to recovery. Her major hurdle now would be emotional healing from the loss of her boyfriend and friend.

AFTERWORD

When the cause of the accident was investigated, Alaska State Troopers spokesperson Janelle Hout said, "It looks like [the pilot] missed the top of the ridge by about three hundred feet." (1)

Joette Storm, spokesperson for the Federal Aviation Administration, said, "Pilots should have someone else do the looking and focus on flying...The pilot's decision-making ability is critical." (2)

It is critical in chartering an air-taxi pilot to have some understanding of the risks involved in flying with a stranger, especially during peak air-flight seasons when many pilots are overtaxed by constant stick time and little sleep time. Your life could well depend upon your decision.

Source: *Danger Stalks the Land*

Jesus and Kids

Considering the roadway ahead and seeing Gaius and his family, I was reminded of my agent's report about the Nazarene's fondness for children. He had told me of his amazement when observing the Nazarene contentedly playing with children. A young boy around seven years of age tugged at the Nazarene's tunic and said, "Come play with us, Yeshua."

The agent was close enough to observe the Nazarene as he feigned a scowl in mock disgust and spun around to face the youngster in a fighting stance, bent at the waist, hands raised in boxing fashion in front of his chest and replied, "I'm too old."

"No, you're not."

"You don't want me."

"Yes, we do."

"Okay. Okay. But you have to promise not to hurt me."

"We promise."

"Remember, I'm pretty fragile, you know."

"We promise not to hurt you."

The boy, tagged the Nazarene and said, "You're it," then ran. During the conversation several children had gathered in a loosely arranged circle and the Nazarene then ran among them feinting toward one then the other. At length he reached out to a girl and tapped her on the shoulder, "You're it."

After that the game gathered momentum with the children tagging one another, all trying to get close enough to tag the Nazarene. He dodged this way and that evading the tag and laughing the harder each time with bright eyes and smile. Periodically he dived to the ground and rolled away from the tag or jumped to the side.

In a short time the game evolved into a game of leap frog, initiated, the agent shared, by the Nazarene. A line of children positioned themselves on all fours and the Nazarene hopped over each in the row until he reached the first. He was immediately followed by the child behind him who followed his example. The agent lost count after the first time through the line and didn't know how many times they repeated the leaps.

At any rate, before he knew it, they were playing follow the leader, the leader being the Nazarene. He gathered them in a group, spoke to them, placed his hands on either side of his head like ears on a camel and hopped along the ground a dozen times before stopping, each of the children hopping along with glee. Next he stuck his arms out to his sides shoulder high and moved in a semi-circle to his left while dipping his left shoulder and raising his right arm; he then repeated the movement to the right while taking long steps. After a few minutes he relinquished the lead to a youngster who took the group on a somersaulting journey before surrendering his lead to another.

The agent recounted that as he watched, it seemed numerous adults viewed the activities in happy contentment, almost as if they wanted to join the fun. In the end, the children gathered in a group around the Nazarene and cheered.

The Nazarene playing with children was a new one. Made me smile when I tried to imagine him playing leap frog in a tunic. Might be a challenge at that.

Source: *Brachan*

Larry Kaniut

Sig Casiano

Several things impress me about Sig's story: 1) Noise did not deter the bear—helped locate the man; 2) large boars are very protective of their food source; 3) Sig's concern that spray would NOT have worked; 4) boar's determination and strength; 5) officials' suspicion/blame hunter—not innocent until proven guilty; 6) chambered round; 7) time elapsed; 8) pistol and lanyard—good advice; 9) being armed always; 10) in your face to anti's and huggers—a man's got to do what a man's got to do (kill a bear if necessary!)—11) shoot till they stop moving!

Gary Shelton, thorough bear expert with three books on bears, says the baddest bear on the planet is the old boar. This bear is not just a brute, it is a brute on steroids. The baddest banana in the bunch.

So, here's Sig's story, in his words:

It was Sunday morning, late April 1998. Hunting season would start in about a week on May first. I had gotten a permit to hunt bear by bait in the Kenai National Moose Refuge and I decided to go out and set up my station.

I drove out to the parking area where I could see the lake. Because it was kind of heavy, I put my 55 gallon drum on a child's sled for transport. I had already cut a hole in the barrel and I had a chain inside it (in order to chain the barrel to a tree for storing bait). My two-burner Coleman stove was in my metal frame pack on my back.

I had my .300 on my right shoulder and my .454 Casul pistol holstered in a chest-shoulder holster. Because I've heard stories about bear's attacking people, I always wanted to be on the cautious side of things. Some of us try to prepare for things like this. Every time I go out, even for a hike, I carry a pistol or a rifle. I don't want to be surprised and not have the ability to protect myself.

I started walking down the trail across from the parking area and the trees were pretty dense. There was still about two feet of snow on the ground. The trail got narrower so I decided to come back down the road about a hundred yards to a trail I could use; it was maybe six feet wide.

I got about a tenth to a quarter of a mile down that trail when I heard this noise to my right. It sounded like I had startled a moose that was getting up out of its bed. I couldn't see anything because the foliage was really thick. I kind of bent down to see what was making the noise and I only saw a brown patch. As I stood back up, I could still hear it and it sounded like it was coming towards me.

The only thought going through my mind was why is this moose charging me? I reached up to grab my pistol and quickly realized that it was coming real fast. I've been around a lot of animals. I've scared moose up and never had one charge me. Bears too. They always run the other way.

I quickly unslung my rifle from my shoulder. I had a round in the chamber. When I'm by myself, I always have a round in the chamber. With someone else, I typically do not have a round chambered. In this case I did.

Right when I got it down, the moose was coming through to the right front of me. I released the safety, pointed the rifle and pulled the trigger. It landed about six-feet away from me, literally right at my feet. Because of the snow cover when the moose hit the ground, snow sprayed up.

That's the first time that I realized it was not a moose, but a bear. I immediately pulled back and put another round in...in fact I short stroked it and the case got stuck in there. I pulled it out and shot the bear in the shoulder. My third shot, I chambered another round and shot it in the shoulder again. He was still breathing so I pulled my pistol out and shot him in the chest one more time and he stopped breathing.

It happened so quickly. From the time I heard the noise till the time I shot him probably three seconds elapsed. I didn't have a lot of time to think about what to do. I had a half a second to realize I didn't want to use my pistol. And the other couple of seconds were taking my rifle off my shoulder, pushing the safety and pulling the trigger.

People asked me, "Why did you shoot so many times?"

I answer that I wasn't sure where I hit him the first time. I didn't know if I hit him in the head and knocked him out or if I hit him in the spine and crippled him. I kept shooting him until he stopped breathing.

I loaded my rifle back up with four more rounds. I heard noise in the brush and thought it might be a sow with cubs. I crouched to see what it might be. Then I realized that the noise was the brush settling from the bear's passing through in its charge.

I took my pack off and left it there and got in my truck and headed down Swanson River Road so I could get in cell phone range to call the Alaska State Troopers. I did not have a camera so I drove to a friend's at Longmere Lake to borrow a camera from him.

On my way I called my wife on my cell phone. I told her I'd be home late. She asked my why and I told her I'd just killed a bear.

She asked if it was hunting season yet.

I said, "No. I had a bear charge me."

She said, "What?"

I said, "I killed it and I'm okay. I didn't get hurt or anything."

She was all worried about my going back out. She didn't want me to go back out any more. I said, "I just can't do that. I love hunting. I won't get hurt."

I explained that it was an isolated incident that doesn't happen to every hunter going into the woods but that it's something that they should be prepared for because it could happen. Nine out of ten times a hunter is not going to be charged by a bear. I kept that thought in mind which kept me from being too worried about its happening again.

When I got in his house, I was able to contact the troopers and inform them of what happened. They were going to meet me out there.

My buddy and I got in my truck, had a camera and got out to Mosquito Lake. The troopers both had rifles. They were both standing there with M 16 style rifles, a shorter model. I thought that their sense of adequacy with the firepower wasn't very good. Their rifles would shoot more rounds, probably.223 caliber. More volume but not as far as fire power. I didn't feel comfortable leaving without my rifle.

They said, "Okay, why don't you show us where it's at."

I asked them, "Do you mind if I bring my rifle?"

They both said, "No. That's okay. You don't need your rifle."

I looked at their rifles and said, "Yeh, I think I'm going to take my rifle."

So we walked out there and got to my back pack. The one thing they wanted to do was ascertain whether I'd stalked this bear before killing it. And it was quickly noted that that wasn't the case. We hiked down the trail in two feet of snow. We could see my tracks walking in and his tracks coming through the woods, making a B-line right for me. So they quickly ruled out the possibility of my being out there hunting.

We followed his tracks for about a hundred yards and found a dead moose. You could see where the bear had bedded down on it. He'd been on it a couple of days but he hadn't eaten much of it. It so happens that that dead moose was on the trail that I'd started on the first time. I was pretty fortunate to be able to turn back and come back down the other trail because I'm not sure how it would have been otherwise.

As we walked through the woods following his tracks back, we noticed a number of broken trees. From the moose to the dead bear was a straight line. He was dialing in on me because of this noise that he kept hearing, this chain that was rattling inside of this barrel. He knew exactly where I was.

He'd knocked down spruce and birch trees that ranged in size from two-inches to four-inches thick, just knocked them clean off. The noise that I'd heard from the brush was all the trees breaking. The bear never went around any trees, he was running full speed. In fact right before I shot him, he hit a spruce tree that was probably five or six-inches in diameter and he didn't break that one—he bounced off of it when he hit it with his shoulder.

Initially they questioned me about my having so much fire power in the woods—both a rifle and a pistol. I thought it was a silly thought because I've read responses from people and results. The situation was exactly why one would carry a rifle and a pistol.

Neither of them knew how to skin a bear. Luckily I did. My buddy had actually brought a knife with him. I happened to have one with me. I told them I would skin the bear I just needed their help moving the bear. There were four of us and we couldn't roll it over. I thought it was anywhere between the 1200 and 1300 pound range.

Federal guys come because it was on the refuge and he had to actually investigate too. It took five guys to roll the bear over onto its back so we could start working on it.

We got it rolled over and I started skinning it. I had them do some things for me like hold the legs and stuff like that. One of them almost cut one of the feet off. I started hearing this sawing noise and I looked up and he was sawing the foot off at the wrist, almost cutting into the hide (with my bow saw).

I told him not to do that. He asked me, "Well, what'd you bring the saw for?"

I said, "The saw is for cutting dead trees I would use for my bait station, not to cut a bear up."

You cut a bear up with a knife, through the joints.

We did a quick job on it. I cut it off at the wrists and the neck. Left the hams and the neck and the hide. I had brought another sled too. We stuffed the hide on the sled, and it probably weighed a couple of hundred pounds. We had a little trouble getting it out because it was so heavy. Even on the sled the rope kept breaking.

We finally got it to the road. Some tourists happened to be driving by at the same time. One of them asked if it was a moose. We told him it was a bear.

The authorities informed me that since it was killed in defense of life and property they would have to seize the bear. One of the things that I did that I kind of got scrutinized for was I took a claw off the bear.

They took the hide back to fish and game and the next day one of the biologists at fish and game called and asked me if I had the claw. I said, "Yes, I did."

He said, "You have to return it with the bear."

I said, "That's not a problem."

He was quite frank to me about it..."It is a big bear. There will be a lot of exposure. They need to really go by the rules on this one." So I respected that decision and got the claw back to them right away.

The Peninsula Clarion wrote a big story that I'd filched a claw which really got under the skin because I didn't steal...filching in my definition is deception and stealing. And I didn't know it was against the law to take a claw. And I gave it back when I was told about it.

Up to that point I didn't mind talking to the press about the incident but after that I wouldn't talk to anybody because I was wasting my time because they weren't telling the story. They reported other inaccuracies such as the size of the bear which was never weighed. I've killed enough bears to know that this one far exceeded their estimate of 500 pounds.

I was prepared to buy the bear at the Fur Rondy auction (usually each year at the Fur Rendezvous celebration in Anchorage furs are auctioned), to put a bid on it. But a couple of weeks after they actually got the bear, the Brigham Young

University museum in Hawaii was doing an Alaskan exhibit and they requested a large brown bear, which I had shot. It squared 9' 6" and the skull measured 28 inches green.

Although the *Anchorage Daily News* reported the story most accurately, they quoted a state trooper implying that because this bear had pellets in its rear end from earlier run ins with humans, that it had lost its fear of people.

I disagreed with that. When I was skinning him, I found some birdshot BB's from a shotgun in his rear end. That doesn't necessarily mean he'd lost his fear of humans. This bear may have been around homes. It was fifteen years old. There's also the possibility that over time a bear hunter in a tree stand tired of the bear's presence, brought a shotgun and shot him in the rear end to get him out of there.

The reason that he charged wasn't because he'd lost his fear of humans. He charged because he was protecting his meal.

I've read lots of articles about bear attacks. A couple kind of startled me. In these articles the charging bear hit them and knocked the rifle from their grasp and they had nothing to protect themselves with. They had to either play dead or improvise. They were killed immediately.

Once you lose your pistol or your rifle, you don't have anything. You can punch a bear all day long and there are no definite results. If you punch him in the nose, you don't know if he'll run away or if he's going to continue attacking you. With a pistol or a rifle there's a definite outcome for the most part. You shoot him and it's going to have a pretty big impact on whether he decides to stay or whether you actually kill him.

That information caused me to buy a .454 Casul pistol, a very large caliber pistol designed for large animals like bears. I carry my pistol on my chest because the first thing you're going to do is jump on your belly and try to protect your head and your neck. If a bear ever got me on the ground, I would have a last line of defense with the pistol. If the bear went for my legs and tried to shake me to death, when he stopped shaking me, I would pull the pistol and shoot him.

If I had a rifle, I would use the pistol only as a last resort. I'm not going to pull the pistol out unless I have to pull it out.

Given the option of using a rifle or a pistol, always shoot your rifle before your pistol, even at six feet. Your rifle with the right round is lot more deadly, more powerful and has more impact on the animal that you're shooting than most pistols.

I recommend having a pistol on a lanyard so that it's always available. A lot of pistols don't have a place to put a lanyard but any gun dealer can weld one on.

For a defensive weapon I recommend a thirty caliber and up. My favorite rifle for protection is my .45-70. It's a lever action with an 18-inch barrel, easy to handle. When I'm fishing, I can put it on my back. It's a lot more effective than a shotgun. It is magna ported with hardly any recoil...anybody can shoot it, even a woman.

Another article pointed out that 90% of people that die from bear attacks where the bear was able to get their heads into their mouths. The people that lived typically were smaller bears that weren't able to do that. That's not in every case of course.

I would probably have died that day if I would have had pepper spray (instead of a firearm) because when I shot him, he was six-feet away and still running. Pepper spray would not have stopped him. I truly believe that pepper spray in my situation would have done me absolutely no good.

One of the benefits I had was I was wearing a metal frame. For me at the time I thought I had a lot of things in my favor. The two burner Coleman metal stove in my pack would have protected my entire back if he had gotten on top of me. He would have taken a bite out of everything he could take a bite of until he got some soft tissue.

The only soft tissue I had exposed is my legs. My thought afterwards if it happened was if he went for my legs and tried to shake me to death, after he was done shaking me, I would have pulled the pistol out and shot him.

Larry Kaniut

A lot of people have said that my military training helped prepare me. That's quite possible. My military background enhanced my hunting abilities—anticipating noises around me and my environment, being aware of animals in the area and it prepared me for being comfortable with handling a weapon. I have no problem pulling the weapon down and popping a shot off when I need to. I've never been in combat but being in the military helped me be comfortable in handling a pistol and staying focused. Being comfortable with the weapon, pulling it down and shooting without asking any questions, without hesitating and without second guessing my judgment helped me. That's my nature too, I don't worry about a lot of things. I've been around a lot of animals. I've scared moose up and never had one charge me. They always run the other way. Bears too.

It was a survival instinct as far as I was concerned. I was very, very lucky that I was not hurt. I've always recognized that. People told me that, especially fish and game people. I recognize that I was very fortunate.

I never thought this would happen to me and I'm sure that everybody who's ever been attacked by a bear never thought it would happen to them.

There are a lot of people out there who didn't understand why I did what I did, what I was doing out there or why I was hunting at all. I think they may understand it but I don't think they accept the reason that we have hunting and regulate the populations of predators and animals.

I recognize that. I enjoy hunting because it's allowed. I eat the animals that I kill. I've hunted black bears and killed several black bears. I've never eaten brown bear. The state doesn't require that you eat brown bear meat. I don't eat small predators like fox, but for the most part I eat the animals I hunt.

I'm comfortable accepting responsibility for my actions totally in every situation. That's why I hardly ever second guess myself on my decisions. If I make the wrong decisions, I'll fess up to it.

I never thought I'd ever be attacked by a bear and I'm sure that everybody who's ever been attacked by a bear felt the same. I'm glad that I was armed and prepared.

Source: *SAFE with Bears*

In Search of a Man-killer

When I first read Frank Dufrene's *No Room For Bears*, I thought it was an awesome book. His story about Hosea Sarber and his theory about the twenty-fifth bear was one of the most hair-raising bear stories I'd ever read. If anything, it's gotten better with each reading…he captures the brown/grizzly's territorial nature, a terrible mauling and a hunter's crafty stalk for a man-killer. I've rewritten that story including the report written by the sole survivor on that fatal trip into the rainforest.

On that dreadful day of October 16, 1929, Jack Thayer and his assistant Fred Herring conducted business as usual. But the day held a far different outcome from their planned return. They spent the day conducting a Forest Service timber survey. Jack was a prominent employee of the service and a Forest Examiner.

While returning to the motor vessel at day's end, they encountered a brown bear. Jack and Fred could almost feel the bear's presence, a feeling that both men had come to know in the proximity with the big browns in the rainforest. Most bears flee the presence of man, however they believed that this bear had chosen to take a stand in the face of human interlopers rather than retreat.

Jack knew that a brown-grizzly could cover thirty feet with two bounds in a shade under two seconds. He knew the impending danger and had decided to shoot fast and accurately should the animal show signs of battle. He would take no chances of endangering himself or Fred, who stood behind him.

Jack pulled his rifle barrel from the crook of his left elbow, slid his finger inside the trigger guard onto the trigger and pushed his thumb against the weapon's safety, all in one single, long practiced movement. He slipped ever so slowly forward. Knowing the speed and power of an aroused brown/grizzly, the one thought that drummed across his mind was You better be ready; this could be quick.

But that black October day was a day for the bears.

The bear was nearby in the foliage.

That's when Fred saw the hulk and hissed a warning to Jack. The big animal had risen off its bed as silently as a silhouette and stood amidst three hemlocks facing the men with its head lowered. A half-minute evolved into eternity while the bear's eyes pierced its antagonists; Fred thought its eyes looked like two red marbles. Slowly the black lips parted and curled back over a set of yellow teeth. That's when the bear came.

Fred Henning later wrote up his version of the tragic event (which I've included verbatim):

STATEMENT OF FRED HERRING WITH REGARD TO THE CIRCUMSTANCES OF THE DEATH OF JOHN A. THAYER

On the morning of October sixteenth, 1929, Jack Thayer and I left the Launch Weepoose to cruise the timber in a creek valley which is located on the westerly shore of Eliza Harbor about 2 miles from the head of the harbor. Eliza Harbor is on the southeastern part of Admiralty Island, Alaska.

Thayer carried as a means of protection a Newton 30-'06 and was using Government steel jacketed ammunition. I was unarmed and carried a light pack containing a compass, increment borer and our lunch.

Leaving the beach at 8:30 a.m. we ascended the mountain side on the north side of the creek until an elevation of nearly one thousand feet was reached, which is the top of the merchantable timber belt on the mountain side. We continued up the valley at this elevation or approximately, depending on the timber. At noon we ate lunch about four miles from the Eliza harbor beach. It was a cloudy day with some rain.

After lunch the timber in the valley near the creek was investigated, the creek crossed to the south side and we ascended to the muskegs at an elevation of approximately 100 feet above the creek, and began our homeward journey.

We walked about a mile and a half, stopping at a large boulder of conglomerate rock, which we investigated, as was our custom, for mineralization. We continued walking and soon came to another muskeg upon which we noticed a bear tree, where bears stop to rub and claw as an advertisement of their size. We remarked on the size of the bear and the freshness of the chewing and clawing marks. We had seen many bear trees during the summer and so attached no importance to it.

As we left the muskeg and entered the scrub timber I, who was in the rear about three or four feet, heard a snort and saw something move behind a clump of bushes about fifteen feet or twenty feet behind me and to the left of our line of travel. I called Thayer's attention saying: "I think there is a bear or a deer behind that clump of brush, Jack" and I started immediately to run for a tree, as that is man's only refuge—the brown bear being too large to climb small trees. As I passed Jack he shot and almost immediately the bear began to bawl. I ran about twenty five yards and climbed a tree which had limbs close to the ground and would afford speedy ascent. From the tree I heard the noise of a struggle and saw movements through the underbrush and then first realized what had happened.

After a few minutes I saw Jack get to his hands and knees but fall again. I descended the tree and crept close with caution not knowing if the bear had gone far away. This was a short time afterwards, probably less than five minutes after I had climbed the tree.

Jack was conscious and said: "Where did he go, Fred?" I answered I did not know. He then said "Save yourself, Fred" and lapsed into unconsciousness.

Jack was badly scratched and wounded, the worst wound being on the left side of his head. A great chunk from the top of his ear to his shoulder was torn loose. He was bleeding but as far as I could see no artery was severed. There were many other wounds but none of them as serious as on the head. The clothing around the trunk and legs was badly torn.

I removed my pack and shirt and laid his head on the packwith the large wound on his head up and bound my shirt around his head to hold the wound closed. I did what I could to make him comfortable and left for the beach where I met Capt. Carl Collen who was on the flats at the mouth of the creek waiting for us to come out. I informed him of the accident and we rowed to the launch Weepoose.

Capt. Collen and I gathered together a first aid outfit consisting of flour, compresses, bandage, blankets, iodine and a piece of canvas for a stretcher. We left the boat about 3:30 p.m. and returned to the scene, which was about two and one-half miles from the beach. Thayer was found only with some difficulty due to the natural condition of the country. When we arrived Thayer was conscious and able to talk a little. We arrived just before dark at approximately five o'clock.

We applied first aid to Jack, built a fire and rigged a stretcher. Jack kept saying: "I am cold, boys, hurry up." He called us by name also. We cut his clothes from his body and bandaged more wounds which were thereby disclosed. He was very restless during the evening and thrashed about, not allowing his wounds to close. We found his broken watch in his pocket, which had stopped and read 2:05 and we supposed that to be the time of the encounter. Some time during the evening Jack passed away. We judge the time as 10 o'clock, neither of us having watches.

During the evening we built a lean-to out of poles and brush for protection from the rain. As it is impossible to travel in the dark due to the heavy brush and wind-falls we were forced to remain till morning. We had intended to remove Jack if he were still alive to the beach in the morning.

At daybreak we attempted to pack the remains to the beach and succeeded in only one-half mile of travel due to our weakened condition from lack of food and exposure. We cached the body and walked to the beach for help.

We arrived at the Weepoose at 10:30 a.m. and left immediately for Pybus Bay, the nearest point where help could be obtained. This was October 17.

After a three hour run we entered Pybus Bay and stopped at a fox rancher's island but no men were home, they being fishing. We continued up the bay to the cannery, where the cannery watchmen, Leo R. Christensen, told us of two trollers, George Moreno, a Mexican, and Dave Johnson, a Native. We then moved to the head of Pybus Bay where they were found and their aid solicited. Another fox rancher, Henry Lietro, and a troller, W.E. Logan, were found, making a total of five men to aid us. The hour was then late and the men wishing to place their boats and ranches in order to be left alone, Capt. Colen decided to stay in Pybus Bay till morning.

We left Pybus Bay cannery at 4:30 in the morning October 18, and arrived at the creek mouth in Eliza Harbor at 7 a.m. and started immediately for the body.

No difficulty was experienced in the transporting the remains to the beach. Four men carried the remains and the others selected the trail and removed what obstructions possible. The packers were relieved from time to time by the extra men. (The burden weighed over two hundred pounds due to the rain.) We arrived at the beach at 11:30 a.m. after four and one-half hours of continuous travel.

All of us left immediately on the Weepoose for Pybus Bay and returned the men to their homes. At Pybus Bay the body was removed from its crude dressings and placed under better conditions.

We left Pybus Bay at 2:30 p.m. on the Weepoose for Juneau. This was October 18. The weather was very doubtful in Frederick Sound and at about 7:00 p.m. a strong northwest breeze and a large sea forced us to seek harbor in Pleasant Bay, Admiralty Island. We laid in harbor for an hour until the wind died and we then proceeded to Juneau. Weather conditions were very unfavorable, having a strong head wind and running against the tide. We arrived in Juneau at 7:30 a.m. on October 19 and reported immediately to the forest Service officials.

The death of Jack Thayer re-ignited and re-opened the age-old clamor to remove protection from the big bears. People preferred living friends to living bears. They suggested re-introducing the use of poison or bounties to rid the territory of bruin.

As Director of Alaska's Game Commission, Frank Dufresne felt the pressure to destroy the man killer. Fred Herring guided him to the scene of the mauling. An Indian tracker located the tracks of the rogue bear and they followed them to the alpine meadows of the coastal mountains without seeing the brute. Finding no blood and eventually losing the tracks, they had no choice but to give up the search.

A year elapsed before the search was resumed.

One day Hosea Sarber, told Frank he believed that one in twenty-five grizzlies would just as soon battle man as leave him alone—he joked that it was too bad that bears didn't wear numbers, like a football player, to warn man of the 1 in 25 odds.

Sarber, a savvy woodsman with years' of experience, told Frank that he had a hunch. He figured that enough time had passed so that if the bear had no serious injury from Jack's bullet, it had returned to its old haunts. Sarber wanted to go after it.

Exactly one year to the day after the bear had killed Jack Thayer, Hosea anchored his gas powered boat in the bay at the mouth of the river in Eliza Harbor. He knew that a wounded, man-killing brownie would harbor a grudge and take no prisoners. And if Jack had injured the bear that Hosea sought, it would be a very dangerous customer indeed.

Before motoring away from the power boat in his skiff, he instructed his boat mate to expect shooting in the late afternoon followed by three successive shots if he were successful. In the event he hadn't returned the next day, Hosea instructed him to wait until noon before following him up the river.

That said, Hosea climbed into the skiff and rowed to the beach. In moments he'd grabbed his gear and ghosted into the woods. Anyone who's ever been in the rainforest of southeast Alaska, knows that a thick layer of moss blankets the ground. Thick huckleberry bushes, alders and Devil's clubs, with maple leaf shaped leaves and spiny undersides growing a foot-and-a-half across, make up the bulk of the bushy ground cover. Moss hangs from thick branches of spruce, hemlock and cedar, nearly to ground level. It is a veritable jungle of the north.

Normally a silver-gray, smoky mist cloaks the scene, tendrils of fog silently swirling around the trees accompanied by the steady drip-drip-drip of falling rain. Winds often lash the forest and a cold chill embraces the land.

Heavy rains had recently flushed spawned out carcasses of pink and calico salmon from the stream's beaches seaward, leaving little for the bears to feed upon. Therefore Hosea encountered nearly no bear sign in the lower regions of the stream. He was encouraged, however, because he knew that the later running coho would be spawning upstream closer to the area where the tragedy occurred the previous year. And he knew that where salmon spawn in Alaska, bears congregate and feed.

At one point he encountered two yearling brown bears and gave them time and room to retreat into the forest before continuing on—he didn't want their woofed warning to alert the target of his mission.

At noon he'd reached the fork of the stream, the physical embodiment of the line Frank Dufresne had drawn on a map for him to follow. Hosea knew that he was getting close to the mauling scene when he encountered a rusty lantern left by the rescue party and pruned blueberry bushes that had been removed to provide better travel for the litter party that had carried Jack Thayer from the forest.

Hosea's approach heightened his senses—he listened more acutely, looked more closely and his sense of smell registered better. He stopped often. He tested the wind and remained motionless for minutes at a time before stealthily stepping forward.

The overhanging branches and typical rainy weather, accompanied by the gray clouds and dampness, added to the spookiness of the affair. The situation was one few men would choose, highlighted by the presence of life-threatening danger and travelling alone.

Because Hosea was within a quarter mile of where the bear struck Thayer down and because he hoped to catch the bear on the river feeding, he had purposely planned to arrive in late afternoon. It would be easier to deal with the animal in the relative openness of the river or the stream bank.

He finally reached the pool known to be the maverick's hangout and discovered partially eaten salmon on the bank. He cautiously eased past fresh bear tracks, wondering if they were made by the bear that he sought. His nose picked up the all too familiar rank odor of brown bear and he knew that he was very close. He felt the presence of death all around.

Quietly and stealthily, Sarber pushed on until he came to the foot of a windfall, a huge hemlock that had probably been uprooted by a windstorm. There he fixed his gaze on the leaning trunk and measured with his eyes the places where he would step should he need to gain elevation in a hurry.

Hosea was packing a .30-06 sporter rifle, loaded with 220-grain open point-expanding bullets, the kind to deliver a fatal dose of medicine in just such a situation. His rifle had an iron receiver sight and open aperture, which would allow quick use in close quarters.

Rain continued to fall and rain drops accumulated on the rifle barrel and stock. Hosea felt certain that the clock was ticking and that the bear was near. He stopped to evaluate the immediate surroundings. Wanting to be as prepared as possible when the time came, he purposely held the rifle with one hand while alternately reaching beneath his rain slicker to wipe water from each hand on his wool shirt.

Feeling the hair on his neck rise, Hosea broke his long practiced rule of carrying an un-chambered shell in his rifle.

He slowly, and as silently as possible, unbolted his .06, eased back on the bolt to activate a cartridge and fed it gently into the chamber. He closed the bolt with a near inaudible metallic *snick*.

Immediately the forest erupted in a trumpet-like rage-filled roar. The heart-stopping noise surrounded Hosea, seeming to come from everywhere and echoing throughout the timber, as if magnified from some giant speaker system. Those horrible sounds propelled Hosea up the leaning hemlock where he stopped only after reaching a height of fifteen feet.

Hosea had found his man-killer, and this brute meant business.

It was then that Hosea's apprehension was realized. The bear had been watching for him. No doubt, recalling its previous encounter with a man who sought its demise. With nostrils filled with man smell, it had been zeroing in on him. It probably remembered the dreadful click of metal against metal from the previous year, which ignited the beast into a fury of rage.

Finally detecting the source of the bellowing sounds, Hosea looked down into the undergrowth and saw the great beast looking for him. It champed its teeth and roared its rage, gyrating about and slavering from its mouth. In all his years in bear country he'd never seen a bear so agitated and determined to culminate an attack. But the bear could not locate the hated man—the action of Hosea's moving up the tree trunk had caused his scent to rise on the air currents, taking his scent from the bear.

Because it failed in its efforts to locate him, the bear's chuffing enunciation soon turned to an eager whining.

Within moments it stopped its thrashing leaps almost in mid-air and remained motionless. It had winded Hosea. Slowly it rose on hind legs and for fully ten seconds stared at its foe above. But it was too late for the bear to affect its rage on Hosea.

The man had taken advantage of his position, raised his rifle, taken careful aim and touched off a shot. With the resonating roar on the forest floor the bear sagged to the ground. The bullet blew up a vertebrate and killed instantly. The brute's reign upon earth was finished. The man-killer would harm no one or thing again.

Hosea waited a few moments to assure himself that the bear was incapacitated, then retraced his steps down the tree trunk to the ground. He edged up to the bear and prodded the animal in the back of the neck with the toe of his boot. Then Sarber grabbed an ear and pulled the head around to look for wounds. Near the shoulder was a long scar that may well have been the result of Thayer's bullet.

Hosea raised his rifle in the gathering twilight and fired three successive shots into the night sky, alerting his boat mate of his success. No doubt, Hosea was greatly relieved that he'd chosen the proper time to run up the tree. His woodland expertise paid off handsomely in his personal safety and in the demise of a hell-bent man-killer.

Source: *Bear Tales for the Ages*

Terrific Fishing

As he watched the water run off the floats of the bush plane and the aircraft vanish in the distance, the lone man savored a week's fishing on Wolverine Lake. Bill McGregor unrolled his bedroll and prepared a quick meal of canned stew and brown bread, eagerly anticipating morning.

At five he was up and sorting through his flies, looking for a tempting morsel for the rainbows or silver salmon that inhabited the waters. By eight he had caught and released two dozen 'bows, saving some for breakfast.

Each day Bill tempted the trout, and each day was equally rewarding, except there were no silvers. While engrossed in this sport, Bill continually experienced a nagging feeling that someone or something was watching him from the lakeside landscape. Bill sneaked peeks and even modified his fly casting style in an effort to get a glimpse of his surroundings, but he never saw anything out of the ordinary.

For a number of days Bill exulted in his activity...and wondered what wandered the shoreline. On his last day he resumed where he'd left of the night before, fishing from a small spit of land. Finally a silver struck. Exploding from the depth, it cart wheeled and tail walked. Bill's pole bent double as the coho fought. Fifteen minutes elapsed before the fish was within his grasp.

At that point the mystery of the past few days was solved. Thirty feet away, a brown bear emerged from the brush. It snorted, gaining Bill's attention. The man whirled to face the bear. The bear rose to peer down at the mere man.

What could he do? He was trapped on the spit. Sweat spread across his brow. He rapidly considered his options—should he swim out into the lake? Running was futile, and what about the silver?

Then an escape plan suddenly formulated in Bill's mind. He raised his hard-won fish ever so gently and in a fluid, slow motion tossed it off to one side of the beast. The bear shot the fisherman a hurried glance, then snapped up the bribe and leaped into the undergrowth.

Bill was astonished. That bear had just watched and waited for a silver until the right time came. A rainbow wasn't good enough. Bill hustled back to camp and spent some anxious moments during the night awaiting the return of his pilot. The next morning the pilot touched down onto the mirror-like waters of the lake and taxied up to Bill's camp. Unable to contain his curiosity, the pilot excitedly asked Bill if he'd caught any silvers: the fisherman replied, "Nope not a single one."

Source: *More Alaska Bear Tales*

Northern Lights

During the night Lane awakened and noticed a reddish glow through the windscreen. "Hmmm," he thought, "think I'll wake Gabrielle to show her." He gently ran his finger tips across her lips. She pursed and puckered her lips a couple of times to the tickling sensation. Lane suppressed laughter and continued. Lane cooed, "Wake up, Sleepy Head. Sleepy Head, wake up."

Finally Gabrielle rubbed her lips with her right hand. She opened her eyes and looked toward Lane. When her eyes adjusted to the dark, she realized that he was kneeling beside her. Somewhat concerned for being awakened in the middle of the night, Gabrielle questioned, "Lane, is something wrong?"

"I've got a surprise for you. It's an aurora alert."

"A what?"

"An aurora alert. My family and a few friends call each other to let them know when we see the northern lights. So they can enjoy them too. Sometimes we get calls at 1 in the morning."

Rubbing her eyes Gabrielle groaned, "What kind of joke are you pulling now, Lane?"

"No joke, Angel Eyes. Can you scoot out of your bag to your knees?" He placed his hands over her eyes and said, "Let me turn your head. When I say 'open,' I'll remove my hands and you'll be in for a thrill."

Turning her head toward the glow he said, "Open."

Gabrielle gasped, "Oh, Lane! They're beautiful. I've never seen anything like them."

Shades of red spread across the vast canopy of space. Pulsating fingers of colors, varying from red to florescent green, intensified in both breadth and brilliance as they blazed upward thousands of feet before trailing off in rainbow arcs, flowing like banners blowing in the breeze. Like a herd of wild-eyed horses, nostrils flaring and sides heaving, carrying men onto the battlefield in a galloping cavalry charge—guidons rattling, bugles blaring, guns spitting lead and sabers slashing—the bright rose fingers swept in waves above the naked snow...only to retreat, regroup then charge again...and again...and again.

Gabrielle gushed, "Oh, Lane. They're so incredibly beautiful."

"Yes, they are. Every time they're different. Those myriad fingers glide like a pianist's hands, frequently accompanied by a hissing, crackling sound. The fingers bend and dance back and forth over the keys of a baby grand, ever probing the purple-black of the keyboard sky."

For several minutes they gazed in awe with renewed appreciation for the raw, natural beauty around them. Then they crawled back into their sleeping bags and went to sleep.

Source: *Trapped*

"There's One!"

Anyone who's heard of the Old West range wars would likely be interested in the bear-cattle brouhaha on Kodiak Island in the mid-1960s. Jim Rearden apprised the public about it in his "Kodiak Bear Wars" piece in *Outdoor Life's* August 1964 edition. The problem revolved around the argument of protecting cattle, bears or both.

To quote Jim, "What is the solution? Can Kodiak Island, and other brown-bear ranges of Alaska, have both cattle and bears? If so, how is bear control to be handled? Which is more important in the long run to the economy and welfare of Alaska itself, and which will best serve the long-range public interests of the whole country?" (page 69)

One of the major complaints involved "strafing" grizzlies from the air with a "machine gun." It was a timely message that I do not wish to reiterate here. However I would like to share what it was like to be a "hired gun" for the game department, going aloft and gunning for brown bears from the cockpit of a Piper PA 18 rag wing aircraft. I thought it would be neat for more than a handful of people to see what it was actually like to hunt brown bears from the air in a Super Cub….

Two guys, one plane, one bear. The Cub driver points out the brownie to his tandem partner. In the same micro-second he jams the stick forward, dumps the nose over and kicks his right rudder. The chase is on. The pilot grasps the dangers. There's a left cross wind and he's got to pick his way among the trees and low knobs to get his gunner close enough for a crack at bruin.

Johnny knows the area. He's flown it often. We're on the deck. Bear's heading for that gully to hide. Got to watch that string of cottonwood trees along the creek. He reminds himself,

Keep an eye on that abrupt hill on the left in case the bear turns that way.

The shooter also knows the dangers of his task/in his lap. How many times have we done this? Mac knows he'll get only one shot. Don't hit the floats. Don't blow off the wing struts. Got to swing the Garand and aim behind him to compensate for our air speed. Jeez, he's bouncing like a top, humping across the grass and dodging around alder patches. Closer. Line up on the running bear. Just about there. Easy. Fire.

Two guys, one plane, one DEAD bear.

That's how it ended...for the bear and for the hunters. But that's not how it started. Since the Russians arrived on the Emerald Isle with their cattle just prior to 1800, there has been trouble in paradise between them and bruin. In the 1960s cattle ranching was confined to a specific area of the island. Less than a dozen ranchers had leases, raising around 2500 cattle, something like 150-200 head apiece.

Wondering what it must have been like to "strafe" a grizzly from a Super Cub, I contacted Johnny Morton and Ovid "Mac" McKinley to ask them how they did it.

Both men had actively hunted bears for the ranchers. The conventional method of hunting the stock killing bears in 1962 was on foot or by horseback.

Mac rode the Cordova from Seattle across the Gulf of Alaska to Kodiak in1946, during an era when a man's word was his bond. He could leave his door unlocked and borrow money from a local bar owner to send for his family in the States (which he did, enclosing $220 cash in an envelope—Mac told me, "Your credit was good till you proved otherwise."). Mac became a marshal, chief of police and fish hawk.

Johnny Morton, a WWII hero and experienced pilot decorated by General George Patton, was a crack rifleman. He'd been a registered guide and outfitter until statehood when he got out of the business because of the red tape. At that time eagles were considered nuisance birds and had a $2 bounty, so Johnny took advantage of that and commonly shot twenty or thirty a day. A 6-foot wing span was common but Mac tells of shooting one with an 8-foot wingspan. Since dolly varden and seals also had bounties, Johnny hunted them, continuing flying and working for the ranchers since he knew them well.

John told me, "Not one bear out of a hundred will attack cattle. But when he starts, he'll never quit. One bear only ate off the ears. If it was a cow, he'd eat the udder. We killed some big ones. One of them was over ten-foot, the other one was about 9-foot."

Mac said, "Those ranchers worked very hard ridding the range of problem bears. Hunting bears was not an everyday thing, but something done when one was spotted. We chased around on foot over there for several years off and on. John and I weren't hunting together at that time."

In May 1963, Morton and McKinley teamed up, Johnny flying and Mac shooting out the side of the plane. Mac commented on the history and the action aloft:

"The only way to efficiently locate bears was from the air. Even though bears were hunted from the ground, eventually the plane was the way to go. Over those few years there were less than a dozen shooters who killed bears from planes. Gilbert Jarvela, Dave Henley, Johnny and I hunted the most; Johnny and I shot the most because we could schedule hunting around our work. We eliminated bears for the ranchers. They were glad to get rid of the bears and we were glad to help them out.

"When the airplane come into being, it didn't come on real fast. We hunted from a Champ, J-3, Zentner's Cub and a 150 horse Super Cub that we chartered from Kodiak Airways. We started in a J-3 with no flaps. Below 68-70 miles per hour it shivered and shook, which didn't help your aim.

"The smaller aircraft burned 7, 8-gallons an hour if we were working it pretty hard. The Super Cub burned 9-gallons an hour. You could bet on it. The 150 horse Super Cub was the one best suited for shooting bears with a tail gunner—it was my favorite.

"Joe Zentner bought the 90-horse Cub and brought it up. As I recall it was damaged in the landing so it was laid up and couldn't get parts and pieces by just going down here and buying them. This slowed down the aerial hunt for quite some time. And when it was re-rigged and we got her back to flying again, we took the door off so I could shoot out of it. I roped myself and tied a rope on the rifle in case it fell out, then I could retrieve it in flight.

"We learned as we went along. To have complete trust in the other guy's ability, you need to come to that quickly. John was the pilot; I was the shooter.

"Disabling bears required practice. We did a lot of work. We used to throw out paper plates on a lake and make a run and shoot at those plates floating on the surface. You've got to get the angle, speed, lead the animal and so on. I got to where I could tear those plates up.

"Our work involved a lot of things. I don't know how you could tell a person how quick this all happened, that bird was popping along there at 80, 85-miles an hour and just flying stable. You're coming up on the target. I can see him. Get ready. Out the door she goes. He's coming up underneath the wing struts. I'm canted just a little bit so that when the time comes and he's right here, I'll touch the trigger. That ought to put it on him.

"I try to lead him, I've got to shoot under him.

"I've got to judge the speed so that when I see a bear at a certain place through the open door then touch one off. I can't think as fast as that animal's moving and by the time I think I should shoot, I should have shot quite a while before because the target is back there.

"After a while, with experience you learn to shoot automatically. You're not necessarily aiming through the sights or down the barrel, you're pointing and judging when to fire when the bear is in that sight picture through the door.

"You've got to avoid hitting the struts and the floats. If the plane didn't have any wing struts, I might get off 8 rounds going by that son of a gun with the semiautomatic Garand M-1. There are a whole lot of things hanging out on that airplane that's inconvenient. You have only a limited amount of space in which to shoot without hitting the plane and a limited time in which to shoot before you're passed the bear. If the bear's far enough away and I can get on him, I might get off as many as three shots before whatever happens. The fact that you could get three shots out there increases your chances of hitting the bear by three.

"You only get one shot. Bear running through alders and humps, trying to escape, and the cowboy up front is trying to keep the bear in sight and get close enough for a killing shot. The bear turns on a dime and reverses.

"Johnny climbs to slow down, turns quickly and keeps up with the chase.

"Never cut power. Keep it on so you can maneuver the plane. To stay in the vicinity, you've got to kill your speed. What better way than climbing? Make your turn up there, drop the nose so you don't stall, and you go right back down after the critter. You're still in the same area. Load the rifle, come right around, put her into a full slip and head her for the ground like a brick, flare out and you're on him again.

"One time Dave Henley got me within 20-feet of a bear which was going like hell. We'd catch up with him. You go right by him and have to turn. Dave was up in the air, around and back and right up on him again.

"Things happened so fast pumping across the grass.

"Sometimes I've shot over 60 rounds and never did a bit of good out the back window. We were high enough because of turbulent weather conditions that I could get off two or three shots. Whenever the weather got to the point where she was bumping us around a bit, all you're doing is wasting gas and ammo.

"There were good days and bad days. You didn't just go out

there and take them on like a flock of quail. You had to hunt for those rascals.

"Johnny and I lived side by side. Word of mouth was the way we got the information from the ranchers. Telephones were in town but they certainly weren't out on the ranches at that time. When word came in that a bear was spotted on a ranch, we got in the plane and went to try to find it.

"Bears don't stay in the same place, they may be here today and fifteen miles over there tomorrow. But when a bear's on his way, he probably wouldn't kill a cow. He might go right through a herd and straight on across, just keep going.

"On a typical day when it looked like we could get down amongst them, we'd go out early in the morning. Many guides will tell you that by 10 o'clock a bear heads for the brush or squats on top of a kill. You'll find a lot more of them if they're moving than if they're parked.

"We'd get in the old pickup and drive down to the plane. Gas was kept out at the hangar at the far end of the lake in town. We always got up on the plane and stuck a finger in that tank on each side to make sure we felt gasoline before we buzzed off the water. Because they weighed a fair amount, we didn't have a starter or a battery and it was a hand prop job.

"'Good' weather in Kodiak is generally rain with fog patches all through these little hills at that time of day. If it's a real good weather day, we've got other things to do.

"The radio was a little hand held thing about ten inches long. We carried it in a case. Even that wasn't a safe thing. If you hit the ground hard, it come flying out of there, might hit you, beat you up if it didn't just pulverize you. For the radio to be effective we would have to talk to somebody on the ground. Of course, where we were, there was no one on the ground.

"Most of our hunting was in the spring when the grass was first coming out. The cattle are close together; the sun hit the top of that hill first and you're probably going to find the critters up there where that fresh, green grass is. That's a rule of thumb.

Where you find the critters, everything's moving, that's when you'll find a lot of bears out and about.

"Any time we were flying, we were looking for bears. We were always prepared. I had some kind of a smoke pole sitting in the aircraft. You set her down the hard way, if you did live over it, the rifle would be a handy thing to have a means of discussion in case you were accosted by a bear.

"We flew high so we could see more country, scoot and scout to see if we could find anything. We tried the rivers first, worked the creeks where trails were packed in for centuries. It seemed to be a better place. It was always easiest to hunt the flats and avoid the hills, brush and trees. If they're moving, they'll be on those bear kills.

"You've got to be able to see anything before you know it's there. We'd go to these places and look. We could be-bop go around and go down these little canyons. We took most bears where there weren't many trees.

"If we couldn't see anything, we'd go back. We were very seldom out more than a couple of hours at the most.

"Sometimes you're lucky.

"We make a flyby and get down in there and look this bunch of cattle over.

"When we'd get this son of a gun in sight, we'd go after him. Being a rifleman, John knew what it took for me to hit that critter. He would do his level best to get me into a position where I'd have the rifle out that back window. He'd be coming up on this target and trying to stabilize that aircraft as much as possible.

"Give me half a chance and I'll try to take him out. Most of the time I was successful.

"The closer you get to him, the less time you've got to shoot him, but the bigger the target is. So you've got two or three ways of looking at this. If you get too far away and there's no possibility of hitting it, you see ground flying up all over the place, and you've got to come back again.

"If we got locked on to something, we'd make a pass at it. I had a short line on the semiautomatic .06 Garand so it wouldn't go sailing out the side of the plane. If all the movement yanked it out of my hand, anything could happen.

"An escaping brown bear could reverse direction in an instant but the plane had to pull up, keep from stalling, turn around and go back after it. If the pilot didn't know how to fly, you'd be a half mile away before you got turned around.

"Even though it wasn't the easiest target to hit, coming up on him and missing him was annoying. You just figure, 'What the heck did I do that for?' If there's a little burble in the aircraft when you touch her off, you're liable to be shooting out across the country...a little flip and that's all it takes to miss.

"We couldn't talk much in the plane. They're a noisy thing. I'd tap him on the shoulder and point, or give hand signals to slow down. We didn't need to talk. I'd just tap him, a little bit of signaling. We understood each other; we carried on a pretty good conversation.

"I'd signal 'going up' and up we went.

"Once I fired, Johnny pulled up so we didn't get so far away from the target. The best way to do that, of course, is to climb and stay right there in the vicinity. Once you fire at that rascal, if he's ever been shot at before, they get pretty cagey. They will run like a turkey down through there.

"John's flying and I'm trying to keep track of the bear. If I try to get John to turn back too tight, that's where you get into trouble. Moose hunter's stall, down she goes.

"All these darn actions get your blood pressure up.

"One time Johnny and I were on a bear and I fired a couple of rounds from my .375. We made a turn out over the water to come back around on the bear and his rudder jammed. While he climbed, I got to work pulling out floor boards. I found a casing from the .375 wedged into the cables, it was all crunched where he'd been jamming on it with his rudder pedal. Who would have ever thought a little slot in the floorboards would let a casing go through and jam the controls?

"I don't recall ever putting in a whole day in on it unless Johnny plunked the plane down on a beach and I took the rifle up after the bear. If we spotted a bear near a place to land, that was a common method to hunt. But a drop off hunter never knew what to expect with regards to the plane, whether the pilot would break it or not before the hunter and pilot saw each other again.

"One hunt it was bumpy under the clouds. Come up on Don Hirst's place over the pass to Salty Cove. We make a usual circle on the big flat ranch area. We flew out over the bay, didn't see anything and circled back towards the cabin. Came to another creek going toward Hightower's place. We saw a big son of a gun along the creek by the trees. John spotted him first, 'There's one down there!'

"We were at 1000 feet and it was running for the creek toward an opening. John dropped down and flew along and I popped him. I thought I got him. The bear got up and run into these trees. We made two passes on floats and couldn't land. We went to the bay a quarter mile away and touched down then taxied to the beach.

"I told John, 'You take care of the plane and I'll go up there and finish the rascal off.' I've got the .06 Garand. I'm on the cow trail going to where I thought the bear was. Rose bushes are thick with thorns as long as a hound's tooth. I'm ready to do battle, alert and looking everywhere for the bear.

"And here comes Zentner in his plane. He drops a note that flutters to the ground. I found out later from him that the note told me the bear got away. It turns out the note fell into the area where the wounded bear was. He couldn't see over the brush on all fours and stood up because he could hear me moving in on him.

"About then I heard the bear click his teeth. That son of a gun rose up and up and up, kept going up to the sky. He was huge. I've had bears stand up but never that close. I sewed him a row of button holes from his belly to his neck. I cut his head off; it weighed at least thirty pounds. I got back to the plane and John said, 'I see you got him.' I threw the head into the plane and we took off.

"We went up to Joe's and landed on the lake. Joe told us he knew where the bear was that got away from us. Then I took the head out of the plane and said, 'He didn't get away from us.'

"Wanting us to know there was more than one, he said, 'There's another one.'

"We discussed the bear that he'd dropped a note to tell us about. He asked me if I rode a horse and I told him, 'I'm not much of a horse rider.'

"John had to go refuel the plane.

"I told John we'd be on the hill by 3; it was 11 then. The horse I rode was named Jughead and was well named.

"We came over the rise at 2:30, still had a ways to go. We followed a cow trail—they were foot wide paths on every hill. Joe said, 'We're there. That bear's right in those alders,' and he points down hill. I'm going to tie this nag up and hopefully this bear will run uphill like most do.

"I walked down, wanting to stay in the open cause John's coming and was going to shoot the air up from the plane. He's got his son Reilly with him. He's no slouch. He leans out the door with his .44 magnum six-shooter to make noise. Boom! Boom! Boom!

"Here comes the bear. It come right across this field and I pumped 6 government issue slugs out and he didn't even slow down. The bear ran right up to Joe's horse—he's as big as the horse—and Joe tried to get his gun. Now it's coming right at me.

"Joe rode up the hill to be above the bear. He's 200 feet away and coming right at me. I shot twice. Hit him but it didn't even slow him down. He's getting closer. I charged a new clip and fired 6 rounds. I must have hit him in the front leg with the

6th one. He went down and was trying to get up. I had only 2 rounds left.

"I ran at him like a P-38 and shot him twice. The bear was full of holes but wouldn't go down.

"Then I waved John off and he took Reilly home and came back for me. He was at the lake when we got back.

"John had warned me to be careful and asked me why I charged the bear like a marine. He was in a box seat watching the event.

"Later Dave Henley came to the island. He was a World War II fighter pilot who flew P-51 Mustangs. Conversation eventually got around to combining the fighter pilot's skill with the ranchers' need to eliminate problem bears. The logical, if not, controversial solution was a 'fighter plane' to strafe the animals. They teamed up to develop a means of increasing the cattle's chances of surviving.

"Then it started to take root, that there was a better, safer way to go after bears...you didn't have to go out and kill yourself. Henley was the man. What he said, you paid attention to. If he said, 'Don't do that,' I'm smart enough to take his word for it. And with the guidance of Henley, a whole lot of us are still around here.

"I don't know of anyone in the group other than Dave Henley with the experience and know how to come up with the M-1 Garand mounted on the Super Cub. It was an effective one-man operation—there was usually only one guy in that airplane. Why carry another 200 pounds when you're going to be maneuvering?

"We mounted the rifle on the top of Zentner's 90 horse Super Cub on wheels. He paid for the fuel, perhaps some of the other ranchers helped out. I never heard that they did or didn't.

"The rifle was mounted on a tripod front and back. It was set up high because you've got a propeller to worry about out here. It shot above the prop about an inch. Your sight was on the screen, set dead on the target at 125 yards. Even at 200 yards you had only a 3-inch drop.

"The weapon was rigged so that the pilot could fire it from the cockpit like the old fighter planes. Attention was paid to the mechanism to allow room to facilitate operation. A button on the stick activated the trigger. Wiring ran up beneath the fabric on the side of the aircraft and through the greenhouse to a solenoid. The Garand emptied herself and threw out the clip.

"A sliding door in the greenhouse allowed the pilot to reload while in flight. When the last shell was fired, the pilot could reach with his right hand to the side-back of the seat and pull a full clip from the cloth pocket. He slid the skylight door open, pushed the end of that in the rifle, gave her a yank to pull the ejector back 4-5 inches (further than the cartridge) to pick up the load, threw it in, let her down and he had a rifle round in there. The Garand will take care of itself until you need to put in another clip.

"He put that clip in, charged the weapon and put the bird back on the critter.

"John was perfect. He had a long arm where he could reach up, open the slide, replace the clip. He was fast. I would have much rather have fired from the back end of the darn thing than to worry about that rifle.

"If you're shooting the Garand on a bear and you miss, you can see the mud fly, a tree fall, and you keep right on peppering and go right in there after him. Everything's happening so damn fast. Dave was telling us about the Mustang P-51. He was doing some low level flying and was getting about 450 and he felt like he was in a wedge. Of course, this doesn't feel like a wedge. Optically everything is out there and you can see it. It's stopped and you aren't. Depends on the plane and the pilot. A guy like Henley got on a bear and there was feathers. He did a lot of damage.

"The mounted rifle was the most effective means of getting a bear that they ever come up with. It's hard to pin down the exact number killed because many weren't counted, and we didn't make a lot of noise about taking them with the Garand.

"It was only a matter of time, however, before the bear-cattle volcano in Paradise erupted and overflowed."

Mac told me, "I didn't think we'd get by as far as we did. The main thing that we were concerned with, is just what happened. We got publicity."

Morton added, "If you have to kill a bear, you might as well do it with a P-51 or something instead of fooling around in the brush for a month and maybe not hit it. Jim Rearden didn't like the machine gun. He didn't have anything bad to say about Mac and me, just how good I could fly the airplane…that we did what he had to do and all that. The whole thing about that machine gun deal on the airplane, it was all legal. Fish and Game and FAA approved it. This was the only time the game department ever sanctioned shooting bears with an automatic weapon from the air over Kodiak.

"Once *Outdoor Life* got hold of it, and people read about it and had a screaming fit. The pressure from the guides shut it down. They used the Garand only a couple of months. After that Mac and me started shooting bears out of the side of a Super Cub."

And so a truly a historic period passed from Alaska, and, probably, from the planet.

Source: *Bear Tales for the Ages*

Keep Dreaming

Who's to say where it started? I thought I was a normal sixth grader, building plastic model airplanes. The Thunderbolt, P-51 Mustang, P-38, Corsair and other vintage War Birds graced my bedroom, either hanging from the ceiling and strafing the deck or parked on the airfield atop my dresser. I loved the Mustang's sleekness and the Corsair's graceful lines. The Thunderbolt roared power and death. While planes rumbled overhead, the *U.S.S. Missouri* battleship churned across another dresser.

Growing up in Walla Walla, Washington, and later frequenting eastern Washington, I marveled while watching crop dusters working the fields. Nearly every time I saw one, I pulled off the highway and watched the low flying acrobatic performances as the gutsy guys of the air sprayed field after field.

I learned about Pearl Harbor and saw movies as well as newsreels about WWII air combat. The Zero was the bad guy, as were the Messerschmitt and the Luftwaffe. The Corsair, P-38, Thunderbolt and the P-51and P-40 Mustangs were the good guys, as were the B-17, B-24 and B-29. My mom had riveted bulkheads for B-29's in Everett, Washington's Boeing plant. Wow, Rosey the Riveter under my own roof!

Later on I witnessed movie versions of the Sabre jet blasting Migs and I cheered for the American flyboys.

When I arrived in Alaska, my air affair expanded.

One of my first aviation experiences was in 1967 when my wife Pam and I drove from Palmer to Anchorage. A Piper flew over a few hundred feet east off the deck between Peters Creek and Chugiak, heading toward Anchorage. A mile beyond he banked right and completed a 180 degree turn, sank beneath the trees out of our vision in the highway corridor and plopped down onto the northbound lane. The plane bounced once or twice, the motionless propeller nearly clipping the trailer of a semi ahead of him, before coming to a complete stop in the middle of the highway.

I pulled onto the right shoulder and ran across the median to help the pilot move the plane from the highway. We tailed it off the east side of the shoulder and onto a little trail. About then a white car showed up carrying a state trooper who left to round up fuel. The pilot dumped it into his plane; the cop stopped traffic and the bird was airborne.

Early on I heard flying stories, one about Harley Buzby of Palmer and one about my friend Bob Tyler's buddy who had the misfortune of parking his plane on a final fatal flight in Merrill Pass. And, of course, our neighbor Tom Kucera had a PA-11.

Hoping Bob Reeves, founder of Reeve Aleutian Airways, would speak to my literature of the North students, I strolled into his office one day with Pam around 1967 to meet the old geezer of glacier and mudflat fame. I thought she was going to run away with him (his patch covered eye and all) in her zeal for his historic aura.

In 1968 I flew for the first time in a small aircraft. While working for the Alaska Department of Fish & Game I left Nushagak Bay at Dillingham with Jay Stovall, hauling a load of lumber secured to his Cessna's floats. We flew to Fish and Game's Igushik River camp at the outlet of Amanka Lake.

Before leaving Dillingham I heard about a local school teacher who flew a plane that moved so slowly you had to sight over a post to see if it was moving. I believe his plane was a Taylorcraft. The pilot beach combed the coastline from aloft. One day he flew out to the Round Islands, landing on floats at low tide, seeking walrus ivory. The tide came in, lifted his plane off its tie down rock and drifted it out into the ocean a quarter to half mile. The wind shifted and blew the plane back to the island where he promptly boarded and blasted off for the mainland.

At the completion of my Fish and Game work in 1968, a summer temporary flew Pam and me in his PA 12 out to Cape

Constantine where we planned to beach comb. Pam told the pilot she'd always wanted to land on sand to see what it was like. He responded, "So have I." Although Pam was eight months pregnant with our first child, we spent the day hiking miles up the beach while stockpiling hundreds of glass floats and awaiting the pilot's return. On his third attempt that afternoon he touched down and told us because of the strong cross winds, he couldn't taxi which curtailed the retrieval of our treasures.

During my first two years in Alaska I flew with the Dimond wrestling team on a DC-3 to Kenai to wrestle and once in a Connie to Homer with West High School for a tri-meet.

A few years later my friend Ralph Ertz invited me to fly in his PA-12 numerous times— landing on the Yentna River, on the rocky reaches of the Chitina River in the Wrangell-St. Elias Mountains and touching down on the tundra of the Mulchatna Hills to hunt caribou. I fell in love with the idea of piloting a plane some day.

In 1992 we went to Oregon and our daughter Jill gave me a Christmas present, one hour's flight from Mac Air in McMinnville. I checked on the flight, learned ground school included flight, paid an additional $180 and enrolled in the first ground school they ever offered. During that time I watched the Spruce Goose make its final journey on flatbed trailers in preparation for its new home at Evergreen Aviation near Mac Air. I passed the pilot's exam and returned to Anchorage.

I called my friend Charley Vandergaw and asked him for a pilot training recommendation, signed up with Arctic Flyers— Herman, Heidi and Rick Reuss— and soloed in November 1994. Wanting to be around planes and hoping I could earn enough money to purchase one, I began an aircraft snow removal project.

About 1997 I told a friend that I wanted a plane. When he asked me if I had the money, I said no. Then he asked me why I bothered looking. I told him that you had to have a dream. I've learned so much about small planes since then and I'm glad I dreamed and researched before I had the money.

The thought of owning my own plane persisted as I drove one day to visit Atlee Dodge, respected and notable Piper modification expert. My friend John Graybill added fuel to the fire when he invited me to fly in his Piper Super Cub from his Peters Creek strip.

The experiences and activities achieved with a plane are those I could never acquire without one:

to fly and experience the un-tethered bonds of earth;

to land on a gravel bar to fish, hunt or explore;

to plop down in a high mountain valley or on a plateau to hunt sheep or pick berries;

to beach comb Prince William Sound or Montague Island.

In 2003 it turned out that one man's loss was my gain. We purchased an insurance wreck, a 1956 Piper Super Cub. After three years of rebuilding it, I've had the immeasurable pleasure of flying the beautiful canary yellow L 21 on 31-inch Alaska Bush Wheels with appropriate cowgirl nose art of her namesake, *Tundra Bunny*, my wife Pam.

Source: *Alaska Air Tales*

When Ice Fishing Got Hot

Flames poured from the shack. Steve Frith awakened and yelled at his buddy then fled out the door, away from the flaming building and into the night. They were on an ice fishing trip which turned nasty.

On December 12, 1990, the two Fairbanks buddies left their homes for an 80-mile trip to Quartz Lake. Steve Frith, 23-year-old university student, and Tom Villa, 35-year-old family man, looked forward to spending the night and fishing for rainbow trout and salmon.

The two swimming instructors reached the lake, pulled Tom's pickup up to the ice fishing shack and carried their gear into the empty 8x8-foot building where they would spend the night.

Villa caught three fish before the men decided to stop fishing for the night. They set up their propane stove and went to bed.

During the night, Frith awoke to fire in the shack. He said, "I woke up and there was flame everywhere. It spewed like a blowtorch." 1

He yelled to alert Tom. Then he fled the flaming building.

Villa said, "I did not think of being burned. I was thinking about all the equipment we had in the shack or leaning against the shack. That's what I was thinking, 'What are we going to do for warmth?'" 1

Once clear of the building, they rolled in the snow to put out the fire that burned their clothes.

Neither man knew what caused the 20-pound propane bottle to explode, but they theorize that it was too close to the heat. Evidently the tank's pressure valve released gas which eventually ignited.

The men were not fully aware of the tissue damage they'd

suffered. Villa had second- and third-degree burns on 60 percent of his body, including his chest, waist and arms. Frith was burned on 50 percent of his body including his face, back, arms and right leg.

Standing in the snow clad only in their underwear, the buddies knew they needed to find clothes and shelter to increase their chances of survival.

The most sensible solution for their problem was to seek refuge in Villa's vehicle.

Fortunately he had not locked it with his key which burned up in the conflagration. Enduring indescribable pain from their burns and knowing they faced the possibility of freezing to death, they climbed into the truck. They found a sweat suit. Villa put on the pants and Frith wore the shirt.

Without Villa's keys they couldn't start the engine. Their time in the unheated truck was frigid. He said, "We kind of assessed the situation and it looked pretty bleak. We decided that we wanted to live." 1

The pain of the burned skin was compounded by the freezing temperatures. The men lay on the truck seat agonizing the night away. Every bump or touch irritated the skin. Hours dragged away.

They could only hope that help would arrive. They continued to reassure each other of their desire to live. Villa continued to coach himself to persevere, "I want to live. I want to live. I want to live. I have a wife and two children. I want to live." 1

Villa and Frith clutched each other for warmth. Their shivering encouraged them because they knew that it was a sign that their bodies were automatically trying to keep warm. They knew that once they stopped shivering, they were in trouble from serious hypothermia, where the body's core temperature drops because the body isn't producing enough heat to keep warm. Hypothermia untreated causes death.

They kept hoping for the dawn. Hoping for someone to come to their aid. For four hours they waited, clinging to hope.

Late that morning Dick McManus of North Pole and a friend arrived at the lake to fish. When they drove into the fishing area, they saw Villa's truck parked in the roadway. The two men were somewhat puzzled, thinking the truck had been abandoned. But then Villa opened the door, stuck his head out and screamed for help.

McManus was startled by the sight of the men. He said later, "I didn't think they were dying, but boy, I knew they were in pain. They begged us not to leave, but there was nothing I could do for them." 1

Rescue required McManus' departure to find a phone. The nearest one was about ten miles away at the general store. McManus reached it and called officials. Medics arrived and transported the burned buddies to Fort Greeley.

Villa and Frith were near death. In addition to their burns the men suffered frostbite and hypothermia.

From Fort Greeley a Lear jet zipped them to Anchorage's Providence Hospital.

Recovering from burns in separate rooms at Providence Hospital both men agreed that they would have died had it not been for the constant encouragement that each provided the other. "If either one of us had given up, lost consciousness or panicked, neither would have made it," said Frith. 1

Villa spent two months at Anchorage's burn unit with second-degree burns over 60 percent of his body. Surgeons operated four times to replace flesh lost from his feet, arms and hands.

Both men wear pressure suits which are designed to protect the tender young flesh of burn victims. Frith said, "It's like wearing Spandex over your whole body." 2 The material is uncomfortable and itchy. However it helps minimize scarring. They expected to wear the suits at least a year.

A year later, the men say they are doing well, thanks to family, friends and a strong will to live.

Villa admitted that even though he knew hundreds of kids

from his swimming instruction days, he was surprised at how many people remembered him and chose to assist in his medical bills (he and his family, including wife Kimberly, and their two infant children were uninsured).

He stated later that, "For three weeks I didn't know what was going on, and for another three (weeks) I didn't know much. When I was able to read the mail it was just amazing." 2

He admits that both mentally and physically, there is much to cope with, "I was talking with my wife about it and crying on her shoulder. I think it's important to talk about it.

"My body looks pretty trashed, my arms, my chest. Getting used to this new body is a little bit different." 2

However he proudly admits, "We are not burn victims, we are burn survivors. Steve and I went out to have a good time. We had an accident...My doctor says you don't get burned twice." 1

A year after their ice fishing shanty caught fire and burned them badly, Steve Frith and Tom Villa have returned to life. However life will never be the same for them.

Frith said that the choice to live was easy, "You either bounce back or you don't, and given that choice, it was pretty cut-and-dried for me." 2

Frith lost his left foot which was replaced with an artificial one. He has adjusted to it and gets around well. He admits that his burned hands are more of a problem. He said, "A lot of people said I'd never use them again. I wouldn't accept that." 2

He discontinued going to physical therapy a month after he started in Anchorage. He types 50 words a minute. He hopes to go fishing again as soon as he sheds his pressure suit.

Frith was a University of Alaska Fairbanks student who wrote for the campus alternative newspaper. He did not experience the financial problems that Villa had with his medical coverage.

Both men chronicled their year of recovery by writing about

it. Frith hopes someday his account will be published.

Villa busies himself these days watching the children, cleaning the house and chopping wood. Although he's not 100% he says, "I just think it's important to look back at where you started so you know how far you've come."

Source: *Swallowed Alive*

Larry Kaniut

Ella May

When four-year-old little Ella May Lindberg left her Sitka house alone July 1921, it was with one thought—blueberry pie. She told her mother if she would bake a pie, Ella would get the berries. Ella wanted a surprise blueberry pie for her papa. She knew about a prize patch of berries where she could fill her pail. Ella had not given any thought to the large bears that roamed the woods near her Baranof Island home. She was really too young to understand anything about bears.

Almost two hours after Ella had left the house, her father Hans, superintendent of the U.S. Horticultural station at Sitka, arrived and queried about "Baby." He was shocked to learn she had last been seen walking with pail in hand toward the woods. He immediately sprang into action, meeting at the blacksmith shop with all available men, distributing his two 12-guage shotguns and .22 rifle. He carried his .30-40 rifle himself. The men spread out in a half-circle and slowly began combing the woods. They were to fire three shots if anyone found Ella May.

A half-hour later Ella's father heard three shots and rushed toward the sound. One of his companions confessed that they hadn't found Ella, but they'd discovered some large fresh bear tracks. In a frenzy Ella's father plunged ahead of the others into the dense brush, hoping against the inevitable. He tried to force all negative thoughts from his mind—she could be mangled by a savage bear, she could be partially consumed, she may never he found. He was overcome by a father's grief for his little one.

He called frantically to Ella, reassuring her that he was near, coming to her aid. Shortly he stumbled from the brush tangle almost bypassing the still, small form lying on the ground.

It was Ella May. She lay in a patch of blueberries, chubby little body peacefully sleeping, with her empty berry pail nearby.

He fired three signal shots and turned to his daughter who was awakened by the commotion. Her first words were, "Where are my berries, Papa? I had a whole pail full of blueberries." Completely surrounding the berry patch were large bear tracks evidencing where Ella's berries had gone.

Source: *Alaska Bear Tales*

Dear Diary

Crap happens. We can either let it define us or use it to better ourselves. It's always easy to blame those around us. It takes a lot of inner strength to accept accountability for what we have done in certain situations, and move forward with a happy heart. Sure, another party may have been a part in some crappy situation, but it's our choice not to dwell on that. We are all human. We all make mistakes. We all have choices. It's that choice that we are going to move forward, enjoy the short life we are given, and make the most of every day. God didn't put us on this earth to be miserable. He gave each of us a passion and a reason to live, and it's up to us to strive for both.

Source: *The B.G.*

One or Fourteen

When an aircraft loses flying speed at low altitude, things happen quickly. Do you have time to recover? Can you recover? Where's the safest place to put down? When I'm at the controls of our plane, I'm always looking for a place to set down if necessary, preferably on the closest thing that resembles a runway—a gravel bar, field or clearing in the trees. I've had a few emergencies requiring a "runway" and when I needed one, I found it.

Such an emergency developed in 1999 on the Yukon River by a commercial pilot who was running mail and cargo for Larry's Flying Service out of Fairbanks. At the time it was a bit of a mystery but as the details became clear, the mystery was solved.

Al Smay, my friend and former student-athlete, invited me to accompany him and eleven men on a construction project. The plan was to fly from Fairbanks, Alaska, to Tanana, de-plane and travel downriver in a long skiff to the Kokrines Hills Bible Camp about fifteen miles east of Ruby. We would spend a few days building a bathhouse at the camp which was populated by summer youth campers studying God's word. In addition to Al Smay some of the volunteers included Bob Arnold, Ernie Byers, his son Brent, Noel Heaton, Steve Machida, Art Mathias, Allan Sanders, Lars Tulip and Bob Wheeler. Most of the men attended Al's Anchorage Grace Church.

Somewhere along the way plans changed. Instead of driving to Fairbanks we would drive to Nenana and fly out of there. Al and four of us left Anchorage Thursday, June 10, 1999, and drove to Bob and Dee Eldridge's home to spend the night. Bob, the founding executive director of the Voice of Christ radio ministry broadcasting from Nenana, had agreed to fly us to Tanana. The next morning we drove to Bob's Piper Cherokee and lifted off to the west, destination Tanana, about a hundred air miles distant.

Since I had a pilot's license, the guys suggested I ride shotgun in the front seat next to Eldridge. On our approach ten miles out of Tanana, I replaced my headset and heard a lady's voice, "...He clipped some trees... look for debris in the river."

A plane was down but I missed the earlier part of the transmission and didn't know the locale of the incident. However it sounded pretty serious.

We landed a few minutes later and while awaiting our boat transport, we discovered that the missing plane had departed Tanana about an hour earlier, heading west. It was a twin engine Navajo PA-31 piloted by Richard Fey, a 35-year-old U.S. Air Force veteran with over 3,200 hours flying experience. He'd worked for Larry's Flying service three and a half years.

President Larry Chenaille of Larry's Flying Service described Fey as a "very experienced pilot" and indicated "We haven't had any information. We're still waiting to hear something from the FAA."

Fey had departed Tanana's Ralph M. Calhoun Memorial Airport's runway two-four at 7:18 a.m. en route to Galena to deliver cargo. He turned to follow the Yukon. The agent for the operator reported normal sounding engines at takeoff from the 4,400-foot by 150-foot gravel strip. But within five minutes of departing the pilot radioed on CTAF that he was having a problem with the airplane, stating he might have to ditch.

About fifteen seconds later Fey reported being over the river, clipping trees and attempting to return to the airport.

Moments later he radioed that he was going down.

Later the agent said within five minutes of the Navajo's departure he had heard a loud noise from the river area followed by a loud bang, screeching noise and then silence.

My co-workers and I sat on the river bank for two hours watching search and rescue efforts downriver a mile and a half away. Locals operated skiffs in the river, a military chopper clattered and a state trooper chopper hovered, blasting dust into the sky where a huge, slow C-130 wallowed in lazy circles overhead.

The crash site was Long Island. Several large cottonwoods 200 feet south of the shoreline had their tops clipped 45-feet above the ground. Broken limbs and portions of the aircraft covered the ground on a magnetic heading of three-three-zero.

Rescuers were able to approximate the location of the plane when they discovered the debris along the river bank. Putting the puzzle together, it appeared the plane cart-wheeled after it struck the cottonwoods, hit the bank and its momentum carried it into the river.

When our transportation arrived, our crew left for Kokrines Hills. Nine boarded the skiff and three climbed aboard Art Mathias' float plane while most Tanana townspeople continued in the rescue effort, either at the scene or in the background. Some volunteers worked on the barge with grappling hooks and ropes, dragging the bottom. Others brought drinks for the rescuers. They worked with the Army's 68th Medical Detachment, the Alaska Air National Guard's 210th Air Rescue Squadron and the Alaska State Troopers.

The Troopers called for a river barge and a team of commercial Anchorage divers. River current disallowed recovery even with the use of a large net.

Rescuers met to discuss other options and equipment for accomplishing their task. They thought they could use a fish finder to get an idea of the bottom of the river and to ascertain the plane's exact location.

Although State Trooper divers did not enter the water which was considered too hazardous because of the river's current, commercial divers arrived from Anchorage and went down into the river on June 12. The strong river current hampered their efforts in the murky, brown water that permitted 4-inches of visibility at best. However a diver eventually identified the wreckage. Rescuers struggled to recover it in 25-feet of swift water on the south bank, about 30 yards from shore.

They placed a buoy on the largest section. A nearby barge with a crane from the Yutana Barge Line was called to lift the wreckage, but was ineffective because it was not equipped for the purpose of lifting planes from the river. Ultimately a steel cable was wrapped around the fuselage and it was dragged to shallow water where a diver recovered the body of Richard Fey.

A couple of hours later the fuselage with the right wing and engine was dragged partially onto shore.

In the interim my co-workers and I completed the bathhouse, loaded up on the river Monday morning and motored toward Tanana. Just below town we spotted the fuselage of Piper Navajo N41078 lying on the south bank of the river twenty yards distant. It was a sinister sight. Silence fell over the crew as we witnessed what looked like a large, white cigar, missing a third of the front. So sad.

The National Transportation and Safety Board report indicated: "About 7:23 AM, June 11, 1999, Piper PA-31-350 N41078 struck trees and cart-wheeled into the Yukon River southwest of Tanana, Alaska a mile from the end of runway 2-4. Having delivered mail in Tanana the pilot was en route to Galena with 1,236 pounds of cargo. The pilot had acquired 3,226.7 hours total time; 861.2 in make and model (611.2 within the previous 12 months in make and model plane; 51.2 in the previous month—5.3 the previous 24 hours). The pilot was the sole passenger and the accident proved fatal for him. The probable cause of the crash was undetermined."

The bad news is that Richard Fey did not survive the crash. His family, friends and community were left with brokenness and grief.

The good news is that thirteen other men were scheduled to be on that flight. But somewhere along the way plans changed… the bathhouse builders were not aboard Navajo N41078.

Source: *Alaska Air Tales*

Lars Monsen

As I sat signing books in the summer of 1997 at Barnes & Noble in Anchorage, a stalwart, blonde Viking stood nearby off to the right of a line of people. I saw him out of the corner of my right eye. Unable to give him my attention while addressing those in line, I completed our visiting-signing then turned to him.

I asked, "May I help you?"

He stepped somewhat rigidly forward, bent at the waist and asked in his Norwegian voice, "Do you accept gifts?"

Taken aback by his question in light of previous signings, my response was, "Well, it would be a first. People don't usually give me gifts at signings."

He then handed me a rolled up 8x10-inch glossy picture of him shouldering a shotgun and a brown bear closing on his dog Toini. I was impressed and told him it was a nice picture. He said he didn't have to shoot the bear. Then he handed me a book, a very nice coffee table book of pictures and text...relating his walk across Alaska. I jokingly said, "Oh, thanks. You give me a beautiful book of pictures and text which I can't read because they're in Norwegian!"

Part of his inscription to me reads:

"Anchorage July 31st, '97...Your book *Alaska Bear Tales* scared the s—t out of my girlfriend, I loved it. Thanks for the inspiration, and do continue writing books. If you ever come to Norway, and need help in any way, contact me!

Best wishes from Lars Monsen."

We laughed and talked. His desire was to get his books translated into English. Over the intervening years we kept in touch and became friends.

Lars is an incredible individual who loves the outdoors. You will discover a great deal about him as you read his summarization of his Alaska bear experience from having travelled solo or with a partner over vast areas of the state.

He provides great advice on how to co-exist with our ursine neighbors. I find it incredible that in all his miles and months in Alaska's wilderness that he has NEVER fired AT a bear.

Enjoy reading about a modern day Viking!

Letter from Lars:

Trout Lake, some 120 air kilometers E-SE of Inuvik, Northwest Territories, Canada, July 28th 2000

Dear Larry!

How are you? I hope all of you are doing fine. You're probably busy writing, and fall is a good time to do so, don't you agree? At the time being I am spending some 20 days by this 60 kilometer shoreline lake in the midst of nowhere, or actually, where the small Kugaluk River starts its way northwards. My days are highly leisurely, I have one base camp (tarp) and canoe around for trips up to 10 days or just stay here, mostly fishing, writing and exercising the dogs. No bears (!), or moose or caribou, but one wolf very close (it was curious, ran away, young one) and another one distant. Fishing for lake trout is excellent, I catch some 10 kgs every day (rod), enough to feed myself and the dogs.

Anyway, I have written 20 pages for you, all bear stuff from my expeditions. I hope you like it. Feel free to use it in your coming book "What's Bruin?", but don't feel obliged to use it. I do have slides if you need that, and also, if you have questions, I'll be glad to answer them.

I'll mail this letter in the beginning of Sept., and I'll probably be in civilisation for a couple of weeks, camp around Inuvik, to do some work for my sponsor. I have one hour's access to the

Internet and email every day, at the library. We can communicate then, if you have received the letter. I'll get in touch with you, and we'll figure it out!

I don't know where I am going to spend Sept-Oct-Nov, it may be here, or maybe up in the Yukon Mountains. I'll probably be back in civilisation in Nov/Dec., when I start up again from Tsiigehtchic (Arctic Red River) with dogsled and all. We can communicate more then, and as I go between Fort Good Hope, Norman Wells, Fort Franklin, etc.

Take care, Larry, and keep on with the good work!

All the best from Lars

BACKGROUND

Born in Oslo, Norway, 1963

Became a teacher (elementary school) in 1988, but quit after two years to do what I love the most and know the most—spend time in the wild woods and mountains.

Today I have spent 2700 nights plus in the open, average is 200 nights a year. More than half is above the Arctic Circle in winter time (Nov-April).

My father taught me to love and respect nature, he let me spend the first night alone in the woods as a 9-year-old, I "slept" under the open sky. Had a terrible night, seeing the axe killer as ever. Wanted more and was allowed to.

Spent every night possible out in the woods during my school years, one year 51 weekends in a row, normally around 40. Lived for weeks and twice months in the woods while attending high school and teachers training college.

All 26 in a row summers (8 weeks) spent in the mountainous terrain south of Bodo (above the Arctic Circle) where my mother was born. The cabin they lived in is my base today, no road leads there, either boat across the fiord or 2.5 hours walk over the wild mountains. Ptarmigan, brook trout, sea trout, (silver) salmon (up to 30 pounds normal), reindeer, wolverine, lynx, rabbits, foxes and lots of eagles in the nature up there. The weather in these coastal mountains can be as fierce as anywhere, and taught me always to be cautious and prepared.

Didn't have much money, learned to use whatever available. Got my first real hiking boots as a 23-year-old, but still used cheap cotton clothes for a few years. After the first long expedition, 365 days and 2542-plus kilometers hike along the Norwegian borderline to Soviet, Finland and Sweden (1989-90), people got to know me because I started writing articles often. This was in 1989. Since then I have more or less been sponsored on all gear, and today I can choose what to wear, what brand to use. This "business angle" can be the other side of the coin, outdoor life is big money today, so I always try to focus on what's really important: the basic skills of surviving all conditions.

I've always wanted to explore new things, and if people say something isn't possible, I get especially interested. Everything is possible with proper preparation respect.

I've been weather bound in snow storms and fog at least 200 nights, up to 9 days (the wind blew me off my feet).

I've survived solely on dog food for a week four times, both in summer while hiking 10 hours a day with a 70 pound pack in the bush (north Finland) and while lying still in a tent in 40 below in December. The latter was perhaps hardest, nothing happened, left with my longing thought for food. You can live on dog food, but with constant headache and a slow stomach maybe a month.

I've lived four winter months in the mountains, half above tree line without a tent, but with a tarp 2x3 meters and a good shovel. Dug a lot of snow caves.

I know physical pain. With experience and will power you can learn to walk two more hours after the "knives start hunting you" (feels like walking on knives) in the end of a day's hike. Pure muscle power is important to a degree, but what really decides survival or not is your mind, your attitude, your ability to always look for possibilities, keep up the good spirit.

To become fearless (not respectless!) you must learn to sense your own fear, your own limits. I deliberately hiked through the woods when 13-14-years-old in totally black October nights to feel what that was like. I crossed rivers in the dark (not swimming much!), felt the bottom with my feet, got soaking wet, dried off by the fire.

In spring time I often don't bring a sleeping bag, only a thick wool sweater, matches and fishing gear, plus salt, bread and coffee. You learn to appreciate the small things.

Skill hour 1 is orienteering. Hour 2 is making a fire under all conditions (one match only, no artificial help). I've lived for months in the mountains above tree line without a stove.

After the 1995 crossing of Alaska (see www.larsmonsen.net for more details on expeditions) I fell in love with one animal in particular: the brown bear. It has it all. Strength, beauty, total control of the environment (boss!), it demands respect, it rules and there's a lot of mystery. So I decided to get more experience, and do it all the way, really thorough. Why not cross all the three areas with the highest brown bear (grizzly, same animal to me because they wander from the inland to the coast and back again) density in the world: canoe through Katmai, walk across Kodiak and Admiralty! Get right in there, into the beast's living room, on its premises as a humble guest passing through. (I had never been to any of the places before, but I hadn't been to Alaska or Canada before '95). Would it be possible to live with a tent, sleeping bag and fishing rod in the thickest of bear country without any dramatic episodes? Without having to shoot at a bear? How close would I come? What could happen in the alders in the middle of July on Kodiak, was obvious, but can one crawl through there on one's knees in the bear trails, and get away with it? Would the bears come to my tent at night? Were there differences in their behavior in Katmai, Kodiak and Admiralty?

General: Katmai bears were habituated and were not afraid

or shy of humans, the Kodiaks and Admiralty brownies were, probably because they are being hunted and/or aren't used to humans around. I have no reason to say one was more aggressive—they would try to avoid us. Always exceptions though!

All these questions burned inside me. I had to find out. The fact that no one had heard about anyone crossing either Kodiak or Admiralty on foot made the project even more exciting. With proper preparation and lots of respect it would be possible! If you are a macho guy out there, you won't last long. I knew from the start that everything I did had to be done out of respect for the bears during the daily hikes and in camp.

Source: *What's Bruin?*

Solo Trek

Plagued by hordes of flying insects, distraught with the loss of her boyfriend and near panic with the prospects of her survival, Lydia Marie Barragan plodded on. The exhilaration she'd felt a month previous vanished in light of her predicament. What should have been a pleasant sojourn in the wilds of Canada, turned into a survival trek which would try her very being, physically, emotionally and spiritually.

In a surreal world she sat upon the beach, immobile. Shock reigned as she gazed across the lake at the haze surrounding the forest fire. Thoughts came slowly, almost lethargically to her. How could this have happened? My life has ended. And even if it hasn't, my life will never be the same.

Through the haze of the growing smoke cloud she saw the arctic sun, a red-orange orb. So close but yet so far. It shone almost as a leering face in the void. Laughing at her predicament. Her sole companion, it tortured her.

The sun had the face of a menacing gargoyle, threatening her very life... challenging her to either suck it up and survive or surrender to the environment and die.

But paradoxically, the sun also provided heat and light. Lydia could either capitalize on those aspects and seek sustenance in her journey or accept the tragic odds of her solo situation.

She chose to live.

Lydia Marie Barragan, 24, and Jean-Jecques LeFranc, 28, of Montpellier, France, planned to spend a year studying caribou seventy-five miles north of the Arctic Circle. They'd spent time canoeing the arctic two years previous and had some wilderness survival training and skills. They had established their campsite

75 miles from the town of Colville Lake in the Northwest Territories of Canada. Their camp at Lake 766, so named on the Canadian maps, was an isolated 8-mile-long body of water two miles wide.

The couple had not left word with Canadian authorities of their plans nor their proposed whereabouts. Any tragedy they faced would be endured by them alone.

As midnight July 14, 1987, approached, the sun hung slightly above the horizon while the angry skies flashed fingers of lightning. Thunder filled the air as a powerful electric storm raged.

Before long a forest fire flamed to life and scoured the earth, hungering for fuel.

At first because the wind blew the flames in the opposite direction, the fire did not concern them. However when they awoke the next morning, they discovered that there had been a shift in the wind direction overnight. A growing swath of fire marched unchecked and steadily toward their campsite.

They were faced with the universal question of what to do in their deteriorating situation. An experienced outdoorsman, Jean-Jacques outlined an evacuation plan. Their only means of escape lay across the lake and they packed their food and gear into their canoe for transfer to a site on the far shore. They hoped to save as much of their equipment and food as possible in order to salvage their project.

In order to survive any emergency the key was to remain calm, and to have a controlled attitude. Should the fire threaten them, they would rely on their experience, their map, compass and knife. Hopefully they would encounter no animal which could pose danger, such as a bear, wolf or cantankerous moose.

Moving camp required two trips. Lydia explained, "It took 45 minutes to one hour to make the first crossing with our clothes and sleeping bags and some equipment." By 1 p.m. they had completed their first trip, ferrying their tent, clothes, sled and snowshoes where they cached them on the south shore.

They returned to camp the second time to retrieve sleeping bags, a knife, photographic equipment and food.

Having loaded the canoe, they launched out into the lake, observing smoke filling the air. They stroked onward assuming all would be well on the other side. A strong wind gust sprang up, sweeping over the lake without warning. Waves pummeled the 16-foot canoe and the couple paddled frantically to stay afloat and to keep from rolling the light water craft. They'd reached the halfway point when a large swell overtook them and tipped the canoe onto its side. Instantly it filled with water.

The slightly built physical education teacher and biology student Lydia Barragan, said, "We were moving our belongings three kilometers (two miles) across the lake to escape the fire when the wind picked up, the canoe was swamped and it capsized."

They tried unsuccessfully to right the canoe in the wave tossed water. Each time they turned the craft over, it instantly capsized. Because they were being carried toward the widest part of the lake, the couple chose to abandon the canoe and swim for shore. They were a half mile from the beach and Jean-Jacques felt it was their best hope for surviving.

He shouted to Lydia, "Swim!"

Frigid water met their effort, smashing into their faces and washing into their mouths, seriously affecting their breathing. Meanwhile the acrid air and falling ash from the fire bombarded them. Lydia experienced stabbing pains in her lungs and sides. Coupled with the water's numbing cold, a euphoric-like hypothermia swathed her pain and enabled her to struggle on, one stroke at a time. Got to keep my mouth clear of the water to breathe. She could not escape the thought that she was drowning.

Instinct took over. She rolled into a floating position and stroked numbly with short strokes. She kept reminding herself, stay in control. Don't panic.

She swam ahead of Jean-Jacques. "We swam together for

45 minutes. He got very cold. He grew tired before I did. I tried to pull him along but could not."

With the beach still some distance away, Jean-Jacques struggled, thrashing behind her in a wild fashion, gagging and sputtering. His efforts failed him.

Lydia swam to his side, reached her arm around his neck and stroked backwards. She could not hold his limp body. Again, with numbness embracing her she attempted to support him and to swim. Her efforts were in vain.

Le Franc drowned.

Lydia summoned her strength and energy and stroked onward toward the beach.

She swam out of the frigid water, effectively beaching herself on the pebbles of the shore. Exhausted and cold, she could not think. She lay sprawled face down on the gravel trying to recall her final moments and wondering. Gradually reality returned. How did I get here? Am I alive? At length she sat up and coughed water from her lungs. That was when she remembered where she was. And she remembered Jean-Jacques. She looked out onto the wind tossed waves of the lake but no one was there. She involuntarily shouted, "Jean-Jacques!" He was gone.

Dejected, alone and crushed by his loss, she said, "I wanted to go back into the lake and join him. I wasn't scared. I was sad to be alive."

Shivering, she awakened the next morning at six. As she rose unsteadily to her feet, she was dizzy from hunger. She considered her chances of surviving without food and the likelihood of overcoming an encounter with a bear or wolf. She clung to the memories of her boyfriend, allowing his spirit and his love of adventure and life to sustain her.

After facing her abysmal situation and resolving to live, Lydia set out for Our Lady of the Snows Mission which lay on the far side of Colville Lake, ninety miles south. Tundra punctuated with swamps and dense forest lay in her pathway. Her wristwatch, compass and butane lighter had survived the swim and would prove valuable to her in her journey.

A mile after starting she found their first cache. The discovery elevated her hope for survival and fortified with some items. She said, "I took a compass, a winter jacket, winter boots, winter pants, a sweatshirt, matches, a cigarette lighter, bug repellent, two packages of dry rice, a small pan for water, a map, our two passports and two photographs of my family."

She carried her equipment in the nylon bag which had held a sleeping bag. "I didn't take the sleeping bag because my jacket would keep me warm, but I took the nylon bag to protect myself from the mosquitoes. It would have been a horror without that bag."

She followed oil exploration seismic lines of Petro-Canada. She stated, "I tried to use my compass but because of the bog and trees I couldn't follow a straight line. Without the seismic lines, I would have been lost."

She became very hot by noon but refused to remove the jacket as it was her best protection from the pesky bugs attacking her in a perpetual black buzzing cloud. I "couldn't take off my winter jacket because of the mosquitoes." Even with the insect repellent the mosquitoes and black flies were relentless, swarming about her all day.

"My clothes were soaking wet. I enclosed myself inside the little bag I brought to rest and decided then to walk at night."

Lydia's difficult survival trek gained only five miles in ten hours of negotiating the wild woods and tundra country. She knew she had her work cut out for her. At this rate it would take nine or ten days to reach her objective. Would her food hold out? Would her energy match her desire to live?

On her second day she encountered a bear. "I was reading my map when he appeared about five to 10 meters away. He got up on his haunches and sniffed twice." She told herself, Don't move! Don't even blink! "I stood very still and he left."

After the bear left, she continued on her journey. The constant threat of survival was in the forefront of her mind and she said,

"I often thought I would never get out, but you can't think of that all the time or you'd never continue. I told myself if I got this far I can get the rest of the way."

She kept reminding herself to stay calm and to stay in control of her situation.

Daytime temperatures in the 80s turned cooler with nighttime temperatures in the 50s.

She struggled on, the flies and mosquitoes dining on her exposed flesh, attacking her eyes and boring into her hair. She was a flurry of constant swatting as she shuffled along the shoreline of Lake 766. An hour of nearly unbearable heat and bugs brought her to the realization that she was going the wrong direction. Her error in direction cost her in spent energy, wear and tear on her body and consumption of her sparse food supply. Soaked in perspiration and covered with bites, she retraced her steps to the cache to reorient herself.

Lydia applied more insect repellent before re-starting her trek, this time in the right direction. She left her sweater and departed.

Early in the afternoon she was nearing exhaustion, pushing herself unmercifully. She was reaching her limits and knew that she needed to regroup and control her destiny in order to stave off panic. She forced herself to stop, dropping to the ground beneath a tree where she removed the items from the nylon bag before pulling it over herself to fight off the flies and mosquitoes.

For several hours she endured fitful, semi-conscious sleep. During that time she dreamed of Jean-Jacques. Her dream was so real that it was as if he were there exhorting her to stick to her plan, continue on without delaying where she was. She knew that walking at night would reduce the hordes of insects, and she could rest by day. She willed herself to continue at all costs. I will not quit or give up.

Lydia arose and continued onward. During winter months when the water and ground surface area was frozen, huge machines had cut a swath through the forest. She followed the twenty feet wide path. In places she met with obstacles in the form of ponds and swamp areas. At one point she encountered a lake blocking her pathway.

Whether she followed the seismic trail or diverted from it, her progress was constantly challenged. When she was forced to leave the trail, thick brush made it difficult for her to follow her compass course. On the trail she encountered more swamp or her compass necessitated an alternate route when the trail deviated from the course. Hour upon hour the difficulty never let up.

With the dropping of the temperature that evening, the insectattacks diminished. Lydia built a fire and ate a handful of rice. She was somewhat rejuvenated and felt hopeful for the first time.

In the early dawn the next morning at 3 o'clock she was up and walking. She determined that a steady, productive pace would accomplish her goal. Convinced that following her compass course would reduce the risk of getting lost, even at the inconvenience of barriers, she trudged on.

When she came to a wide stream, she followed the compass, took off her clothes, placed them in the bag with her other gear and stepped into the water, holding the nylon bag over her head. Within minutes she emerged from the cold, neck-deep water, shaking uncontrollably.

She took time to build a fire which dried and warmed her. Then she was off again, more confident than before. She remained hopeful but still wondered about her endurance.

Because of her knowledge of the human anatomy and the body's nutritional needs, she acknowledged her rice supply would only last so long.

She conserved her food, planning to eat as a reward at given points on the map. She ate unripe, sour berries that she found along her pathway. Water was plentiful and she frequently drank to lessen her hunger as much as to replenish her lost fluids.

Hour by hour she plodded on, developing a routine. When

she was overcome by the insects, she robbed them of their objective by covering herself with her nylon bag before pressing on.

She met water barriers such as ponds and rivers with her steeled will to strip naked, carry her gear overhead and continue on the far shore. Swamps contained slimy goop into which she sank up to her ankles.

Light turned into dark. Dark became dawn. She moved resolutely onward. Day turned to day. The days slowly, painfully turned into nearly a week.

She held to her southeasterly course, always reassessing her route. She determined from the map that she was twenty miles from Colville Lake and another twenty-five to the Mission, her objective. Possibly a day away from Colville Lake and two more to the Mission.

With the possibility of reaching the Mission in three to four days, Lydia's condition included blistered and infected feet. And she had only a fraction of food left. But she chose to live. She pressed onward.

Euphoria embraced her as she identified Aubry Lake, only ten miles from Colville Lake.

The next morning tragedy struck. The day became unbearably hot. Lydia stopped time and again to drink water and to apply insect repellent. The flies and mosquitoes were relentless. The pesky bugs had taken their toll upon her physical and mental reserves. The lack of protein severely weakened her and she stumbled along on bloody feet. It was then that she discovered she had made another mistake in determining her exact whereabouts.

She was going in the wrong direction, north. She's mistaken this lake for Colville Lake. Lydia was near physical and emotional exhaustion. Although she took refuge with her nylon bag, she could not sleep. Lydia took solace in the faces of her family and friends as she studied their pictures. But she couldn't help wondering if she'd ever see them again.

The next morning, July 21, she retraced her steps. Dizziness nearly overwhelmed her. Eating more unripe berries, she stumbled onward hour after hour until at last she came to the shore of Colville Lake.

While resting on the shore and attending her feet, she experienced some stomach pain. Probably from the green berries.

She didn't think she could go on. Closing her eyes and resting momentarily, she suddenly reminded herself of Jean-Jacques and his exhortation. Lydia told herself to get up and to move.

At that point she opened her eyes and discovered what appeared to be a cabin. Is it real? She realized that it was.

She approached the dwelling and found the door unlocked. Though swathed in agony, she moved on bloody, swollen feet into the cabin. She found tea, rice and pancake mix. She prepared her first meal in nearly a week.

For twenty hours she slept, barely moving.

When she awoke, she saw a wolf standing near the cabin. Every day for the next four the wolf was there, almost as if awaiting her departure. But perhaps it was a positive omen which kept her at the cabin. On that fourth day, July 26, she did not see the wolf. That day as she prepared to leave the cabin after writing a note for the cabin's owner, a man arrived.

A deliverer in the form of Gene Marie Oudzie motored along the lake in his boat. He discovered Lydia at his father's cabin. And the manager of a cooperative who was duck hunting marveled that he had come upon the only person ever to walk on foot to this cabin.

He helped Lydia into his boat and rushed toward Our Lady of the Snows Mission, twenty miles across the lake. Lydia had covered over 70 miles in her solo trek from Lake 766, accomplishing one of the most courageous survival achievements in recent years.

The next day she accompanied the Royal Canadian Mounted Police in a helicopter to the site of the canoe accident. They recovered her boyfriend's body and discovered canisters of film at their charred campsite. The canisters contained pictures of the couple's last days.

Cpl. Malcolm MacKinnon of the Royal Canadian Mounted Police commented on Lydia's journey, "Most people couldn't have survived. She did because she's one tough lady."

Source: *Swallowed Alive*

Nearly a Statistic

I received a story of unusual proportions from Ben Forbes, a Sitka, Alaska, registered guide with extensive search and rescue credentials:

When I was working at Excursion Inlet, one of my men owned a cruiser, an every chance we got we would go out and look the country over for bear sign. One time we went over to Mud Bay, across Icy Straits from Excursion Inlet. As we came into the river mouth and anchored, we saw another fishing boat there. There was no skiff around so we assumed that the man was ashore. It was in the fall; deer hunting season was open, so it was very likely he was hunting. And just as we anchored, a skiff drifted down the river, out into the ocean where the fishing boat was anchored.

While we thought the hunter had probably forgotten to tie up his skiff securely, something may have gone wrong. We decided to rescue it and see if we couldn't take it up the river and give it back to him. I rowed over to intercept this skiff. When I got over to it, I looked in it; a man lay unconscious in the bottom of the boat, in a big pool of blood. I tied a line on it real quick and rowed it back to the cruiser.

We got him aboard, dried off and undressed and found that he had been mauled by a bear. He had been bitten through the leg in the thigh, and the leg was broken. The leg was badly lacerated from the bear's teeth. And the bear had also clawed him on the back, ripped his back open a little bit, tried to bite him on the head and tore part of his scalp loose. He was a real mess to look at.

So we cleaned him up, dried him off, got him warmed up and bandaged. He regained consciousness after a while and told us about what had happened. And as we pieced the story together, we filled in some of the details that were pretty obvious.

He said he's shot two deer up on the mountainside. One fell right where he hit it, and the other one ran down the mountain and into the brush and timber. So he dressed the first one out and started down the mountain to get the second one. He found the deer down in the thick brush, and as he was going down the hillside to it, he stumbled onto a bear that had claimed it.

As he came through the brush to the deer, the bear jumped him, grabbed him by the leg and just shook him like a cat would shake a mouse. The bear broke his leg, dropped him, and clawed him on the back with his paw and tried to bite his head. The bear's teeth just snapped across the head, and then he picked up the deer and left.

The man lay there for a while, and then managed to crawl down to this boat. He had pulled the boat up on the beach. The tide had gone out, and the boat was tied up to a tree. So he untied the line, crawled over the side and got in the boat, knowing the tide would come in after a while and float the boat and then the river current would take him out the river. He figured when he got out close to his boat, he could row over to it and get on board and probably take care of himself.

As it happened, he passed out, and if we hadn't been there to see his drifting skiff when he went out the river mouth, he would have been another mysteriously missing fisherman; the tide would have taken him out to the ocean, and he'd have probably never been seen again.

Rather than waste time towing the stranger's boat, we split up. The owner of our boat took him into Hoonah to catch a plane into Juneau. I rowed over to his fishing boat, picked up the anchor and took it into Hoonah and left it with the U.S. Marshall. Then we went right back to Excursion Inlet and back to work.

Later we heard the man was in the hospital for about seven weeks before returning to Hoonah to reclaim his boat. And he apparently got along okay. Too bad. I don't remember his name at all; in fact, I'm not so sure I even knew what his name was, and none of us over at Excursion Inlet ever did hear from him. I don't think he even knew who picked him up and brought him into Hoonah.

Source: *More Alaska Bear Tales*

Larry Kaniut

Quick Thinking Archer

I met Jack Muir in the spring of 1996 and was impressed with him. He was 48-years-old, stood 6-feet-1 and tipped the scales at 190 pounds. For thirteen years he'd been a sales rep at V.F. Grace in Anchorage. He showed me his hunting photo album then told me his tale:

I've been a bow hunter all my life.

I've taken quite a number of animals with a bow and arrow, including Dall sheep, mountain goat, caribou, two black bears, seven moose, elk in Oregon and Montana, mule deer, black-tailed deer, Sitka black-tailed deer, coyotes, and brown bear. I went on safari to Africa in 1993 with a bow and arrow where I took kudu, eland and impala. I've spent some time in the woods.

I like to have a hunting partner with me in camp, but when I'm out hunting, I want to do it alone because I think bow hunting should be a one-on-one experience. I'm not a sitting hunter. It kills me to sit and wait animals out. Sitting in a blind or tree tests my shooting ability but does not really test my hunting ability.

I did very little blind hunting, even in Africa. My guide took me out and let me loose and let me walk. I always want to see what's on the other side of the next ridge or around the next bend in the river. I would rather walk and not kill them, see the country and test my hunting skills to their survival skills, than sit in a blind and wait for them to walk by or come to water.

In the fall of 1995, my hunting partner Mike Manning and I left Anchorage to hunt brown bear. Since I had arrowed a nice bull moose the year before and my freezer was full of big game meat, salmon, and halibut, I didn't have to worry about chasing moose or caribou. I was hunting bear.

Hunting the same area five years earlier during a four-day solo hunt, I saw eight bears and took one, an eight-footer. I was shooting a 75-pound bow, and the arrow passed clear through him. It was a one-shot kill at twenty-five yards. I now shoot a Browning Maxim compound set at 76 pounds, shooting 2413 aluminum hunting arrows with Bear Bruin Lites for broadheads and using a fletch hunter release.

I have an eighteen-foot travel trailer that I normally take hunting. I park it five or six miles away from the trail to my hunting area. Traditionally I hunt a ridge above the stream. Five salmon species spawn in the stream, and the ridge affords a good vantage point as well as keeping man-scent away from bears. Their noses are so superior that you have to take great care to avoid them scenting you. You've got to get elevation to do it right.

Spruce timber blankets the low hills, while prolific devil's club and alders cover the ground. This year we went in ahead of time and cut a trail that would enable us to get in and out in the dark. I no longer fight my way through the alders. I never go into the brush without my little Sierra saw, made by Coghlands. It's a twenty-dollar saw that folds like a pocketknife, the niftiest brush-wacking tool there is. Cutting a path through the alders might take a bit longer, but when I get to the other end of an alder thicket, I'm not whipped from bending and stooping and trying to drag a backpack through the brush.

Mike, who manages Kenai Supply, and I headed up the trail on the opening weekend of brown bear season, 15 September. The first day we sat on the upper end of the stream and saw fish and bear signs, but there were no bears around.

Sunday morning we went back in and sat again. Nothing came by, so around noon we decided to walk downstream to the mouth to see if we could figure out where the bears were. When we got to where the stream flows into the main river, it was obvious that the bears were there. The water in the main river had dropped, and the bears could catch a better quality and quantity of fish in the stream.

I wanted to hunt on the ground from one of the high banks, but my hunting partner wouldn't have anything to do with it. He loves to hunt bears, but he's more cautious than I. He wanted to be in a tree. We also wanted to videotape and felt it would be better if we were both in a tree so we could tape each other shooting a bear. We looked around and found only one tree that we thought we could get up into and shoot from. We then cut a new trail from that spot back to the main highway.

We came back that evening and crawled up the tree. As we were trying to figure out how we were both going to sit in a small spruce tree without tree stands, three bears walked out into the stream about a hundred and fifty yards below us. I got the video camera out of my backpack and videotaped the bears. I didn't want to shoot any old bear because the price of having a rug made is one hundred dollars per foot. I've already got one bear, and I'm looking for a pretty hide. We got some great footage of bears chasing fish.

I let the first two bears go by. On the ridge across the river about one hundred yards away, we heard bears fighting, and we saw a pair of cubs go up a tree. Shortly after that another bear came down to the river and fished his way toward us. He came along the near bank and smelled where we had come out of the water. He then tracked us step-for-step to the base of the tree. I got a video of him as he worked his way there and I've got a picture of him looking up at us, eighteen feet above him. He saw me moving, figured something was wrong, made one "woof," crossed the stream, and went up the bank the way he'd come. That was a good-looking bear, light on the back and dark-legged; his coat had some character to it. I should have taken it.

About ten minutes later a sow with two cubs came down to the water about one hundred yards upstream and started fishing. It got dark and, even with all those bears around, we crawled out of the tree, slipped into the water so we couldn't leave any scent, and quietly left, hoping that we wouldn't run into any bears in the dark.

The following weekend my partner couldn't hunt with me so I went back by myself and hunted for two days, but didn't see anything. The next weekend we went back. One seven-foot bear came past. It was solid brown, not the bear I wanted, so I passed up a shot at him from about thirty-five yards away.

The fourth weekend my partner was working again, so I went in alone. It had snowed on the mountaintop the night before. The morning dawned a cool, crisp thirty-five degrees. When it got light enough to see, I shouldered my backpack and took off down my trail. There was blue sky and sunshine, an absolutely gorgeous fall day.

As I reached the ridge above the stream, I saw a bear downstream chasing fish where I expected to hunt. It had probably been in there all night fishing. I laid my bow down, took my backpack off, pulled out my video camera, and started videotaping this bear that was about three hundred yards away. He had no idea he was a camera subject. The wind was blowing downstream, but I was eighty yards above him and three hundred yards away, and there was no chance of him smelling me. I was concerned that if I went down to the creek, my scent would blow down to him and he'd disappear.

I was wondering about how to get in there without spooking him, when I heard something to my right. I looked in that direction and saw a bear coming along the edge of the ridge fifteen to eighteen yards away. I hollered, "Hey!"

When I hollered, the bear had two choices: run away or attack. She chose to attack. With no hesitation she charged me. A few alders separated us, so she couldn't do a flat-out run. She kept her eyes on me as she threaded her way through the alders, and I never took my eyes off her.

I thought about grabbing my bow, but there was an overhanging tree-inch alder limb that would have stopped me from drawing it. I could have done it if I'd gotten down on one knee to shoot, but there wasn't enough time.

Still, on she came. I dropped my camera and grabbed my Ruger .44 Magnum out of my shoulder holster and cocked it (on the video you can hear the cylinder roll). I hollered again, "Hey!"

She kept on coming. I backed up my trail two steps, hoping she would go past me or turn and go down my trail the other way. I stood there looking at her as she continued her resolute charge toward me. I raised my handgun with two hands and looked at the sights, following her with the barrel. She made a ninety-degree left-hand turn onto my trail, only eight feet from me.

She was so close and her head was so big that I touched one off. It hit her in the forehead above the left eye. She dropped like a sack of potatoes. The gun recoiled. It's a double-action weapon, but I drew the hammer back single action again and put it back on her. She was dead still.

By then I realized there were two cubs following her. I hollered at them. They kept coming. They stopped. I cocked the gun again and swung back on the sow. She hadn't stirred.

I grabbed my bow and started backing up the trail, and the cubs came up along the side of their mother. They were two-year-old cubs. The larger of the two, probably a boar, weighed approximately four hundred pounds. The mother should have kicked them loose by then. They were old enough to be out on their own.

As they moved up alongside, I backed up the trail about fifteen yards to where it made a left-hand turn. From there I could see that the sow had fallen on my video camera. Lying in front of her nose was my backpack full of hunting gear: binoculars, spotting scope, tripod, range finder, still camera, all my bow hunting paraphernalia except my bow.

Bears will chew up anything that has man-scent on it. I could see that they were going to chew up my stuff. One of the cubs walked up and pawed at the backpack while the other sniffed at the camera.

I hollered at them and shot my gun again. They just turned and looked at me, not showing any signs of aggression. They were probably still waiting for their mother to lead them, because up to this point in their lives she had been in control. The mother wasn't doing anything and they weren't either.

After seven minutes (timed on video) I decided I wanted my camera and hunting gear back. I reloaded my gun, yelled, and I fired two rounds. If they attacked I needed at least four rounds. I kicked the alders and made noise to sound as big and bad and nasty as I could. I hoped my bluff would work.

I got very close. I never showed any hesitation and kept coming right at them. I began to think I had made a mistake because I got closer than I thought I would have to get before they started backing off. Finally they turned and backed off the way they had come.

I was able to grab the camera out from underneath the sow's head. I grabbed my backpack, opened it up, dropped the camera in, and headed up the trail. I walked ninety steps and stopped. I put the backpack down, reloaded my gun, and put it back into my shoulder holster. I pulled the camera out to see what damage the bear had done and realized that it was still on. The camera had landed on its side facing in the direction of the river rather than down the ridge, but the sounds of the entire bear attack were recorded. It was then that I realized there was a piece missing off the end of the camera. I shut it off, put it in my backpack, and headed back to camp.

I reached my truck and drove to my trailer. My camp companion and camp cook was still in her sleeping bag in the trailer house.

She said, "Why are you back so early?"

"Well, I had a little problem with a bear."

"Did you get one?"

"Yeah, but not the way I wanted."

We made a pot of coffee and I explained what had happened. Finally about 11:00 I said, "Let's go in. We gotta get this hide off of her. By law you have to turn the hide into the Fish and Game." I grabbed my Model 70 Winchester .375 H & H Magnum that I had brought as a backup for my brown-bear hunting with a bow and arrow. We drove up there, parked the truck, and headed down the trail.

I gave her a can of bear spray because I didn't figure she could handle a rifle. When we got to the bend in the trail where I could see the downed bear, we started videotaping. As we walked in we heard something off to the right-hand side, and one of the cubs was back in the brush about ten yards away.

I videotaped it and decided we'd better chase it off. I walked around the sow in an open area. I wanted to stay in the open in case I had to move the gun around quickly and shoot. I tried to chase the cub off. It started to move off and I was following it along, when suddenly the larger cub got up to my left. He was standing broadside looking at me.

He was twelve yards away. And boy, he got my attention. I put the .375 to my shoulder. There was a downed alder between us. We looked at each other for a minute as I talked to the bear in a conversational tone, trying to convince him to leave. He just stared at me, eyeball to eyeball. I leaned into my .375, so that if I touched it off the recoil wouldn't tip me over backward. I looked like a shot gunner ready to take him on.

Finally the boar started to move. I told him, "Don't come around that alder. You come around that alder, I'm gonna kill ya." He started to come around the alder, then stopped. He slowly turned and went in the direction the other bear had gone. They wandered off just out of sight, which was about twenty yards into the alder thicket.

By that time I had a charge of adrenaline. The long eyeball to eyeball encounter with the big cub had me charged. We took some still pictures and video. While we were doing that, the larger cub suddenly came walking in behind me. I jumped up, grabbed the .375 and confronted him again. He stood and looked at me. I took a few steps toward him, and he turned and reluctantly moved off.

I took two more still pictures and he walked in again. That did it. This bear wasn't going to leave. There was no way I could get the hide off the sow safely. I didn't want to shoot the cub or put the woman with me in jeopardy, so we packed up our stuff and got the heck out of there. Later that evening I went back. The cubs were still there. I couldn't get them to move away.

The next morning I circled, got in the creek below them, and shot more video of them as they looked down on me. I returned to camp, loaded up the camp, and got ready to head out. I decided to go once more about 4:00 P.M. to see if the cubs had left.

This time I was in luck. The bears were gone. I scouted within twenty yards in all directions. I cut some alders down, opened the area up so I could see better, and started skinning. I did a record job of getting that hide off.

I had the hide about three-quarters of the way off when a bear came walking down my trail. My friend was holding the .375. I jumped up, grabbed that .375, hollered at the bear, and it turned and went charging off through the alders. I don't think it was one of the cubs because it shot out of there.

It surprised me that the bear had walked down the trail we had just left, because of the fresh scent. Obviously, the bears I that area are not afraid of human scent.

I finished getting the hide off, tied it onto my pack frame, and we boogied on out of there. I threw the pack into my pickup, and we headed back to Anchorage. The next morning I took it down to Fish and Game. I told them my story. They said I had some forms to fill out. I said, "Well, let me tell you a little more about it. I got it on film."

"What? You got the film with you?"

I had the film in my hand, so we went to the back room to a VCR and watched my film. Eleven seconds had elapsed from the time I was videotaping the distant bears until the sow was dead—only eleven seconds!

The sow was a 7 to 7 ½-foot bear. I'm a bow hunter, and because it was taken with a handgun I didn't want it as a trophy. I know taking a trophy with a handgun is a challenge, but that's not the way I intend to do it. I'll be back in this area next year, and I hope to arrow a pretty bear for my wall, and maybe on film as well.

I do a lot of hunting in Alaska without carrying a pistol. When I'm in the woods, I figure I'm the king of the beasts and they need to watch out for me more than I have to watch out for them. After this incident, I realized an attack can happen with amazing speed, so I won't go into the woods without my handgun. That Ruger Red Hawk has earned its trip with me from here on out. It's not because I'm afraid, it's just that things happen quickly.

My Red Hawk has a 5½--inch barrel. I had two loads in the gun. One was a handload done up by my hunting partner. It's the locally made hard-cast, lead bullets made by Ace Dooby. It's a 328-grain hard-cast bullets loaded with 21½--grains of H110 behind it. The other load, made by Arctic Ammo, is specifically for our Alaskan bears and is a 265-grain Barnes solid with a velocity of about 1,400 feet per second. It's a bullet machined out of solid brass, designed for breaking big bones or shooting through the head.

The bullet penetrated the skull and shattered the first vertebrae on the neck where the skull and neck are attached. When I cut her head off, that area was a mass of bone fragments. The bullet was lying underneath the skin on the right side of the neck. It weighs thirty-nine grains less now than when it was in the pistol.

Source: *Some Bears Kill*

Shark Attack

By Eric Larsen as told to Larry Kaniut

When I first read about Eric Larsen July 3, 1991, I wanted to pursue his story from the angle of its rarity and of man's will to live. I called information then contacted him in his hospital room requesting his address so that I could send him a copy of one of my books and my intentions. I assured him over the phone that the land sharks would soon be arriving in large schools and suggested that perhaps we could write his story for *Reader's Digest*. He replied that "they were already here." So much for the major players' ability to respond instantly.

Over the years I've lost contact with Eric but am enclosing his story as I think he would have wanted it to be written. Primarily to state that sharks do not regularly seek humans as prey and that the news media does not normally endeavor to tell the victim's story (the way he'd like it told).

Imagine sitting on a surfboard, dangling your legs and hands in the water. You're facing north and looking over your left shoulder for a wave. It's a pleasant and peaceful morning but you feel some apprehension because you're alone. One second you're on your board, the next you're in the water. A great white shark has you in its massive jaws.

What do you do?

My brother Nick and I decided to go surfing and planned to leave early on Monday, July 1, 1991. He was on vacation and I was on a leave of absence from my job. We got up about 5:30 in the morning and went out to Davenport in my Toyota 4Runner truck for "dawn patrol." We arrived later than I had wanted to due to the fact that I had slept through my alarm wrist watch. It was already light when we were suiting up. We both were wearing full length wetsuits, booties, and web fingered gloves due to the cold water

Having worked with the Bridger Bowl Ski Patrol in Montana where I acquired an Advanced First Aid and CPR certificate, I modified my attitude towards taking risks in the outdoors. When I first started patrolling, I thought that taking more risks meant that you were "advancing" in your efforts--a person who knew more and was more experienced was a person who was in a position to take more and bigger risks.

Since watching and listening to the professional ski patrolmen however, I have concluded that this was a false perception. I learned that the people who are really "in the know," do things essentially the same way every day, day in and day out, with very minimal risk, accomplishing a very dangerous activity in such a way that it is very safe and routine.

When we arrived at the beach, we saw a couple of guys out in the water and we spent some time observing the surf. We had a quick talk about how we would enter and exit the surf zone and where we would position ourselves to wait for the waves. We stretched out and checked leashes. I always try to put my leash on in the same way, so that I can remove it quickly should it snag and hold me underwater. I discussed this with Nick and we practiced unleashing. We timed out a couple of sets and then hit the water at 7:20 a.m.

Nick rode my 8' 2" Agua tri-fin in a long board shape while I used a 7' Taylor tri-fin short board.

We bobbed around for a while and waited for the intermittent waves. Conditions were not very good. We were on the "outside," trying to ride the rights—after picking up a wave, the normal move would be to make a right turn. Nick caught a couple of waves, which he rode on his chest. I only stood up one time, and did not get a very good ride. I had not been surfing much due to canoe commitments and was not surfing well, especially on my short board.

I observed seals a number of times that morning. It may have been the same seal, seen repeatedly. About thirty to forty-five minutes prior to the attack a seal came close by and I slapped the water with my glove.

A boat was seen not too far offshore. This boat left after the emergency response happened. It is suspected that the boat may have been discharging some fish entrails (chumming) into the water in hopes of attracting a shark.

About 9 a.m. Nick indicated he was not feeling very good due to taking on salt water while being held under by waves. Since the other guys had gone in and I was out there alone, I planned to follow Nick in, after catching just "one more wave." It wouldn't take long to surf the hundred and fifty yards to shore.

About twenty minutes later I was sitting on my board facing north and looking over my left shoulder for the next wave. My legs and wrist were dangling in the water. Although I had surfed the area many times including once alone, I felt some apprehension about being out there alone, the only one in the break. Since the surf was small, I was not too worried.

While awaiting a wave I had the feeling that I was in the presence of a very large marine mammal. I felt sort of a strange quality to the water in that it seemed to be swirling a little and I felt like I was being spun around. I remember hoping that an elephant seal or whale had come up under me.

I felt a clamping force on my left leg and looked down to see the shark's jaws on my leg. The shark had come up between my legs, under my board and clamped onto my left leg. My left knee was pointing into his mouth and his teeth were biting in just above the ankle and about six inches below my buttocks. I looked down at the jaws and gum line. I remember a distinct visual image of large triangular white teeth, and a very red gum line.

I remember my first thoughts being, "How can this be happening? Shark attacks are very unlikely!" Then I concluded that I needed to deal with the situation somehow, because it was happening to me, unlikely or not. The shark was motionless for a few seconds and lacking any better ideas, I tried to pry him off my leg by placing my left hand on his top jaw, and the right hand on his bottom jaw. This was futile due to not being able to get much mechanical leverage and the strength of the shark's bite. At this point I should have hit the shark on the snout with my left hand.

The shark opened up slightly and I was able to extricate my leg. I think the shark flicked his tail and came at me. At this point I think I was pushed off my board into the water. Snce my hands were essentially in his mouth, he got both of my arms in his mouth at this point. The left arm was in up to the elbow, and oriented for maximum thickness. The right arm was in at about mid-forearm, oriented flat. My impression was of a fairly large cavern inside his mouth.

I was able to pull the right arm out. At this point, I was still near the surface, sort of thrashing around. I remember a lot of bubbles in the water. I pulled back in my right arm and used it to hit the shark with a "hammer blow." By this I mean that my right arm hit with the little finger next to the shark's skin, along with the forearm. I was very "pumped up'" with adrenaline at this point, and hit with sufficient force that I later had a lot of muscle soreness and tightness in my (uninjured) right shoulder. The effectiveness of my strike was limited by difficulty in winding up and hitting underwater.

The shark released my left arm and I remember thinking that I was coming out of this maybe okay. My next recollection is of a violent pulling on my leash, which was attached to my uninjured right leg. The shark was somehow entangled in my leash and pulled me under for a few seconds. The sensation was very violent. It was like being hooked to a ski boat. I came free and got to the surface. I got a fast breath and got right onto my board in one motion. On the first attempt, I happened to hit almost exactly the right spot on my board and I started to paddle in.

I remember trying to stay calm, paddle very efficiently and thinking that everything had to go right from this point onward if I was going to make it. I was surprised at being able to paddle almost normally, even with my arms being very ripped up due to the injuries. This is due to the fact that the flexor muscles and tendons were relatively intact, whereas the extensors were damaged.

I remember looking down at my left forearm and noticing the yellowish fatty tissue. At the shark seminar I attended the instructor mentioned that sharks were supposedly attracted to yellow color. I surmised that this is because seals have a lot of fat, and it might be yellowish, like mine. I also observed blood trails coming off my arms. I remember looking over my shoulder for an oncoming fin.

I was about 150 yards offshore at the time of the attack. About two thirds of the way in I was able to catch a small wave and ride it in on my belly. I got to the shore and picked my board up and carried it over some small rocks. I set it down and looked at it quickly to check for dings or bites. I remember thinking that I should probably not worry too much about it. I started to feel weak, so I sat down and looked at my arms. I could see blood spurting out of the left arm near the crack of my elbow. I clamped the wound closed using my right hand and elevated the left arm. I was feeling very weak and at this point the thought occurred to me that I might die soon.

The beach was empty and I was around the corner of a small cliff from some beach houses. Nick was up at the truck at this time, over a mile away and out of sight. I knew that nobody would see me for at least a half hour, perhaps more. I concluded that I was going to have to walk up the beach to the houses or to where Nick could see me. At this point I had a sensation of some important events in my life passing before my eyes, like a movie projected at one hundred times normal speed. I tried to motivate myself by thinking about how I had motivated myself in long distance canoe races.

Walking was difficult due to the fact that the shark had transected (completely cut in half) my left quadriceps lateralis muscle. This is one of the main walking muscles. I knew that crawling was out of the question due to the possibility of getting sand into the wounds on my arms. I lost energy at least once and had to sit down. I did not want to pass out because then I would have released the grip on my left arm wounds and a lot of bleeding would have occurred.

I got to a point near the houses and started to yell as loudly as I could. I was yelling, "Help, SOS." I saw someone come out of one of the houses and I yelled at him. I was very anxious at this point. I told the person to call 911 right away. This person turned out to be Ben Burdette, a 16-year-old surfer who lives in the house near the beach.

Ben's mother, Michelle Tummino, came out, with some towels. She indicated that she did not know much about first aid. I instructed her to apply a pressure point to my brachial artery, to apply direct pressure using the towels to the wounds, and to elevate my good leg to drain some blood into my abdomen. I think I also asked her to keep the left arm elevated. She asked me what I did for a living and I told her that I was a programmer on leave of absence, and that "real surfers don't have real jobs."

I asked someone to go up and get Nick at the truck. He came down and saw that I was pretty cut up. I told him I was glad that he was there. At this time, the paramedics and emergency response people started showing up.

The last blood pressure they got on me was 50 over 30. They started oxygen and fluid IV's on both arms. They used mast trousers which inflate and then compress your legs to force more blood into your abdomen and brain. I felt a lot better when they were on. Nick was holding an oxygen mask on my face since I felt like I wasn't getting enough oxygen without his pushing it against my face.

The Army had a helicopter ready to land and everybody put on goggles to protect eyes from blowing sand. It was a Huey. At the time we took off, it was unclear to me (and Nick) where we were going. We landed at Dominican Hospital in Santa Cruz.

Essentially they slammed the doors shut and took off. This resulted in a very fast response. I think that the elapsed time between the 911 call and when I was in the air was only forty-five minutes. This is very fast, given the fact that Davenport is fairly remote. It is also good that a helicopter was available, due to the Fourth of July holiday traffic.

I am also told that the Stanford Life Flight helicopter was unable to land on the sand. The army guys landed close and picked me up. They had a winch that they could have used to send down and pull up a litter, as well as the capability to put a medic in a wet suit directly into the water. The Army unit that provides this service (free of charge) will be relocating within the next year or so, and at that time it is unclear how these vital services will be performed.

A lot of X-rays were taken in the emergency room (of me, transition). While I was being moved around and positioned for these, I got a lot of pain. A couple of ER guys helped me out by holding my arms in a static position relative to my body while I was being repositioned. This helped a lot. While waiting for surgery, I started to get very cold due to having lost all the blood. They turned on warming lamps and I started to feel a lot better. These two guys were starting to really perspire. They were local surfers. I thought it was so good that they were willing to hang in there and give me some good moral support even though it had to be very uncomfortable and hot under the lights.

I don't remember much about the surgery, since I was under general anesthetic. I think I took 350 sutures internally and 135 staples externally to close thirty inches of wounds. I received three units of blood. The doctors decided not to give me more blood to reduce the risk of hepatitis and AIDS. I was placed on iron pills and told to eat hamburgers and drink orange juice. This is my normal diet anyway.

The surgeon that worked on my arms (Dr. Tomlinson) had treated three shark bite patients previously. He had been a doctor in the military stationed at Tomales Bay. He had a very fast, precise and accurate method of operating and dealing with situations. I think he might have developed this as a result of dealing with a lot of patients in a military hospital. One move he made that was pretty good was when he was removing a drain (a section of tubing installed to allow fluids to drain from the repaired wound), and observed that it was not quite normal.

Later, he made a short exploration and found that a section of the drain had indeed broken off inside my arm during the removal process. He removed the extra section of drain. Had it been left in, it would have caused complications. This is a case where expertise, and experience proved invaluable A less experienced surgeon might have missed this.

My first memory is of waking up in intensive care and talking to my nurse. I think her name was Tracy. I told her the shark story. We spent a lot of time that first night trying to get a sand grain out of my eye. Dr. Tomlinson was able to quickly remove it the next morning. I took this as evidence of why surgeons deserve to make the big bucks.

Tracy asked if I wanted to watch TV. I remember seeing a clip advertising the National Geographic specials which showed a diver testing a chain mail wet suit. The clip showed a shark clamped onto the diver's arm. I think I changed the channel!

The worst pain and problems were in being able to urinate. I had a lot of problems. They pulled out a Foley catheter that was inserted into my penis. I had trouble relaxing with all the nurses fluttering around. A local surfer and doctor, Dr. Scott, was visiting me, and he was able to apply a sort of relaxation-hypnosis technique which allowed me to urinate over 1000 CC's. This is about a quart! I felt a lot better. Dr. Scott is a general practitioner. Even in the ICU with all the high technology equipment, there is still no substitute for the human touch.

I got pretty good care when I was transferred to the normal part of the hospital. One of the best things I got was a massage. I was able to sleep very peacefully for about three hours after this. I got physical therapy from a guy who had been in the Navy. He had worked with the Navy SEAL teams. It was good to work with him, since he motivated me to get out of bed and walk up and down the hall with my walker.

I remember very distinctly the first time I was cleared to walk around unsupervised with my walker. I was able to brush my teeth myself for the first time, and it took about twenty minutes. I had to get the brush and the toothpaste and a cup for the water as separate operations. It felt very good to make small steps towards being more self-sufficient.

It was very hot the week I was in the hospital, but not too bad in Santa Cruz. The sun would beat in the windows in the late afternoon, so I would roll in my wheelchair over to the deck area and get some sun and fresh air. I would lift my casts over my head to let the blood drain out, then hold them down to let the blood drain in. It felt good to hold my arms up in the cool evening air.

Doctors make you survive and live, therapists make you healthy and normal. I enjoyed PT, and I had a very good physical therapist, Susan Happe. She knew a lot of things. I was in physical therapy for about six weeks.

Although the attack occurred on Monday, but the real feeding frenzy took place on Wednesday when the hospital finally allowed a press conference. There were about fifty journalists with TV and still cameras. I was completely encircled. I think it went well. One newspaper account described how I "calmly described the attack." Given the drugs I was on at the time for pain, I would have been very calm about just about anything.

I conclude after my experience with a lot of TV, newspaper and magazine journalists that a person has the attention of the press as long as he is saying something the press perceives to be a good story. I thought that I might be able to use the spotlight to give some attention to environmental issues such as offshore oil drilling on the northern California coast or over fishing of sharks, or mindless killing of sharks by "sport" fishermen.

In general the press did not carry these stories. They were basically only interested in the attack itself. Possibly the worst press was a TV show called "A Current Affair" which had a interview with me interspersed with footage of a simulated shark attack. This footage portrayed sharks as mindless, blood thirsty killing machines. One of the shark researchers I talked to indicated that he always got upset when he saw things like this in the media because the sharks are not actually showing natural behavior. They are showing artificial behavior in the presence of bait.

I spent over six hours with the crew from "A Current Affair," and the segment was cut down to about ten minutes.

I received no money for my exposure to the media, however I did receive some gear. I got two free wet suits, one from O'Neill and the other from Hotline. O'Neill gave me a T-shirt, some booties, gloves and a new leash. I agreed to appear in an ad for Rip Grip, and received some free product in return. The ad should be fairly humorous since the essence of it is that the whole thing is a publicity stunt by a low budget company.

The fundamental lesson is that a person has very little control over what appears in the press, and once you talk to a reporter, you are taking your chances. The standard of truth and accuracy of press coverage is not the same as that of the engineering world. What is discussed in the interview and what appears in the article may be very different in emphasis. Facts can be presented in a very slanted way.

As a result of all the publicity, I got a lot of letters and phone calls from people I had never met. A number of people called who had been in terrible accidents and recovered. A woman called who had been attacked by a bear. A number of people wrote in with religious messages. I got one photo from a model. One woman wrote me a number of very nice letters because she thought I looked attractive on TV.

An important question is: when shark attacks are statistically rare, why did the shark choose to bite me at that time and place?

Years go by when no shark attacks occur. The exact reason for the attack is something that can never be completely known, but a number of theories arise.

This simulates the sound of a fish's tail slapping the water and will occasionally draw a seal up close to investigate. The sound was unexpectedly loud, and may have attracted the shark since they are reputed to have very good low frequency hearing.

This has never been substantiated.

The underside of my surfboard is pure white. This may have looked like the white underbelly of something delicious. I was also wearing a wetsuit with black sections on the legs, and black booties with white bottoms. This coloration may have mimicked that of a seal to some extent.

I was alone in the water. This may have caused the shark to proceed, when he might have been deterred with more surfers in the water.

I vaguely recall someone saying that at that particular time of year, the elephant seal pups are taking their first swims up at Anyo Neuevo (four to five miles north). It is possible that extra sharks might be in the area to gobble these seal morsels. I am not really very sure about this.

One of the shark researchers I talked to mentioned that in a shark attack on an elephant seal, the shark will sometimes bite and then come back when the animal has weakened by bleeding. The fact that I got right onto my board and paddled out of there may have been significant.

Also seal bones are rather porous and "crunchable," whereas human bones are dense and hard. When the shark bit into me, he left striations (tooth marks) on my bones. Encountering my bones may have given him a clue that I was not a seal and possibly hard to digest.

A number of precautions have been suggested by the experts for avoiding shark attacks:

Don't enter waters known to be frequented by large sharks.

Don't swim, surf or dive alone.

Avoid murky water or water with sand churned up

Don't go too far offshore or near channels or drop offs.

Don't go into the water near seal colonies.

Avoid the water at dawn, dusk or at night.

Short surfboards are worse than long boards since they look like a smaller seal from below.

Note that I was in violation of all these precautions.

Four factors were very important for my survival: 1) the emergency response team, 2) my physical condition, 3) my mental condition and 4) my First Aid knowledge.

First, the emergency response and medical system works very well in the Monterey Bay/Sanata Cruz area. Had this happened in Mexico, things might have worked out very differently.

Second, I was in very good physical condition. I had been paddling outrigger canoes almost every day for the two months prior to the incident, and I had been running a lot. This was important in my ability to paddle in and hike up the beach, even though I had lost a lot of blood.

Third, I was in good mental condition. I was relaxed and unstressed due to having been on leave from my job. Because I was relatively comfortable in the water from surfing and swimming a lot, I didn't totally panic, even when the shark pulled me under water when he was hooked in the leash.

Fourth, I had good basic knowledge of First Aid. I had learned this as part of my experience on the Bridger Bowl Ski Patrol. I had a (now expired) Advanced First Aid and CPR certification. I never expected to have to use it on myself.

One other thing that I think about is that the shark bit me, but didn't eat me, or bite off big chunks even though he could have. It might be more accurate to categorize what happened to me as a couple of bites, rather than an attack.

In retrospect the shark was almost gentle. As gentle as he (or she) could have been with his teeth. Once he concluded that I was not a seal, he swam off and left me alone. Humans should similarly give sharks some slack by not killing them for sport, or unnecessarily. Sharks are an important part of the natural environment. Any animal that is that big and that strong, deserves respect.

I have concluded that every day is important. Life is short, and every day is a chance to do something meaningful, and important. This can be surfing, or writing a new operating system for a computer. But in any case life is too short to spend a lot of time on things that are stupid, or don't lead on to anything else. Sitting in traffic and working on engineering projects that get discarded are two of the things that I hope to not spend much time on in the future.

Basically I think this incident resulted in a reinforcement of previous attitudes, rather than any new revelations. Life is deterministic, and a person has a lot of control over what happens. There is a need to be prepared and to be tough. All a person can do is to be as ready as he can be, and then go out and do whatever it is he was planning on.

Five separate emergency response organizations were involved. These were:

Davenport Fire and Rescue

California Department of Forestry

Santa Cruz Paramedics

U.S. Army 237th Medical Detachment Helicopter Crew

Stanford Life and Flight Helicopter Crew

I learned later that the Army guys were in their helicopter and doing a check when they got the call.

The Davenport Fire and Rescue guys were great. I went to a picnic that they held later on in the summer. In some years they have performed fifteen cliff rescuers. Their specialty is rescuing people that fall off the cliffs near Davenport. While I was at the picnic, a rescue call came in and they all suited up and went to rescue a woman that had fallen off a cliff to the north.

Source: *Swallowed Alive*

Larry Kaniut

Pam and Her Sunday Visitor

Unsalted peanuts in the shell cluttered themselves about a fifteen-inch circle on our green metal table on the back deck in December 2005. As Pam stood with back warming to the kitchen fireplace and looking out the bay window, a beautiful dark Steller's jay with black head lifted off the table flying toward the horseshoe pit, nut in beak. I'm wondering if it is Stanley from the summer of 2003 coming to renew his friendship. He hid the nut and returned to the table for more booty.

Then he launched east over our neighbor Steve Couture's cedar fence. In a short time he harkened back to the "come and get it" venue.

He coasted in, landed on the flower pot in the center of the table then hopped onto the table for another morsel. His next designation was the lawn adjacent to the iris patch and rose bush. There he rearranged a few dead leaves and deposited his peanut.

From the bay window Pam witnessed his next mission to the flower box outside the freezer window for another deposit.

Then she opened the back door and began putting on her boots and coat preparatory to going outside to feed the animals—Prince the horse, Diogenes the mixed breed canine and Banana, the Holstein painted cat, the latter two "adopted" to us by our son Ben. While looking out the opened door Pam watched Stanley fly to the tree fort, its floor twelve feet off the ground and fifteen feet behind the deck.

Pam walked out and sat at one of the four green metal table chairs. In moments he flew in, landed on the flower pot again and hopped onto the table for a nut before flying off toward the power line bordering the back lawn.

Pam moved her chair closer to the table and wondered how long it would before Stanley returned. Just about then she felt something on her head and jumped, not knowing what it was. It was Stanley who had flown in from the front west side of our house.

She must have startled him as he flew away without a nut. Since he didn't return right away, Pam decided to do her chores. While at her work Pam saw him return, grab another peanut and head for the loft opening of the barn. He landed on the floor just above the ladder and disappeared for a couple of minutes.

In the meantime Pam went about her duties as chief animal husbandman, feeding and watering the animals, including the currently non-laying chickens.

When she returned to the table, all the peanuts were gone. And so was Stanley.

Source: *Heavenly Rose*

Salmon and Bears

Sixty-knot winds blasted the little tent. With each gust the nearby alder clumps whooshed and shuddered, flailing their branches wildly. A steady drizzle fell in the fading twilight. Below the bank, Frosty Creek meandered through the tundra toward distant Izembek Lagoon, near the small community of Cold Bay on the Alaska Peninsula. Dead decaying salmon littered the banks at water's edge; and bear day beds, circular pockets of bare dirt eight feet in diameter dug into the tundra, cluttered the banks. A damp chill filled the air, but the lone camper who occupied the tent entertained high hopes for the morrow.

Jay B.L. Reeves, 38 years old and single, looked forward to the coming seven days during which time he would attempt to photograph some large brown bears to add to his wildlife photos and footage at home. Jay was more than prepared for this long awaited opportunity. He'd stocked up on food and film and brought his photo gear to this Frosty Creek setting.

Jay prepared a light evening meal and polished it off while pondering the events of the day. He's spent an hour that morning talking with Robert L. Jones at Izembek National Wildlife Range's office in Cold Bay, seven miles away. Jay queried the Fish and Wildlife Service about the most likely place to find bear subjects, and he'd decided upon the Applegate Cove/Frosty Creek area. It was an area bears frequented along the salmon stream and had sufficient alder cover for the creatures.

Reeves and Jones had also discussed and agreed that a .357 magnum handgun would not be adequate to stop a bear. Jones advised Reeves that, although he shouldn't consider the pistol as adequate protection from a brown bear, if carrying a pistol gave him peace of mind, he should lake it. Jay decided not to pack the pistol.

Reeves had gotten a ride to Frosty Creek and managed to set up his tent in the blowing wind and steady drizzle. His tent was near Frosty Road where he'd been let out earlier in the day, and he felt safe pitching it along the bank of the stream.

Now he doffed his boots and clothes and slid into his sleeping bag whose cold nylon cover temporarily gave him goose bumps. In minutes he was toasty warm. With seven days to film, where should he start tomorrow? Before he knew it, slumber had overtaken him and he slept in solitude, though the tent occasionally shuddered from a blast of wind.

The drizzle continued as the salmon wove their way upstream, and the bears fed along the creek's banks. One bear, annoyed or drawn by the flapping of the tent fly, approached Jay's refuge, gathered in the man smell and the faint odor of some form of food. The bear was accustomed to scaring off lesser animals with a guttural grunt as it waked the stream bank.

Bears that heard this cough, left his fishing territory to wait their turns. He began coughing and chomping his teeth as he reared the tent.

Reeves awakened from his reverie, thankful that he'd escaped any danger from the bear in his dream. But the coughing outside the flimsy shelter continued. Was that the wind or a bear that moved his tent?

The grunting noise he heard was definitely a bear, he'd heard it on too many other filming missions to mistake it.

Maybe he should have brought his .357. Perhaps he shouldn't have set up his tent so close to the bear's feeding grounds along the stream bank.

Jay slid from the warmth of his sleeping bag. Fear welled up within him. Maybe the bear would leave. Maybe the food would placate him and Jay could make a run for it. The bear probably only wanted his food. If he had to leave the tent, the bear probably wouldn't follow him down the road.

An ear shattering roar interrupted the flap, flap, flap of the fly; and the lightweight tent gave way under 600 pounds of brown bear. Somehow Jay managed to slip though the tent's opening. As he cleared the nylon fabric and sprinted barefoot toward the road, a fear of death gripped him. He ran faster than he had ever run; then he looked back.

The bear was chomping and ripping the tent and its contents. Then the animal saw Jay. Escape was too much to hope for. Jay had seen these creatures run, and he knew he couldn't outdistance one; and he knew his chances of surviving a hand-to-hand confrontation were slim.

The bear was five years old and in prime condition. Its paws were eight and a half inches across, it had good teeth and wore an eight-and-a-half foot pelt. The bear charged Jay, overtaking him in seconds.

A single swat of the brute's paw knocked Jay to the ground, then Reeves had to contend with its jaws. A few savage, ripping bites and it was all over for the photographer. He never had a chance.

The bear clamped onto Jay's left leg and dragged him to the nearest alder clump and began feeding. All through the night the bear fed upon his human victim. A couple of times he left the alder thicket and wandered back to Jay's tent, ingesting some of the food, wrappers and all. By morning there wasn't much left intact of Reeves' camp.

Frank Snodgrass of Cold Bay drove by the camp about noon the next day and noticed the collapsed tent. He saw no human activity and reported his discovery to officials at the office of the U.S. Fish & Wildlife Service. They began an immediate investigation.

It was August 3, 1974, and the Fish & Wildlife Service officials at Cold Bay were concerned for Jay B.L. Reeves's safety. John Sarvis and John Stimpson climbed aboard a helicopter chartered by a geophysical firm and searched the length of Frosty Creek and the outlying area. There was no sign of human activity near the photographer's camp. Chewed and flattened cans of food were strewn about, and the trail of paper and other articles led toward an alder thicket.

Sarvis checked out some alders from the ground while Stimpson and the pilot flew to another spot. On the chopper's first pass 25 feet above the ground a bear erupted from the brush. It hid itself quickly in more alders. Sarvis was picked up, and they continued trying to find the bear.

On one pass they discovered some blue clothing and noticed the alders were torn up. The chopper moved to one side, and the men saw the deceased man's skull. They obtained a rifle and flew above the alders again trying to locate the bear. Suddenly it lunged from the alder cover 300 yards away. The chopper zeroed in on the animal which Sarvis dropped with one .30-06 shot.

It was getting late, but the crew landed to check the dead bear. Sarvis opened it and examined the stomach which contained some plastic bags, pieces of human bone, skin and hair. The party left as darkness fell.

Several men returned the next day to check the camp, examine the bear and look for Reeves's remains. The scene they found was grisly. All that remained of Jay B.L. Reeves were his belt and belt knife in a sheath, T-shirt, shirt, pants, some ribs, part of his pelvis and his head.

The Jay B.L. Reeves incident above is based on official reports I obtained from the United States Fish and Wildlife Service. Most of the information came from a report written by John E. Sarvis who was a biologist then working at Izembek. John is now the refuge manage. Since I wanted all the known facts regarding the fatality, I sent my account to John asking him to comment on it. He edited it and wrote me, "Many of the details in the account are fictitious since no one was with Mr. Reeves at the time of the encounter. The known facts (upon which this account is based) are that a bear was found by Mr. Reeves's remains which were located in alder several hundred yards from his campsite. Mr. Reeves's remains were found inside the bear when it was killed. No one knows what actually happened that night, whether the bear that ate him was the one that killed him, or how Mr. Reeves died. Mr. Reeves made two errors which contributed significantly to the odds of having contact with bears. He had food in his tent and he camped on a bear trail on the bank of a major salmon stream, rather than camping away from the stream."

Source: *Alaska Bear Tales*

Tom's Last Flight

God had a buddy on earth who loved flying. From an early age Tom Kucera built balsa model planes. When he reached his teen years, he saw planes on Palmer's airport and figured "I can fly if those guys can." He got his ticket when he was seventeen and bought his first bird, a Champ, shortly thereafter. Over the years he owned a score of planes, including an experimental that he built. His love of aviation took him to work for the F.A.A. From those early beginnings around 1957 to 2002 Tom soared above terra firma, living a dream as few can.

On Sunday May 19, Tom was at home nestled on the shores of Beaver Lake, Alaska, his airplane hangar and gravel strip back of the house. That's when God dropped in for a visit.

"Tom, I'm here for your final flight. Need to kick some tires and do a walk around. It will be a brief pre-flight but I want to make sure the bird's ready to go." The Big Guy quickly assessed Tom's control surfaces before He popped the cowl cover over the engine to check plug wires, oil and things in general.

"Oil looks good, Tom. I'll do a quick check of the fabric and gear. Wheels and brakes are okay. Fabric's good.

"I'll check the gas then fire up the engine." God called out, "Clear prop!" and switched on the key to start the bird. It coughed on ignition and rumbled to a solid start. "Mags are okay, Tom. They test out good." While looking back to check the elevator, God pushed the stick forward and the tail feathers dropped. He pulled back on it and the elevators rose. He pulled the stick to the right and left to check the rudder. "Control surfaces are good, Tom. Engine run up looks good. Trim is set for take off. You're flight plan checks out and I know the weather's good. You're cleared for take off, Tom. Catch you on the Other Side, buddy."

Outside the hangar in his accustomed Kucera style, Tom gave his bird full power, walked the rudder from side to side while eyeballing the takeoff point through the windscreen over the nose cowl and lifted off...on his final flight. Destination, Back of Beyond on the Other Side.

Source: *Alaska Air Tales*

Ten Most Asked Questions

When I interviewed Sky, who had an unfortunate run in with a bear, he told me that he had come up with a standard line of answers to those who asked him questions. Here they are:

1. How do you feel?

   I feel fine, but the bear feels better.

2. Was the bear big?

   In comparison, it was smaller than a service station, but bigger than a tow truck.

3. Weren't you really scared?

   Not really—it was quite reassuring knowing the bear was ten times my size and there was nothing I could do.

4. What were you thinking when the bear was chewing you up?

   She was ripping my brand new Pendleton hunting shirt and had tore my lucky suspenders.

5. Did the bear do much damage?

   Other than ruining my shirt and suspenders, my back pack is full of holes and small items such as granola bars fall out.

6. Were you in a lot of pain?

   Actually it was a warm sensation similar to being dragged over cactus bushes.

7. I'll bet you never want to go through that again.

   It was quite rewarding. I learned a lot from the experience and I would recommend it to any outdoorsman.

8. When you feel better, are you going to go out and get the bear?

No, I have a system where the bear gets me.

9. Are you afraid to go out into the woods again?

I get flashbacks as soon as I step of the pavement. I am considering moving to Detroit where I can walk around without fear of being harmed.

10. Will you ever get over this traumatic experience?

What experience?

Source: *More Alaska Bear Tales*

Jerry Austin and Iditarod Mushing

During the 1996 Iditarod Sled Dog race some mushers saw polar bears along the race trail. One such musher was Jerry Austin. Since I've corresponded with Jerry in the past, I wrote for his experience, which he graciously supplied.

Wednesday 3 April 1996

When I reached Unalakleet, the town was abuzz with polar bear sightings by pilots and locals. I didn't think much about it since I see their tracks between St. Michael and Unalakeleet fairly often, especially in years like this when all the ice in Norton Sound shifts around and mixes with pack ice from the Bering Strait. A couple of villagers told me they had seen tracks near their crab pots offshore.

I left Unalakleet at dark, traveled past Blueberry, and was about ½ mile from Egavik, which is right on the ocean, when my headlamp picked up some movement about three hundred yards ahead on the trail. I thought it was only some trail markers reflecting back, so I went on. A few seconds later I realized that among the reflectors was a pair of eyes staring at me. I stopped and set my hook and was trying to remove my .44 magnum from a military-style holster when the eyes stood up, and I realized it was a bear I was dealing with, and probably a polar bear.

A number of grizzlies had also been seen, and in fact one of my neighbors had chased two off a dog trail just a week or so before the Iditarod began. I have a couple of lead dogs that bark a lot, Diamond and Rebar, so I spoke with them and got them barking, but the bear did not seem fazed by it, like most grizzlies are, so I concluded this must be a polar bear. It stood for several minutes and then moved off the trail several hundred feet and started sniffing around again. Several of the teams in front of me had females in heat, and I had one, so I thought this is probably why the bear was several hundred yards inland.

I didn't want to turn around, not just because I was racing but because I didn't want to show fear to the bear, so I pulled my hook and eased on by and down the trail with pistol drawn. The bear never paid any attention to me, and I'm glad it didn't since a dogsled is no place for accurate shooting. I've shot at a wolf before that was running right in the front of my team, and you don't get an accurate shot. At any rate, I took several deep breaths then proceeded to the mouth of the river where the trail heads inland. I was now almost a mile from where I had left the bear.

I crossed the river, and just as the trail made a sharp 90-degree turn to the right, another set of eyes opened up about fifty feet from me on the left. Apparently this bear had been sleeping or waiting for me and stood up on all fours and immediately started padding toward me. The dogs didn't see it because they were completely into the turn. I drove the sled with my left hand and aimed at the bear with my right. But it pulled up and hunkered down at about thirty feet. I was a second or two away from firing and was greatly relieved that it had pulled back.

I never saw either bear again. They were about a mile apart and both of them were a stone's throw from the beach. The second one was larger than the first, which led me to believe I was dealing with a sow and a 3-year-old cub, probably a male since it was a pretty good size.

I only saw one set of bear tracks in the area, which other mushers also saw. One of the teams a few hours behind me passed close to one of the bears but it did not move. Snowmobliers who were out looking for them did not find them in the dark. I was very shaken by the incident, and for several hours, until I reached Shaktoolik, I looked over my shoulder to be sure I wasn't being followed. I immediately told the race officials who passed the word back to Unalakleet to warn my friends behind me.

Source: *Some Bears Kill*

Three Fateful Days

By Amelia Hundley

When I read about this story, I tried unsuccessfully to acquire it for over two years. Then I received a letter from Amelia who agreed to share her unbelievable story with me.

That day in September 1975, the life of Amelia Hundley shifted into another gear. For the next three days she would experience an amazing ordeal, unexpected and profound. It had started as a one-day round-trip airplane flight from Hoonah to Haines, Alaska, for Pat Sawyer, Don and Evelyn Arbuckle, and Amelia. Here she tells the story of what happened instead.

To truly understand my story, you must know that it is rooted in a uniquely twentieth-century experience of faith. The limits of my Christian being were about to be defined exactly, and I was to discover God waiting for me at the place of my limitations.

Air and water transportation is the only means of travel between Hoonah and Haines and many people own small airplanes or boats. When some friends came to visit in two small planes, we seized the opportunity to make a trip to Haines to view some land that had been purchased sight-unseen before leaving Charleston. A second group planned to establish another Bible center there in the spring.

Back at our cooking and eating lean-to, Sam and Lee Fife, Tom Rowe, Don and Evelyn Arbuckle, Pat Sawyer, and some of the other pilgrims enjoyed a hot breakfast of oatmeal, scrapple and steaming coffee. We laid out our plans for the trip.

We would take both small planes to Juneau and fly from there to Haines to walk the land. We would then fly back to Juneau for fuel and return to the landing strip at Hoonah. We had to be back to our island home before the Alaskan darkness closed in.

Sam would fly his plane, taking his wife Lee, Tom Bowe and Mike Lopez from our farm. I would fly in a Beechcraft BE 35 Bonanza with Don and Evelyn and Pat, our pilot. She was one of our best pilots and the plane was new so I felt quite safe.

We were excited about our plans as we started the thirty-minute trek across the mud flats to our skiff, which would ferry us down Icy Straits to Hoonah. Half an hour after reaching Hoonah we were airborne.

Great happiness filled my heart as we cruised above the verdant timber and the glacial rivers of the Chilkat Mountain Range. Icy fingers of Pacific Ocean waters poked inland along the coast and countless tree-studded islands showed their heads above the blue waters. The panhandle of Southeast Alaska runs along the Canadian border, blanketed by sprawling Sitka spruce forests and myriad glaciers, streams and mountains.

At Juneau we filed our flight plan and took off for Haines. We touched down on the dirt landing strip at Haines around 11:30 a.m. A friend drove us out to the 160-acre parcel, which turned out to be set in majestic mountains with a stream running across the back. I would have a good report to take home with me!

By 3:30 in the afternoon, we were back at the Juneau airstrip. It was overcast and the forecast indicated possible fog. We filled the main gas tanks and the tip tanks of both planes. We had to fly by sight as there were no radar stations to bring us in by instrument. But we knew that we could fly low and follow the water channels if need be. After some discussion, we decided to go ahead with the twenty-five minute flight to go to Hoonah.

We left Juneau at about 4:30. But less than fifteen minutes later, we had reason to regret our decision as we found ourselves engulfed in fog.

The pilot of a small plane must be able to see in order to avoid Alaska's mountain dangers in fog. A pilot will sometimes choose to stick to his course and count on using charts. At other times the risk is so great that climbing above the peaks proves less dangerous. Sam Fife chose to stay in the fog and follow his instincts.

We heard his quiet voice through the white gloom over the radio giving our pilot, Pat, instructions on how to set her course. But when Pat found our plane enveloped in the thick fog, she feared hitting a mountain and climbed out of the fog.

Once our plane was above the mountaintops, Pat encountered a hazard of high-altitude flying in bush planes — the lack of oxygen coupled with the cold. The Bonanza was now above the fog, providing visibility to ensure avoiding the mountains, however, frost began to cover the instrument panel, forcing her to plunge back into the fog.

Visibility was zero. I couldn't even see our wing tips. It seemed like fog was in the plane with us. But it was not fog that was in the plane; it was Someone, and He chose that moment to make His presence known: "Amelia, you're going to crash." I heard the words clearly. "You won't be killed. You'll suffer for a while, but you'll learn many things as a result of it."

"Lord," I prayed. "I've always wanted to know You as my God. And if this is what You've planned for me, I'm willing. But if I'm not willing, I'm willing to be made willing."

I laid my head on the back of the seat and relaxed. When I did, everything in me associated with natural fear disappeared.

Moments later we slammed broadside into a mountain in the remote area called Lynn Sisters. It is next to a glacial mountain and is a haven for all kinds of wildlife.

At the moment of impact we had our seat belts on. When the plane stopped, my body kept going. The force of impact stretched my five-foot-two body, tearing muscles and separating bone joints that clicked together as we came to rest.

Our main fuel tanks exploded on impact, engulfing the plane in flames. Don was slumped forward, blocking the only door out of the cabin. We had to get out. Our bodies were afire and the wing tip tanks were still full of fuel.

"Don! Don! Open the door. Open the door, Don! We're

burning!" Those panic-filled words will ever be branded in my mind. Don was too injured to respond to my desperate cries. Behind us the flames tore through the tiny plane. My balaclava, that warm foldable mask meant as protection from extreme cold, was melting into thick goo and felt hot and sticky under my fingers. I frantically tried to put out the flames that were burning my hair.

I kept calling out to Don to rouse him. I saw flames coming from my hands. At one point I dragged my hands over my face and was shocked to find that my whole face seemed to slip under their touch.

Then Don rallied and got the door open. He lurched and lunged awkwardly but the door and immediately fell away, falling down a steep embankment.

Evelyn and I were next. We were fortunate to get solid footing, escaping a fall down the mountainside. Once we were safely out, Evelyn said, "Oh, my God! Pat's still in the plane!"

Evelyn climbed back into the plane to get her. Though Pat was nearly incapable of movement, we managed to get her out. Running and stumbling together down the slope, the three of us fled the aircraft, which was burning brightly and threatening to explode again.

At last the four of us came to a stop in the fog between the utter stillness of the mountain and the violent burning of the airplane. The flames on our clothes were now extinguished. The air suddenly rocked with a second and a third explosion and the rest of the plane burned up.

We had about three hours of daylight left. We didn't know where were. My face was badly burned.

Evelyn did what she could to make Don comfortable, and I did what I could to help Pat. As night drew near, we settled down to try to sleep. We prepared our minds for what might come next.

I thought of my family and their response to the news of our disappearance. Two of my daughters were waiting for me at Game Creek. I prayed for them and for my friends at Game Creek.

The air was very cold because of the nearby glacier and I was painfully aware that I was wearing only a cotton jumper with a cotton blouse. As darkness fell, so did the rain, which never completely stopped throughout our ordeal. Our clothing never dried again.

We now faced a new danger, hypothermia—a condition where the body loses more heat than it is able to produce, resulting in a core of the body getting colder and colder until one dies.

The next morning Pat asked Evelyn and me to move her to a more comfortable place if we could. In our earnest attempt to do so, the three of us slid farther down the steep slope. Here we found a wing that a tree had sheared off before the plane hit mountainside. We dragged the wing to where Pat lay and jammed it between some trees where it shielded her from the rain. I tucked my shirt over her.

Evelyn and I stayed near the plane so we could be seen if someone spotted the plane. By nightfall, search planes did fly over. We found an open space and we waved furiously at them. But because we were surrounded by tall, thickly grown trees, we were not seen.

We spent a long Sunday on the mountain, thankful to be alive and expecting to be rescued. As the day wore on, it became clear that Don was failing fast. We began to think we were not going to be found and that we would have to get off the mountain by ourselves.

That night as we tried to sleep, I suddenly thrilled to the soundof footsteps, like the sound of men tramping through the woods. Rescuers! I thought. We've been found!

Suddenly I realized with concern that the ground shook as the footfalls approached. These were not the footsteps of men. It had to be bears! I recognized the distinct smell of bears drifting through the rain and fog. They were drawing close to us, circling as they approached.

My mind flashed back to a childhood Sunday school lesson in which the Israelites were going into battle with an enemy they could not conquer. God told the king to put praisers and musicians at the head of the army to advance on the enemy. This so confused the enemy that they fell on one another in their haste to retreat, giving the victory to the Israelites.

So I began to sing and to praise the Lord with all my might, singing loudly into the quivering darkness. Sure enough, the bears ran down the mountain.

We fell into some needed sleep. It was a fitful night of thoughts and awakenings. It was apparent that we could not be seen from the air. We were not going to be found. Our only hope of getting off this mountain alive was by the help of God Himself. I determined that at daylight we would leave the crash site and start trekking down the mountain.

I was intensely aware of the constant rain and cold but didn't understand at the time how necessary these discomforts were. Our damaged bodies required both the water and the cold. Without the water we would surely have perished of dehydration due to burns; without the cold we would have become badly swollen and lost the use of our muscles.

As dawn approached, Don died, leaving three anxious survivors. I removed two pieces of cloth from Don's clothing to use as cushions for my burned hands. We monitored Pat, who was still conscious but incapable of travel. When it was light enough for us to discern shapes, Evelyn and I left Pat and started down.

Before us lay the dangers of further injury, hypothermia, wild animals, cliffs and waterfalls. Centuries-old fallen trees blocked our progress and thick branches impaired our visibility. But I had an assurance that we would certainly get out and return home.

As we began our descent, I grew uneasy. I somehow knew that we would first have to ascend the mountain before we could intelligently descend it. It took several hours, but at last we reached the top of the mountain, where we could see the lay of the land and chart our course.

It was still raining steadily and we were cold to the bone, but we rejoiced in the discovering that we were being led by the Spirit of God. We could see an impassable river below in the direction that we had chosen. Had we not ascended the mountain, we would have spent half the day getting to the river and the other half returning to our poor little camp. We picked a course for us and with stiffened muscles and aching joints, started downward.

Not long after, we saw a bear across from us on the knoll. Blueberries were in season and he was raking through leaves and berries with his paws and shoveling them into his mouth. The bear was huge.

Between us and the bear the ground was covered with deadfalls and boulders. Our chosen path lay through the deadfalls and across the knoll. We made our tedious way over this terrain and when we reached the other side, the bear was gone.

Conquering obstacle after obstacle, we continued on— crossing gushing streams and detouring around cliffs, brush and devil's club. We forced ourselves on, pulling off a few blueberries to eat as we went.

We came to a stream and my intuition told me we needed to cross at the top, where there was a waterfall. After we crossed, we poured the water from our boots, put them back on and kept going. We walked and sometimes we crawled. At some places we slid down the mountain on our buttocks. We even slithered on our bellies through some tight spots.

It became too dark to see. Exhausted and still suffering from the rain and cold, we prepared to spend another night on the mountain. It was now about 9:30 p.m. on Monday, September 15.

It was too cold to sleep that night but I remember marveling that both Evelyn and I felt no pain from the crash. Our only suffering came from stiff muscles and from the wet, penetrating cold. We knew that back at Game Creek, our small community would be in constant prayer for us. On the mountain we carried on a compelling prayer life with our Maker.

We rose at daylight on Tuesday and passed another long and arduous day traversing the mountains. As night drew near, we crossed a thick muskeg bog very carefully because we knew there could be sinkholes. We then pushed through dense woods. Suddenly we stepped onto the firm sand of a beach. Looking out over the open water, we saw a boat less than one hundred feet from shore!

The men on board were lowering a skiff over the side. "Yell, Evelyn, yell!" I said. "Yell for all you're worth."

I fashioned a flag by attaching a piece of cloth to a stick. I waved the stick back and forth in the air, yelling all the while. The men heard our cries and came to pick us up.

As I boarded the boat, I told one of our rescuers, "I dreamed last night that two hunters were going to pick us up but I didn't know they would be two fishermen."

"Lady, we're not fishermen," he said. "We're hunters. We were just fixing to go into those woods to hunt bear. If you had come out of the woods just a little later, we would already have been in there. If you had chosen any different point to come out, we would not have met you."

I was shaking uncontrollably from hypothermia and was in shock. By the stroke of mercy, one of the passengers on the boat was a registered nurse, who gave me emergency treatment.

The captain of the boat radioed the Coast Guard, which dispatched a helicopter to us. Evelyn got on the helicopter to guide the pilot back to our crash site.

One of the hunters wrapped me in his down parka, and his body heat in the parka began to penetrate my body. In an attempt to warm me up, they forced me to eat some hot moose stew. A short time later the helicopter took us to the hospital in Juneau.

The FAA later told us it was unbelievable that we survived the crash. We were told that a plane going at that speed and impacting directly into a mountain would have caused the seat belts to penetrate our bodies, killing us.

In the day after Evelyn pointed out the crash site, several attempts were made to reach it by foot to retrieve the bodies. But no one succeeded in getting to the site.

Finally on the sixth day, the fog lifted and a helicopter recovery team was able to get to the crash site, accomplishing what trained, able-bodied men with equipment couldn't. Pat was where we had left her, under cover of the Bonanza's ruined wing, having passed on to her heavenly home.

Evelyn and I were able to work our way off the mountain through terrain that turned back the mountain-trained men who tried to get back up to the crash site. They failed to accomplish what two little ladies in their fifties could, through the strength and direction of God. Surely this is His story.

Source: *Cheating Death*

Larry Kaniut

Boat Guy

To put it bluntly, he was peeved. Ticked off. Truly upset. He decided that mankind was vicious. Evil. Maybe even criminal. He decided to remove humankind from the planet. He selected the only righteous man on earth and told him his plan. Or…

What triggered his thoughts? Annihilation. Could I destroy humankind and start over? Man is not what I planned. Maybe I'll destroy everyone on earth but a few…and use them as "seed crop."

Some say there is only verse in the Holy Bible about baseball. Some wonder where it. That's easy…Genesis 1:1… "In the big inning." Ha, ha. But baseball is not what Genesis is about. There is a story about God's frustration with mankind. The condition of the earth broke God's heart. That story features Noah, the only righteous man alive at that time.

Anyone in his right mind would have to wonder. You're kidding, right? You want me to build what? Four-hundred-fifty feet long, seventy-five feet wide, forty-five feet high. Right! And how am I to do this with an axe? Surely you jest.

So, what would you think if you were tasked with building a watercraft over one and a half football fields in length? And no power tools? With the crudest of hand tools? You have to wonder what thoughts assailed Noah when God told him to build an ark.

Noah tried to conduct his affairs according to God's will. Because the crime rate was rising and the earth was rotten to the core, God acted. He saw man's vicious, depraved behavior and told Noah that he had decided to destroy mankind because of his corruptness. God instructed Noah to build a boat and gave Noah the blueprints.

The boat was to be constructed of resinous wood and sealed with tar. It would have three decks—top, middle, bottom. It would be 450 feet in length and 75 feet wide and have a height of 45 feet. That's some kind of boat for a man with an axe and minimal hand tools. The boat would have a skylight eighteen inches below the roof running around the boat. There would be a door in the side.

What? No power tools? Noah must have thought you're kidding, right? Looks like I'm going to have some serious work ahead of me. Building a boat this size could be a bit of a problem... could require some serious scaffolding. *Hmmmmm.* 450 x 75 x45. *Hmmmmm.* Gonna take some major tool sharpening. Who is going to help me perform this task?

Consider a boat one and half football fields in length. What kind of scaffolding would that require?

Can you imagine how much easier it would have been for Noah if he'd had some power tools, maybe scaffolding and ladders. Maybe even a lift truck such as Genie? What about some glue for splicing wood?

What must have been Noah's thoughts to be the only righteous man on the planet?

How could Noah know and how did he feel about being selected by God to start the human race all over (again)? When God told Noah to collect all the animals in pairs so that they could reproduce AND the food for them and his family, how did he plan to accomplish those tasks for the voyage?

Noah complied.

I don't know how many animals there were nor how Noah collected them. I don't know the extent of the boat's construction. It must have taken years with no modern tools.

So Noah set about collecting materials for the boat—lots of wood for scaffolding and the boat body.

When the boat was completed and the animals collected, God told Noah he was going to let it rain for forty days and nights, to destroy every living thing on earth. At God's appointed time he unleashed the rain. Rain came down in torrents and subterranean burst forth. The boat rose with the water level until water covered the mountains. All living creatures died in the flood…except Noah and his family and animals he'd collected.

God also promised Noah that he and his family and the animals would be safe. And God said he would leave a sign from that day on…that a rainbow would appear in the sky as a sign of God's promise to never end life on earth with a flood.

Source: *Snatched from Death*

The Jaws of Death

By Mike Harbaugh

Waiting for daylight through a February night in Alaska can seem to take forever. I thought about family and friends. They were probably beginning to feel that my chances of survival were dim.

Mike Harbaugh shook his head, rubbed his eyes and puzzled at the stark scene before him. Snow flurries pelted his exposed skin. Bone-chilling wind pummeled him. He got to his knees, lost his balance, tumbled forward and started rolling downhill. When he stopped, he saw what remained of his aircraft. Red and white chunks of the Cessna 182 littered the ground. Gradually Mike remembered what had happened.

We woke up that Sunday, February 9, 1986, to cloudy skies in Flat, Alaska, 300 miles northwest of Anchorage. We wondered if we could make it today. I listened to the radio at the cabin with my friend Glen, a retired Assembly of God minister. The weather forecast was for partly sunny skies.

We went outside and took a look. Even though the wind was up a bit, the ceiling was reasonable—forty-five hundred to five thousand feet. Since Merrill Pass summit is about thirty-five hundred feet, we felt we'd have adequate clearance.

We had been waiting since Tuesday and we were eager to get to Soldotna. I had gone to Flat to help Glen in exchange for a little bit of equipment and an engine. In the process of helping Glen ferry some things to Soldotna, I would return with the engine.

After waiting for four hours for the weather to improve, we decided to take off.

We fired up our two Cessna 182s. I took off first in my 1957 model but about twenty miles out of Flat, Glen passed me in his newer aircraft. I lost sight of him after that but didn't think anything about it since his plane cruises ten to fifteen miles an hour faster than mine.

Flying over the Kuskokwim Mountains toward Merrill Pass, I was pushing a heavy headwind. It took longer than usual to reach Merrill Pass, our chosen route through the Alaska Range. I hadn't had any radio contact with the FAA so I didn't have a weather briefing.

I assumed Glen's plane had made it on through the pass. I tried to reach him on the radio but got no response. Buffeted by increasing winds that slammed snow off my windshield from every direction, I fought the controls. The ceiling was still up around five thousand feet. As I entered the pass, I felt confident I could make it through without incident, even though the turbulence bounded me around pretty good.

As I neared the summit, I was surprised to find it socked in with blowing snow. Approaching the Razor's Edge, that section of the pass flanked by sheer rock walls, I scanned the summit for an opening. Maybe I can squeeze through, I thought. Visibility was negligible, so I did a 180-degree turn and flew back to the mouth of the pass.

On the return I did some soul searching. I was thinking, Fuel's low. I'll take another look at the summit. Maybe the weather's cleared a path. I applied left rudder, left aileron and banked into the pass.

Pilots familiar with Merrill Pass know its history. More than a dozen airframes dot the pass, a graveyard of planes sucked into the walls by wind shear or by the inexperience of the pilot.

I approached the summit again at about forty-five hundred feet. There was no opening. I decided to fly a little closer to confirm the situation. It was immediately obvious I couldn't get through, so I banked to leave the pass. It was around three o'clock.

A large pinnacle rock guards the summit. As I came from behind that rock, I looked back down the pass and everything was going fine.

Then I woke up.

The last thing I remember was flying a thousand feet above the pass and coming around the pinnacle. When I banked into the turn, I was at forty-five hundred feet elevation. In a microsecond I lost a thousand feet.

I thought later, probably bought the farm on a wind shear. That pinnacle sheltered me from the wind. But as soon as I came from behind it, that mountain wave coming over the summit sucked me down and gobbled me up.

By the time I gained consciousness and started to figure out what had happened, it was about 5 p.m., with darkness an hour and a half away. At first I didn't' realize anything was wrong. I didn't hurt. It was just like a new day. I looked around. I was sitting out in the snow with wind blowing in my face. It didn't look like Soldotna. It sure wasn't my airstrip in Wasilla.

I noticed the pinnacle a quarter of a mile away. Eventually it came to me that I was on the west side of the summit of Merrill Pass.

Though the area of the crash looked steep, my Cessna 182 was not near cliffs. It was toward the bottom of the pass on the only fairly level spot in the summit area. The Cessna had just skidded across the bench, hit rocks and shed pieces of airplane as it went until it dumped me out into the snow. I was on the uphill side of the fuselage, some fifty feet away.

I saw my coveralls, down mittens and parka hood out in the snow. I put on the extra clothes and started to drag myself down to the fuselage. But I was now feeling pain so intense that I blacked out again. When I came to, it was starting to get dark. I was getting wet lying in the snow. I managed to drag myself the rest of the way to the fuselage.

I threw a mattress into the fuselage and crawled as far up into the tail so I could to get out of the gnawing wind. I stayed there shivering and awake most of the night, dozing off from time to time.

I realized it was up to me to just wait it out. If the Lord wanted me dead, I'd already be dead. There was a good chance I'd be rescued in the next few days, as soon as the clouds cleared and rescuers could get into the pass. My friend Glen knew my chartered course. I felt confident I'd be found right away.

I worried about my family, knowing they would be concerned when I failed to show up and would have no way of knowing whether I was alive or dead. People lose hope quickly for those who go down the wintertime in Alaska. I didn't want my wife to suffer, thinking I was out here dead or dying. All I could do was pray for my family. I was sure they were praying for me.

As the morning broke, I realized the wind was still coming in the open end of the fuselage where it was sheared off from the baggage compartment. I knew I had to do something.

Apparently filled with blood from a cut on my nose, during the night my eyes had frozen shut. In the morning I had to pry them open. I tried to assess my injuries. I had stopped losing blood. My ankle was white and stiff and I couldn't move it. My collar bone gave me sharp pain every time I moved. I had some cuts and my face was messed up. I couldn't feel my teeth with my tongue; I couldn't tell if my teeth were knocked out or just what problems existed in my mouth.

I decided to see if I could find any food or gear. With the injured ankle and collar bone, I couldn't get around too well. Sharp strips of shredded aluminum clung to the fuselage opening; to avoid injury, I crawled out through the baggage compartment door.

My agony and efforts were compounded by the fact that I had lost my boots—I fly without them to better feel the rudder pedals. They were somewhere on the mountain.

I examined the fuselage. The seats had been ripped out and all the equipment and every piece of paper was gone. How did I survive? I felt like a shipwreck victim scouring the beach for survival debris.

The plane was scattered for half a mile along the hillside. It appeared the stoves, sleeping bag, food and everything else had gone down the canyon. I did find a small cardboard box. Not far away was the airplane door.

I wanted to bring my finds back to the fuselage. In agony I pushed the door and the cardboard box back to the airplane. I placed the door across the open part of the aircraft to shelter me from the wind, which continued unabated from the east. The temperature was staying in the twenties. I knew I couldn't afford to get any wetter than I was.

I passed that day trying to figure out ways to stay alive. I opened the cardboard box as if it were a Christmas gift. Having no idea what was in it, I was delighted to find wool socks, a dish, rags and some Tupperware cups. After my down gloves got wet, I used the socks for mittens.

I had read articles describing how Eskimos use oil skins next to their skin to melt snow when they're out on the Bering ice pack. I took a cup, filled it with snow and put it next to my skin to melt water. It produced a few sips of water every hour or two. I was very dehydrated and I knew I couldn't go on for long without more water.

I kept thinking of my family. If I don't make it back, how will they be provided for? I don't have any insurance. We've got no savings to speak of. What will become of them if I don't make it? How will Linda handle the emotional stress, not knowing whether I'm dead or alive? Fortunately we have good friends and a good church; they will take care of her, give her emotional support.

I rested to conserve my energy. I didn't want to doze off for a long periods of time, so I only took cat naps. I tried to stay dry. I was so deathly thirsty by the end of the day that I ate small amounts of snow and ice, even though I knew it would increase the danger of hypothermia.

That night was a long one. Waiting for daylight through a February night in Alaska can seem to take forever. I continued thinking about family and friends. They were probably beginning to feel that my chances of survival were growing dim. I was hoping, and had faith, that someone would find me the next day.

I awoke to bad weather. A tremendous wind was blowing the snow off Chakachamna Lake and up into the pass, forming a big whiteout cloud that spiraled upward. Visibility was poor and a pilot wouldn't be able to see a thing.

That morning I worked a little harder to melt water. I remembered that a generator belonging to Glen was strapped to the floorboard in place of the passenger seat. It probably had some gas in it.

I searched my pockets and came up with some matches. I got my hopes up until I realized the matches had received enough condensation from the blowing snow to get wet. They wouldn't light. Then I saw that the battery was still in the tail of the airplane. My hands were getting stiff because of cold and exposure but I managed to remove the cover without any tools. Wiring was still there, running back to my tail strobe light. I thought that with a piece of wire I might get a spark across the positive and negative battery poles. I stripped a piece of wire with my pocket knife and I got a spark from the battery.

I took a Tupperware dish and crawled up to the generator, splashed some gas from the generator's tanks into the dish and returned to my cubbyhole. I decided to make a fire right on the aluminum floor, hoping to get a little warmth from it and to melt enough snow to make two cups of water.

Feeling it would burn pretty good, I cut the cardboard box into small pieces. Holding a piece of cardboard in my fingers, I soaked it in gasoline then sparked the soaked paper. A small explosion ignited the paper. I burned my fingers, a small price to pay for a drink of water.

I fed a couple pieces of cardboard onto the fire and it took off. I packed my ceramic cups with snow and placed them tightly to the fire. Eventually the heat rendered a couple of cups of water and I called it good for the day, saving the rest of the cardboard and gas so I could melt more water later.

I was becoming weaker. I prayed and again thought about my family, fortifying myself for another long, dark, cold night on the mountain. I prayed that the Lord would assure my family I was still alive. I prayed that God would help the Air Force and the Civil Air Patrol find me.

That night the skies began to clear. With clearing skies, temperatures plummeted. The colder it got, the weaker I became. As I got stiffer and couldn't move, I knew I had to stay awake to survive. I fought sleep.

Morning dawned clear and cold. Though the sheer granite walls of my gray prison seemed to mock me, it was a beautiful spot. Mountains stretched as far as I could see. The azure blue sky was crystal clear. Iced-over waterfalls and pearly white snow and glaciers glistened. Snow covered the ground in places.

I got a perfect view of the perpendicular walls of Merrill Pass. Their very steepness is one reason I didn't mind flying Merrill Pass in the winter. Not much snow sticks to these steep walls, so a pilot gets the benefit of that gray rock contrast in a whiteout. You can almost always see the walls.

I decided to melt some more snow for water. I went through the same process, including burning my fingers. As I worked at melting snow, I was surprised by an airplane flying over. He was so low that I hardly heard him before he passed. He quickly disappeared down the pass.

The plane looked like a Cessna 180, but my eyes were hurting so badly that I couldn't tell for sure. I thought that perhaps I had gotten some Plexiglas in my eye or that I was suffering from a form of snow blindness.

A few minutes later the plane came around again. I swiftly headed out the baggage door and waved at the plane.

He returned a third time. I was able to focus my vision better. I looked right into the cockpit at the pilot. We made eye contact and I knew for sure he saw me.

We were a few hundred feet apart at the most. The plane came right down into the pass. I was looking right in the side window at him.

I felt really buoyed and confident that I was going to be rescued.

I dozed off. When I awoke around noon, I heard airplanes overhead. I looked out my door and recognized the bright orange-and-white beavers of the Anchorage Civil Air Patrol.

I figured the planes were circling the pass as they waited for a helicopter to arrive. I could also hear a C-130 up there. I crawled back into my haven to rest, feeling very good knowing that rescue was only hours away.

By 3 p.m. it had been more than five hours since the first plane flew over. Still no helicopter. I was sure I had been spotted but I still became a little concerned. I decided to get out and wave at the airplanes. Maybe they hadn't seen me.

Wearing the long wool socks as mittens, I started waving. Nothing happened, so I climbed back into my nest.

Soon after, a small private plane cruised through the pass, low and slow, just as the pilot had done that morning.

I made it to the door, but I didn't have enough strength left to get out of the airplane. All I could do was prop myself up in the baggage compartment and wave. The pilot came through a second time. I looked right in the window at the pilot. I know he saw me.

My hands were so swollen and had no feeling. My legs had lost feeling too. But I still had pain that made movement almost impossible.

Now it was dusk and I heard no more planes. But I knew they had seen me. I figured the helicopter would arrive in the morning. One more night, I told myself. I can make it one more night.

But about 6:30 that evening I heard the droning of an airplane far overhead. Suddenly a burst of light lit up the canyon like daytime. It was a parachute flare coming down. It never occurred to me they would come in at night. I had assumed I'd have to wait until morning.

Mike Harbaugh's disappearance set in place a massive air search that included Alaska State Troopers and the Civil Air Patrol. On February 12, the third day of the search, an HC-130 Kingbird overflew Merrill Pass to coordinate the efforts of thirteen small private aircraft.

A grueling day of search had revealed nothing. Then word came to the Rescue Coordination Center at Elmendorf Air Force Base that Mike Harbaugh had been sighted by two separate pilots and that he was alive.

Knowing that chances for survival in such severe weather diminished by the minute, the rescue team scrambled. Humanitarian concerns dictated a night flight. Major Merle Perrine called the 71st Aerospace Rescue and Recovery Squadron, requesting a chopper and crew immediately.

Helicopter pilot Captain Scott Sommer, a veteran of 2,100 hours of flying time, responded with pararescuers Sergeant Ryan J. Beckman and Airman First Class Patrick Keller. They loaded a bolt cutter, picks, axes and medical supplies. Joining them were the co-pilot, Second Lieutenant Kevin Churchill and the flight engineer, Sergeant Richard Proctor II.

The HC-130 Kingbird returned to refuel before joining the chopper crew in the pass. Crew members of the Kingbird were excited but apprehensive.

The strategy was for the Kingbird to overfly Merrill Pass, dropping flares to provide light for the helicopter. The two-million-candlepower four-minute flares would be dropped every three and a half minutes, the overlap in time ensuring constant light.

The chopper crew's lives depended upon the supply of light; it would be impossible to navigate the gorge in the dark. If the light failed, it would be tough to climb straight back up the pass without hitting the rock wall.

Blackness engulfed the plane and the helicopter as they neared their destination. At the site, complications developed when some of the dropped flares didn't ignite. The chopper hung in the blackness, fighting air currents and the invisible black canyon walls.

At one point a flare dropped onto the floor of the kingbird threatened to ignite the fuel supply, but Senior Airman Bradley Brown kicked it out the door. The flare dropped into the void, cascading light earthward.

Aboard the helicopter, Captain Sommer spotted the downed plane. The helicopter hovered near the plane's wreckage as Sergeant Beckman prepared to exit. Knifelike arctic wind sliced through the open door as Beckman launched himself onto a snowdrift. He put on snowshoes and crossed the slope to Harbaugh's Cessna.

Beckman called out and reached for the door shield to pull it away. He saw an inert mass bundled against the weather. He radioed to the crew, "He's alive. Send a spine board and cervical collar down with Keller."

They could hardly believe I was alive. I didn't look alive. I figured I would crawl out to them, but I was too weak to move. All I could do was watch them rescue me and enjoy it.

I didn't know they were racing against time and a limited amount of flares. There were no wasted efforts. The two guys ripped the aluminum away from the door and strapped me into a Stokes litter. After securing me, they pulled me through the opening in my plane.

One of the men pressed against me to shield me from the churning rotor wash before signaling for the crew to hoist me. Up I went, into the chopper. After three nights on the mountain I left my tomb, resurrected.

The helicopter crew gave me oxygen and administered intravenous fluids. The helicopter flew toward Anchorage, dangerously low on fuel. It was my first helicopter ride. I was flat on my back but I was thrilled.

When I arrived at the emergency room, it just so happened that Dr. William J. Mills was there. He is a leading frostbite and orthopedic-bone specialist. His presence further confirmed my belief that my survival and rescue was a miracle by God.

I'd lost thirty pounds. My core body temperature was down to about 80 degrees (and that's after my body had been warmed on the flight into town). It was one of the lowest core temperatures the hospital had ever recorded in a patient who survived.

I was put in the burn unit, where they ran me through the whirlpools so slowly warm my body. I was completely helpless that first week. After the first three or four days, they managed to elevate my core temperature and got me rehydrated and stabilized.

My leg never hurt me; it had apparently frozen completely. The swelling cut off the circulation and made it freeze fairly quickly, probably eliminating more serious problems. The doctors waited a week to see if I would regain circulation in my leg. I never did. They finally had to amputate the leg.

The hospital's medical staff did a tremendous job in treating me. I got the best care that was available during the three weeks I was in the hospital.

I didn't move around much for six months. I had no money to pay for salvaging my plane. At first the FAA talked like I might have to retrieve the wreck, but eventually I found out I could just let it rest among the other ghost ships in the pass.

Looking back on the rescue, I just praise the Lord that something urged the rescuers to come for me.. The night they snatched me from the mountain, the temperature dropped way below zero. I probably wouldn't have made it through the night.

As far as I know, I'm the first crash victim who has ever come away from the summit alive. The same crew that rescued me had moved the bodies from another crash site a few months before my accident. When they found the bodies, brown bears had been feeding on them. This crew didn't want to leave me overnight and come back the next day for a body. They were divinely motivated.

Source: *Cheating Death*

The Rest of the Story

Over the years since our books were published, I've had the good fortune of having participants in those events contact me. One such was from *Cheating Death* wherein Mike Harbaugh slammed into and skidded across the slope of Merrill Pass, pockmarked with fuselages of other planes where the pilots weren't prepared to leave the bone yard. Some of the stories in my books were finished...until years later when the following information emerged regarding those "finished" stories.

KEN E. GRIFFIN

I received an email from Ken E. Griffin in June 2005 about his participation in the Harbaugh event. He wrote:

I realize the book has been out for over 10 years but I just read an excerpt regarding the rescue of Mike Harbaugh from Merrill Pass in the chapter titled "Jaws of Death."

I was the radio operator onboard the HC-130 aircraft that initially located and then directed the rescue operation on scene. You'll never know how close Mike came to remaining there overnight if not permanently. Snippets of a conversation I overheard over monitored radio frequencies between the civilian aircraft which spotted him and a Flight Service Station he was communicating with clued us in as to his whereabouts which subsequently led to his rescue that evening.

I say it was a close call because we had already sent the various search aircraft home for the day and were ourselves heading back to Elmendorf. We decided to drop a flare in order for Mike to know he had been spotted and that help was on the way.

I radioed the RCC at Elmendorf and requested our needed

supplies including fuel because there was no way we were leaving him there for another night. We also requested the launching of the helicopters noted in your story.

We returned to Elmendorf and took flight again as soon as we were provisioned. We caught up with the Jolly's on the way and led them to the location.

Everything else is in the story except our crew had put in a 14 ½ hour flying day but to a man agreed we had a job to do and we did it.

Just another insight into the story. Just file it away.

Thanks for your attention.

Ken Griffin

CYNTHIA DUSEL-BACON

Call me clown, nuisance, panhandler, habituated, menace, killer, man-eater. I could be any of these. Or all of them. I'm your average North American bear and I come in three flavors— black, grizzly or polar. Most of the time I mind my own business, making my living scrounging grub, resting, protecting my cubs, looking over my pecking order shoulder or finding a mate. I'm not interested in people…usually. However every once in a while I rock your world and things get ugly.

While listening to the radio in 1977, I learned about a lady who had been frightfully mauled by a bear. I hoped to acquire the details of the event. Her tale of confrontation and survival is one of the most amazing I've ever heard…so much so that other authors have included it in their books or magazines.

I wrote Cynthia at the Stanford University Medical Center to which she'd been transferred and suggested if she were willing to share her story, that she call me collect. After all, how could a person without arms write?

Imagine my surprise when a short time later I received her cassette taped story and a letter. She had typed her letter with a stylus between her jaws. She was eager to share her story in hopes of sparing others the dilemma similar to hers. And she stated, "I couldn't be more pleased about your efforts to amass all available information about bear maulings in Alaska. I can't think of a greater contribution one could make to educate people about the potential danger of a bear encounter. I believe very strongly in what you are doing."

Cynthia decided that her tape recorded, off-the-cuff, account of her experience needed to be written up as a complete article so she, helped by her father, wrote it up and sent it to me to include in *Alaska Bear Tales*, which took me five years to research and write.

Subsequently we met on a couple of occasions. The first time our family met her was a couple of years later when I was on my way to commercial fish Bristol Bay...so I missed Cynthia. Our 6-year-old son was most impressed that she could squash a paper cup with her artificial split-hook, which she chose as the most functional replacements for her hands.

We met about five years after when Cyn travelled to Alaska with an assistant and I drove them to Girdwood. I told her that she and her assistant could come to our home for dinner instead of staring at the four walls of the hotel. She agreed; I called my wife and we headed home.

Once inside our house, Cyn told me that her shoulders and neck were sore from wearing her artificial arms and wondered if it would be okay to remove them. I told her that we did not normally allow it but that we would make an exception in her case. Her assistant helped her remove her prosthetic devices and she put on a poncho.

I had some concern that our children might have a negative reaction to a handicapped person, but it was one of our most awesome experiences. My brother-in-law and sister Lester and Laura Lee Smothers were visiting and while Les ate peanuts at the kitchen table, he asked Cynthia if she wanted some. She assented and Les removed peanuts from shells, placed them on a napkin and slid it across the table to her. She bent at the waist and ate the peanuts, much like a cat or dog would do.

Amazingly beautiful.

We receive Christmas cards every year from Cyn and Charlie, usually with their son Ian and his wife included. They live very productive lives. In 2017 when Ted Gorsline, former animal handler for Mutual of Omaha's TV show "Wild Kingdom," contacted me about his plans to write three bear books, he requested usage of some of my Alaska stories. He later provided a cover quote for *SAFE with Bears* in which he claimed "Larry Kaniut is the dean of bear book writers…" When I realized he was writing not three books but a nine volume set, I sent him his complimentary copy of *SAFE with Bears* to Germany, I inscribed it "From the Dean of bear book writers to the King of bear book writers."

I've just finished his volume number nine. On page 24 Ted has a picture of Cynthia Dusel-Bacon which I've never seen. He includes her story from my *Alaska Bear Tales* AND Cynthia's comments. From her "How my accident could have been prevented," I've cherry-picked three paragraphs:

…"I believe what would have prevented my accident from happening was to have had a gun and not been alone. Had I been with another person, we might have been more intimidating to the bear or one of us could have been on the radio calling for help while the other tried to scare off the bear…

"My boss had a strong belief that guns were more dangerous than they were helpful, and I was talked out of my original request to carry a gun. I should have insisted and proactively got firearms training. As a result of my accident, the U.S.G.S. subsequently provided firearms and bear-behavior training annually and made a firearm available for anyone working in Alaska.

"I can't say that I would've chosen the exact right moment to shoot the bear, which maintained a 10 foot distance from me prior to attacking, but if I had been trained in bear behavior, I would've recognized the bear's raised hair and chomping teeth as sure signs that the bear was going to attack. It would've been an easy shot."

Ted has done an incredible researching bears and the need for protection against them. His website is Ted-Gorsline.com. I suggest you buy his books.

The day after Thanksgiving 2021 Cynthia responded to my request for an update with the following e-mail:

Summary of post accident for Larry K.

Since my losing my arms to the bear in 1977, I have been able to live the happy and lucky life to which I had aspired as a newlywed. My husband, Charlie, took my lack of arms in stride and saw me as the same woman he married. Being an outstandingly competent husband, who always enjoyed cooking, he took it over full-time, along with grocery shopping, which he also enjoys and looks forward to seeing his cashier friends during his weekly shopping excursions. Being a go-getter myself, I had to get used to being taken care of and have done very well at accepting and enjoying being a "kept woman". Charlie refers to me as "management", which I try to do well. Such duties have been managing our son's care, driving him everywhere before he turned 16, planning vacations, dealing with home improvement projects, etc.

I'm also happy to report that I was able to continue my career as a USGS Research Geologist specializing in the geology and mineral deposit potential of east-central Alaska. Having my husband come with me as an exemplary (overqualified) field assistant made all of this possible. I planned and supervised fieldwork, but my husband was the gun-bearer and sample collector. I've published almost 70 scientific papers and maps, starting out by typing one key at a time with my left hook, then, since 1995 dictating everything with voice recognition software. Because my managers at the USGS gave me a chance to see what I can do using my brain, and with my husband's support in the field, and my own publication record, I was able to be promoted through the years to the top of the Research Geology grade hierarchy. I retired in 2014 and still am writing scientific papers and working with the next generation of geologists working in Alaska as a volunteer (Scientist Emerita).

As far as my hobbies go, losing my arms caused me to have to look elsewhere for my musical passion, since playing the guitar was no longer an option. Instead, I took up playing the chromatic harmonica and learned to play jazz standards, which I have enjoyed since childhood hearing them played by my musical father. After evolving to a modified hands-free harmonica in a neck rack, I was able to join a jazz quintet and play that kind of music for senior groups – even for money! I've regularly attended and occasionally played at the annual international convention of the Society for the Preservation and Advancement of the Harmonica (SPAH) and am the Chair of the Youth Committee, which gives scholarships for young players to come to the convention. For the past year, I've been taking harmonica lessons on Skype to learn to improvise in jazz – not an easy task, but I'm really enjoying the journey.

I stay in shape through hiking and swimming and have enjoyed backpacking in the High Sierra of California with my husband and son. At 75, we've evolved to staying in mountain cabins and doing day hikes. In addition to geology, all aspects of nature interest me, especially butterflies and birds. Every year on "bear day", August 13, I thank my lucky stars that I've been able to have another year that I almost didn't get to have.

Source: *What's Bruin?*

ROBIN CANDROW

I heard about Robin's story and contacted him. He responded with the following email.

Email received 1/1/2004

Dear Mr. Kaniut,

Here is my story, as promised. I hope it's what you are looking for, and if not, I hope you can at least enjoy it. You asked me what I did here in Whitehorse, well, at the moment I am an unemployed Class 1 driver, but just recently got out of employment as a mover for a local moving company here. It seems as if I may be leaving the north soon to go work for a trucking company in Labrador, but rest assured, I'll be back. The north is my home, and could never stay away.

hope you enjoy,

Robin Candow

My story begins in the summer of 1998. It was an exciting summer for me, as I had just finished school, was turning 19, and planned on doing a little exploring of the Yukon. That was also the summer of the great Fox Lake forest fire. Some friends and I drove through some real bad smoke filled spots on our way up to the Dawson City Music Festival. On the drive back from Dawson that weekend, I showed my friends, where just a few weeks earlier, I had my very first encounter with a huge grizzly bear. At least, I thought it was huge.

It was getting around the end of June, and I had decided to take a trip up to Dawson City, just for kicks. Not having any money for gas, I figured I would just hitchhike. So I packed my tent, clothes, a couple cooking pans, some food, and an old hunting knife I found to attach to my belt. In a way, I'm really glad I hitchhiked. I wasn't getting rides all the time, and those that did pick me up, were only willing to go a short distance before dropping me off again. Normally, this would just irritate me, but every time I got dropped off somewhere, I would walk along the road until somebody picked me up, and would get a really good view of the Yukon's great outdoors. It was really exhilarating; as I've driven this road many times, and never felt the freedom I felt that day.

Well, I finally made it to Dawson City in the early evening, just in time to find an old friend and set up camp in "Tent City". You had to catch a ferry across the river to get to Tent City, and then back again to get back into Dawson. So I did, then my friend and I went to a local diner for some grub and hot coffee.

My whole weekend in Dawson City was quite memorable, as I was able to see all the great historic sites of the old north and see how much life has changed from the gold rush. I even met some really nice people while I was there, including a small group of people staying in Tent City that I would talk to long into the nights.

Then on Sunday morning, I packed up my tent and clothes, and threw my cooking pans and left over food back into my bag. It was time to head back to Whitehorse. I grabbed my old hunting knife and went to strap it onto my belt, but the sheath snapped right at the belt attachment. I tried to rig it up so it would just hang, but every time I walked it banged against my leg and started to hurt, so I just took it off and put it into my backpack.

Sunday was worse for rides. Out of the entire 533km between Whitehorse and Dawson, I truly believe I walked 200km of it. There was next to no one on the road that day, and I was starting to debate whether I should keep going, turn back, or find a place to set my tent back up and camp the night.

I had passed the Dempster Highway cut-off, where someone had dropped me off, and walked down the road for a little over an hour without seeing a single car traveling in either direction. Boredom began to really sink in, and I was trying to find things to keep myself busy. I started picking up small rocks and began tossing them into the trees that lined the side of the road. After awhile, the trees seemed to be going away from the road, as a small ditch began to form. So I threw the rocks harder.

Every once in awhile, I would hear a noise in the trees like a squirrel, and would aim my rocks in that direction, knowing I would never hit anything, or so I thought. I threw a nice rounded rock as hard as I could towards the sound of a snapping twig. I heard a thump, a grunt, and then the bushes began to move.

I knew immediately I was in trouble, and whatever was down there was big. I hadn't seen a vehicle in about an hour and a half, maybe more, I was in the middle of nowhere, and all I had to protect myself was an old hunting knife that I...MY KNIFE! I tapped my hip, and remembered I had put it into my bag. Just as I started to take my bag off my back, I looked down into the ditch to see this huge Grizzly staring me right in the eyes.

My mind raced faster than it ever had. Don't move! Play dead! Run! Don't look it in the eyes! Help! Dear God, please help! I was frozen with fear. Sweat poured down into my eyes, but I didn't dare even blink.

I tried to think if I should go for my knife, and risk this bear coming right at me, or to just stay still, and hope he goes away. As it turned out, this bear had no intentions on just going away. He began to saunter slowly towards me, and I could feel my heart stop, or so it seemed. I started to slowly back up, now more scared then I thought possible. I didn't know what to do, I mean, I've never taken courses for this kind of stuff. I wished someone could have yelled out what I needed to do, cause my brain had just shut down.

The bear was about 50 feet away, but continued to walk slowly towards me. Suddenly, I saw a slight flash out of the corner of my eyes. I looked up the road to see, to my amazement, the first vehicle I'd seen in almost 2 hours. A blue pick-up truck came around the bend up the road and was heading right in my direction. My heart began to beat again.

As the truck came closer, the bear stopped and looked at it. Then, I did the one thing that could have gone either way from saving my life, to ending it. I threw my backpack back around my shoulders, and ran to the middle of the road and began waving my arms as hard as I could. I wanted more than anything for that truck to stop, but as it got closer, the driver turned and went around me.

I just about started to cry.

The bear, now triggered by my sudden movements, came towards me again, only this time, faster than before. At that exact time, I cursed to myself as I turned and ran towards the departing truck, which slammed on its brakes once the driver saw me turn and run in his rear view mirror, as at that time, the driver finally saw the bear.

Now I've heard stories that bears can outrun any human, but this day I won the race. I probably broke a speed record that day as I ran for the opening door of that beautiful rusted blue truck. Within what seemed like an eternity, but must have been a split second, I reached the door, threw my bag around my shoulder and into the truck, and jumped in myself, yelling for the driver to go. He had his foot burying the pedal the second I had hopped in the truck.

Suddenly, just as the truck began to move, we felt a huge jolt. I looked back to see that the bear had hit the side of the truck, before deciding to stop its chase. I couldn't thank the man driving that truck enough.

A little while up the road, we stopped at a rest area for a quick pit stop. I was surprised I held it in as long as I had, and didn't leave any for the bear to sniff in my tracks. Once I had jumped out, I looked to the rear of the truck to see where the bear had hit. It was quite obvious as there was now a nice sized dent about the size and shape of a football in the side of the truck.

The man gave me a ride to Pelly Crossing where I had to walk again, this time though, I stopped within sight of town, and had my knife tucked into my pants.

I'll never forget that day as long as I live, and haven't hitchhiked any great distance since then. Every once in awhile I get the opportunity to take a drive up back up to Dawson for a quick visit or for work, and every time I do, I shiver at the spot where I was sure I was a grizzly's lunch.

Source: *What's Bruin?*

A Moo in the Night

On a night in 2009 Pam asked me if I'd heard the sound of a tugboat moaning on the river

"No. What did it sound like?"

"A low moaning. I've heard it a few times."

"When?"

"Today."

"What do you mean?"

"I've heard it a few times at different places in the house—by the water heater and in the kitchen and the bedroom."

We retired to the family room to watch a video. That's when I heard the lamentably sad moaning, "mooowwwaaaahhhhh." Momentarily stunned, our eyes riveted on each other.

I suggested maybe it was a moose outside the window. Or since I had worked on the incoming phone line earlier, maybe it was coming from that line.

Mooowwwaaahhhh.

Thinking it might be coming from the radio between us, I unplugged it and held it to my ear. No moan. Then I gave it to Pam.

Picture this: two geezers alternately holding a "dead" radio to their ears. No moaning.

I replaced the radio on the stand.

Mooowwwaaaahhhh.

Not from the radio.

All of a sudden I detected the culprit. "Oh, it's Jill's cell phone on the stand by the radio."

So our daughter's cell phone tricked us both.

Source: *Heavenly Rose*

People Say The Darndest Things

I've been accused of many things by people who have read or heard about our books...even been told I needed to see a shrink. Hmmmm. The following vignette captures one of those events.

STUDENT: "What do you do with all your money?"

In the mid-1980s a student asked me that question as I sat before my tenth grade English class. I laughed so hard I nearly fell off my little stool. When I stopped laughing, I asked Kim to explain her question.

She said, "Well, you told us you had a Leer jet agency with offices all over the world."

I agreed, "Yes, I said that."

"And you said that you made 1.5 million dollars last summer on your lawn mower business."

I concurred again, "Yes, I told you that."

"And you're rich and famous," she concluded.

I fought the impulse to ask this tenth grade brunette if she were wearing a blonde wig. Then, without insulting her by asking if her hair were dyed, I said, "Yes, I told you all those things. I assumed you students knew that I was only joking about owning a leer jet agency and a lawn mower business."

Source: *What's Bruin?*

Larry Kaniut

Date with Death

I first heard about Paul Coleman over the radio news about Wednesday the eleventh of November, 1992. As always my ears perked up and I wondered and hoped that searchers would find him. His disappearance was compounded by the fact that his insulin and syringes were found in his pickup.

I wanted to help in the search but had committed to take Laura Lee (sister) with Pam (wife) and me to Lewiston, Idaho, on the 13th. The following week the official search was called off. I wanted to help out, but I was committed to help Pam wrap up her Christmas shopping prior to leaving for Anchorage the 20th. When I heard the news during the week, I decided to go help on Saturday the 21st.

I called Larry Coleman the evening of the 20th to make sure I could get to the searcher rendezvous efficiently the next day. He informed me that I needed to go to mile 31 east of Estacada and turn left at the marker to space 1 of the Silver Bow RV Park. He told me to look for Bruce or Barbara Coleman or Curtis Bunch. I set the clock for 5:40 in anticipation of a little over an hour's drive.

I got up and awakened daughter Jill (as she'd requested— to make me breakfast and lunch, but I told her I had some things in my pack already). I headed out in a driving rain and wind, listening to the radio for news as I traveled 99W to I-5 to 205 and ultimately the Estacada off ramp.

Black enshrouded everything, rain hammered the land, puddling on the roadway. There was little traffic. As I rolled along, country and western sounds honkey tonked from the radio--Tanya Tucker belted out "Two Sparrows in a Hurricane" and Alabama crooned "I'm in a Hurry and Don't Know Why." The weather man warned of strong 60 or 65 mile per hour

233

winds along Oregon's north coast with strong gusts to be felt in the Portland-Cascade Mountain areas. At the I-5 overpass at Tualatin, I got my first glimpse of light—layered gray clouds blanketed the eastern sky.

Windshield wipers rhythmically thumped. I increased my speed to 65 and the Suburban shuddered side to side with sporadic wind blasts. A ghostly eighteen-wheeler loomed ahead, crowned with amber lights and lumbering along, water spewing from its tandem wheels.

I kept a steady speed toward Estacada and when I'd left her eastern boundary, I enjoyed the rural scenery in the lightening dawn—farms, barns, outbuildings. Highway 224 snaked along, large trees dotting the shoulders. After half dozen miles the 45 mile speed limit evolved into 55, and I stair stepped up into the Cascades through a few fog patches.

I didn't see the milepost at 32 but caught the RV sign out of the corner of my eye and made a hasty turn, zoomed up the asphalt to the park, discovered three or four dozen vehicles scattered along the roadway near camp trailers. A guy told me to head up to the recreation center.

I slogged through the muddied ground under the fir trees to the center. A Red Cross wagon and an ambulance were parked outside. I entered and discovered a gathering of nearly fifty people—mostly men. Two guys were informing the searchers about the search plan. Spread before Curtis Bunch (?) was a large black and white topo map with grease pen markings designating the area that had previously been searched.

A lady (maybe his sister ?) came in showed the searchers a syringe like Paul's and made some comments about it and being careful. Announcements were made about where to get pancakes for breakfast and sandwiches to take along.

Two groups of seven men were to work together in a grid search where Paul's pack had been found. I caught a ride with Robert O'Brien, a builder from Aurora, and we joined a caravan of eight other vehicles driving east toward Detroit. Ten miles before we got to a mountain road we encountered snow along the roadway (and hit one thirty to fifty yard stretch of four inches in the road).

Due to a miscommunication we lost Greg, our leader. After several minutes he appeared and we went on ahead. By the time we reached the search area a mile and a half from the highway we were in six to eight inches of very wet snow, and it was about 10:30 a.m. We exited our vehicles, put on our raingear and walked down a side road, spread out twenty feet apart and started into the woods. There were fifteen of us spread out over 100-120 yards.

A flagger was on the end to mark our path, and we kicked along in the snow for a half mile to the next road. Then we regrouped, moved another length up the road and started back for the first road. We covered more territory and regrouped about noon. After a brief consultation it was jointly agreed to eat lunch, warm up and resume the search after returning from a newly located base camp closer than the RV park.

We drove back down the mountain into snowless country, found the new camp, pulled in to a roaring camp fire. The Red Cross wagon was dispensing chili, hot dogs, coffee, hot chocolate and pop. As Robert and I surmised, the search was over for the day. It was after 1 o'clock; and we figured we wouldn't get back on the road until 2; it would be an hour to the search area, and we'd have only a half hour to search.

It was disappointing to us as we had wanted to continue the search. Robert and I had mentioned we could gobble a sandwich at the search area, eliminate the long drive to and from base camp and stay with our objective. But the officials chose to return to camp.

We left that camp for the original base camp and checked out. At that time we learned from a woman that Paul's car had been moved from his hunting area (or at least somewhere up the highway where he had made a phone call to his wife) to a lower area (Memaloose) which had been the object of the original, thorough search.

In introspection I was amazed by the apparel and mind set of those who came to assist in the search. Their volunteerism was admirable, however their wilderness skills were greatly lacking.

At least three men did not have gloves. One wore tennis shoes. Most wore rubberized-LL Bean type rubber boot packs. A third wore Helly Hansen type rain gear. Others wore rubber coats; one had a GI olive drab coat; many wore fabric coats; I was the only one wearing a poncho.

People periodically wrung rain water from their gloves as it continued to rain hard the entire time.

From *The Oregonian*, February 2, 1993, appeared the article "Missing hunter's body found," by Dennis McCarthy and Steven Amick.

This article highlighted the recovery of Paul Robert Coleman's body and theorized about the cause of his death. The body of the 28-year-old Portland man was found on the bank of the river by a man and his son while they prepared to pan gold near the confluence of the north and south forks of the Clackamas River.

Deputy medical examiner Jeff McLennan indicated there was no evidence of foul play. It was uncertain whether Coleman's death was caused by his inability to medicate himself with insulin. A diabetic, Paul Coleman left his insulin in his pickup ten miles southeast of Estacada. It was found the day after his proposed return from the hunting trip. The pickup was originally parked a mile upstream from where the deceased was found.

Captain Donald A. Vicars of the Clackamas Country Sheriff's Office theorized that Coleman "might have fallen from a steep embankment above the river and become entangled in some tree." Vicars said "the victim could have been picked up by the river when the water was high from winter storms and carried to the spot where his body was located." Vicars theorized "it would have been very possible to have missed Coleman because of the steep terrain and the trees and bushes, making it difficult to get tracking dogs to the area." (page B-3)

I was saddened by the loss of this young man and wish he

could have been found. His loss further decries the need to have a partner when you go into the field, because, all too often, the common place evolves into catastrophe.

Source: *Swallowed Alive*

Jesus and the Temple

In spite of the dismal thoughts about the men who were supposed to be aiding the worshippers, it was difficult not to notice my surroundings. Countless open air markets dotted her cobblestone streets and merchants hawked their diverse wares—from live creatures to breads, milk, vegetables and fruits. I decided to stop to purchase a few items for Gaius, including a pomegranate for his daughter. It was a beautiful cosmopolitan city.

Before I could accomplish that task, however, I was surprised by the din of voices and footfalls on the roadway just beyond the temple.

That was my first time to see the Nazarene. I heard before I saw. The steady drumbeat of voices and sandals on the cobblestones gave warning of an approaching throng.

I saw him from a distance. But as the gap narrowed, the stories I'd heard about him piled up in my mind. He took on a different, if not more meaningful, appearance.

Clad in his long tunic, striding erect, almost military fashion yet gazelle-like in his robust gracefulness, the Nazarene occupied the forefront. Each step brought him closer, allowing me to more fully assess his features.

He wore dusty, leather sandals. Tanned arms extended from his tunic and his hands were those of a skilled tradesman—in this case a carpenter.

Dark brown, somewhat wavy hair, brushed away and back from his face and forehead, framed his face. It was two to four-inches long, in places the seemingly bleached and tinted blonde by the sun. His healthy cheeks and lips were somewhat hidden by his well groomed and symmetrical full beard, one to two inches long with corresponding shorter mustache. Bold, dark and thick eyebrows highlighted his clear, greenish-blue happy, bright eyes.

His eyes. There was something about his eyes. They spoke volumes…of knowing, of suffering, of experience. And I must admit, compassion.

He looked peaceful enough but somehow his appearance belied my assumption. He walked upright, eyes ahead, his gaze missing nothing. And his features—the healthy look of cleanness shone from his face. His motions were robust, demonstrating a physical power, a rawboned toughness developed by his hours in the building trade and his miles of walking.

There was something about this man—a presence, an overpowering magnetism. That presence commanded my attention, causing me to focus on Him and to question the source of his power. A silent calm gripped me where I stood. A silence greater than a canyon full of empty.

Everything about this man compelled me to notice him and to question his comportment and bearing. I've observed military men. I've seen businessmen throughout the "new east"— in caravans, in tight spots, in tough times and in plenty—but I've never observed so complete a man, so accomplished and confident, so stalwart in stature and in control. What was it that directed him, elevating him to complete command?

Try as I might, I couldn't put my finger on it. As monumental as it appeared, my job was established…my mission became sharper edged, more suspenseful and more significant…even more urgent. Who is this man?

The Temple's ivory majesty, pure white marble walls, gleamed, rising fifteen stories and was accentuated by gold capped columns. Corinthian pillars rose a hundred feet in the air. Near the entrance was a vine of gold and silver with green leaves and clusters of grapes depicting Israel as a prosperous vine.

The crowd entered the building, providing me firsthand

experience in observing this man from Galilee and I entered with the others.

Promiscuous throngs filled the temple courts. A chalky haze of dust rose above beasts in the outer courtyard. Cattle contentedly chewed their cuds. While caged doves and pigeons cooed in the background, an occasional ox bellowed and sheep bleated.

An increasing murmur intermingled with the din of animals and the hubbub of their movement coupled with the angry altercations of traffickers permeated the atmosphere. Merchants and money changers haggled over prices. Boisterous chatter and clamor rose to fever pitch. Words addressed to the Most High were obliterated by sounds and the uproar of avarice. The Jewish leaders had become estranged from the worship of Yeshua, drawn away by greed.

The word on the street was that the Galilean knew all too well that centuries of abuse had taken place, that the priests had no intention of meeting the needs of the worshippers. There was no effort by the priests to inform the worshippers as to the particulars of the process of worship.

When I next saw the Nazarene, I read disgust and anger on his face. The peaceful, joyful countenance he'd exhibited outside the Temple vanished. I also noticed he had acquired a cord. As I watched him surveying the scene, he braided the cord in his hands with controlled movements, weaving it into a whip of sorts.

Next he confidently strode toward a temple merchant. The startled seller saw the Nazarene in time to avoid the swirling swish of the whip. The Nazarene's eyes flashed. He raised the whip and as he swung it, his opened sleeves disclosed his rope-like muscled forearms.

His demeanor reminded me of a disciplined military man determined to see a job through. I was impressed with his bearing. His movements were precise—every move calculated, not a single wasted motion.

Girded with the love of his God and sheathed in muscles groomed over years in the building trade, eyes afire, the Nazarene lashed out with the whip. He then overturned heavy merchant tables of wares, the whip in constant motion as he told the money changers they were a disgrace to the God whose temple they desecrated.

He was thorough in his mission and in his execution. One after another he upended table after table, reaching his hands under each and twisting it over...all the while berating the violators for corrupting the Temple and themselves. Thrusting his whip overhead his right arm rose again and again, wielding it against the spineless swine at the table. No one seemed willing to rise against him. I wondered what kind of challenge that arm and body would present to my friend Alexius in the arena. Could be interesting.

He moved among the stalls of penned animals—bleating sheep and cattle and doves... releasing or driving them from their pens and cages. The air filled with flapping and fluttering doves, the dust from the stampeding sheep rising to co-mingle with them.

A look of righteous indignation overshadowed his brow. He shouted to the pigeon dealers, "Take those things out of here. Don't you dare turn my Father's house into a market."

He drove out the animals and upbraided the priests with words of wrath, "You will not make this temple, my Father's home, a trading center! Get these things out of here." He tossed bird cages and sacks of coins and trading tables out onto the courtyard.

Pandemonium reigned. The scene was electrifying.

Unbridled fear shook some of the priests to the core. They wondered if Beelzebub himself had come in the form of this mad man...or if he were a demon. Others shuddered in anger toward this man who threatened their positions, their power and chances of advancing their agenda, not to mention their wealth.

Though the Galilean's actions were quick, the priests

wondered who he was, why he dared doing what he did and where he'd come from. Above the melee I heard their angry shouts: "What gives him the right to act this way in the temple, affecting an age old tradition?" And, "Who does he think he is?"

After witnessing this performance, I was dumbstruck to say the least. The Nazarene left the building. I followed him directly but lost him in the crowd. Knowing I could catch him eventually if I pursued, I chose rather to continue to Gaius' to relate this event and, again, try to gain a perspective as to this Nazarene and my mission.

My military connections with Rome provided much access and made me privy to the Roman records including scuttlebutt about various Roman leaders as well as many subjects, accounting and business matters.

Source: *Brachan*

Mouse Caper

Having spotted the quarry, the hunter raised his rifle and drew a fine bead on the animal. He hoped he could make a one shot kill and keep things as tidy as possible. It had been several years since he'd had a similar situation. He drew a deep breath and released it slowly as he pressured the trigger. Pop! The quarry vanished. Was it a hit? Or a miss? He comforted himself knowing that the target had been no more than six feet from the end of his barrel. He must have hit it!

Did I mention that he was shooting in his bathroom? A pellet gun? At a mouse?

Well, anyway, he discovered upon further viewing that he had cleanly missed the quarry…which hid behind the toilet next to a Victor mouse trap which was baited with bird seed—glue gunned onto the trigger by the shooter's wife Pam.

Let's see. He spread a pair of socks beneath the door so the mouse couldn't get away. Since he couldn't see the critter, he moved a gallon vinegar bottle with the barrel of the rifle and saw the rodent. Another carefully aimed miss and the mouse was out of sight again. He wondered what to do. He was pretty sure that he'd hit it as he saw red and assumed it was blood. On further review he realized it was the red of the Victor trap and not blood. He didn't want to approach the little fuzz ball and scare it into escaping beneath the door. Was it still in the bathroom or had it found an escape route?

Next thing he knew he heard his wife outside the door asking what the rifle was doing leaning against the hall wall. He explained the situation and asked if she'd like to assist. He thought he could guard the door with his rolled up T-shirt while she moved toward the quarry—that if it got past her in its effort to escape, he could thump it with the shirt. She wasn't having any of it.

Minutes ticked away with no further mouse sighting. Finally Pam said she'd help and she started into the bathroom but suddenly asked if the mouse had run past her through the door opening.

The master of the house noticed that the little fur ball was hiding in a corner by the shower and had quickly skittered to the corner between the vanity and the toilet.

Pam started moving stuff from the shelf on the end of the vanity when the mouse barreled into high gear right past her legs and toward the master of the house who thumped, saw the mouse reverse course, thumped again and again as the critter scratched for a foothold on the ceramic tile floor when there was a Whap! from the sandal in Pam's hand.

The mouse quivered. "He's dead!" the master confirmed as he saw another striking sandal.

"He's dead."

Whap!

"He's dead!"

Whap!

She stopped abusing the little fellow and I congratulated her for her good aim.

Did I mention that it was 5 AM, early Halloween morning when we enjoyed our little mouse caper?

Source: *Heavenly Rose*

Berry Bad Trip

This is a rough draft of which I listed several possible titles. I thought it might be interesting for the reader to get a view of the process of "writing" a story. You may wish to see a few other rough drafts in Appendix 1. In the fall of 1992 I interviewed Dennis. His story follows, in his words.

A Mountain Tragedy	Getting on with Life
You Can't Take it Back	Mistake on a Mountain
Berry Trip Gone Awry	One Man's Mistake
Know Your Target	Know What You're Shooting At
Tragedy in the Woods	

chapter quote:

"I struggled-frantically stabbing with my elbows and pulling... stab, pull; stab, pull...I felt no pain, but my mind was bombarded with thoughts..."

"'Vengeance is mine saith the Lord.' I'll let Him deal with that because I'm pretty busy with the important things in life."

A solitary figure sat beside the forest access road, taking in the grandeur of the surroundings. It was another gorgeous Montana Big Sky day. The fact that he'd just rolled his truck and had to hoof it back to camp wasn't so depressing in light of his freedom and gratitude for life. It was a great day! He was happy to be alive.

Dennis Williams had left camp that morning to pick huckleberries. He was a 47-year-old self-employed seed collector. He headquartered in a mobile home on the Montana-Idaho state line, but he spent days on end camped in the woods to facilitate his work. Ten years previous he had left his office overlooking the Windsor Bridge in downtown Detroit. He'd been burnt out on the politics of working in the human services field as a psychologist. With a vague concept of going to the West Coast, he left Michigan behind in search of some alternative things for his life.

The same day Dennis rolled his truck and on the same road, two hunters bounced along in a pickup truck. They were Larry Bowman and Rodney Cymbaluk. The 38-year-old Bowman maneuvered his pickup down Southside Road just north of Troy, Montana, talking with his 40-year-old buddy Rodney Cymbaluk. The country teemed with deer, bear, mountain lion and elk. Bear abounded in this vicinity (a hundred bear have been shot within twenty miles of here). It was opening day of bear season. Bowman and Cymbaluk scanned the roadside and forest in search of their prey. The sun had dropped behind a mountain, and they knew dusk was not far off. Their plans to fill a tag were inching closer.

It was September 7, 1991. Wearing a pair of light forest green, denim pants and a long sleeved brown and white checkered shirt Dennis Williams rolled up his sleeves because it was so hot. His other attire included a white T-shirt, a baseball hat and lace up, light tan woods boots.

He jostled along in his old International Harvester pickup looking for huckleberries. He was about ten miles out of Troy on Southside Road which follows the Kootenai River downstream to Bonner's Ferry, Idaho. It was a typical single lane, dirt mountain road used by the U.S. Forest Service, loggers, hunters, berry pickers and other outdoors people. Five miles from his base camp, he played thoughts across the big screen of his mind, about his past, seed prospects and his future plans.

When I went to college, I debated whether or not to go into forestry or psychology. Kind of a strange combination. Back in the '60's forestry was a very hard thing to get involved with.

For instance Michigan Technological University, an engineering school, was the only formally registered forestry school in the state of Michigan. I was tired of numbers and all that stuff. I wanted to do something else. So I did.

I spent every free moment in the woods or in the garden. Every summer while I was going to school I landscaped. Since I've always been into nature, it just seemed to dovetail into my lifestyle. Now, jokingly, I say I can get trees to talk to me.

Suddenly I'm jarred alert to the business at hand. Failing to make a slight turn, my pickup left the shoulder of the road and struck a tree.

I fought the wheel and jammed on the brakes. The truck did not respond. I bounced down the embankment, careening off fir trees. In a heartbeat my pickup turned over, smashing onto its top. The windows shattered and gas spewed from the tank of the still running engine. Knowing that my lit cigarette could ignite an explosion given the right circumstances, I scrambled from the truck cab through the passenger's window. How could I know that the truck's left front hub had fallen apart, rendering the vehicle un-steerable?

Fortunately the only damage was to my truck. I headed down the road for my base camp. I'd gone probably three quarters of a mile when I decided to take a cigarette break. I sat down on a rock beside the road in a clear, straight stretch that couldn't have been a hundred and fifty yards long. Grass grew probably eight inches to a foot high on that east slope.

I had just lit my cigarette when I heard a vehicle approaching. I went, "Haaa. Boy! It's really going to be great. I'm gonna get a ride to camp." Theoretically woods people help others.

It was maybe six, six-thirty in the evening. The sun was over the edge of the mountain. It wasn't dark yet, but after six o'clock in September it starts getting dark really quickly. It had been a really hot day, probably 90 degrees in Troy; and it was probably still in the 70's where I was.

I looked down the road to my left and saw the vehicle coming with its headlights on. The vehicle stopped. Then it started forward again. I just looked down the road and thought, "Well, they see a deer. They're gonna shoot the deer or take a picture of it." It was legal hunting hours.

The truck came forward five, ten, fifteen yards...and eased to a stop.

I didn't move. I didn't know where the deer was. I figured if I stand up and scare it off, these guys will get ticked off and won't give me a ride back to camp. I turned back and was looking directly across the road.

I heard a shot and simultaneously a bullet ripped into my left knee cap. The bullet mushroomed and hit my right leg at mid-thigh, all but blowing it off—the leg was hanging by a thread of meat and skin. "Holy shit! I better hide," I thought.

When you're sitting on a rock in grass, there's no place to hide. My only hope was to get to the timber across the road, so that's where I headed. I dropped into the grass and started crawling, using my elbows to paddle-drag myself across the dirt road.

I struggled--frantically stabbing with my elbows and pulling... stab, pull; stab, pull...dragging two useless legs and trailing a stream of blood. I felt no pain, but my mind was bombarded with thoughts...Who's shooting? Why are they shooting at me? Can I hide? Will I live? What will I do in the woods when I get there?

I was almost a third of the way across the road when I was hit again. I couldn't believe it. I had taken a slug in the back. I decided I better just be still...I was still alive and still conscious. And I was not pleased!

I'm thinking, "Ah, shit. What's going on here?" I didn't move or do anything. I held my breath. I heard the vehicle coming. I was lying in the road diagonally with my back to the vehicle. I thought, "I wonder if they're going to come up here and finish me off or what the hell's going on?"

But I wasn't moving. I didn't want to move at all. If I move one more time, they shoot me one more time; and then I'd be dead. The way those bullets were tearing chunks out of my flesh I thought, "Oh, man, this is not cool."

I heard men's voices through the open windows of the pickup. I heard something about, "Oh, my God, it is a man!" Then I heard the door open.

I thought, "Maybe I can look now and see if he's gonna kill me. At least I can see who's gonna kill me." I looked over there and the guy didn't have a gun. It was Rodney Cymbaluk. He came running up and yelled, "Oh, Jesus Christ..." He said, "Oh, my God, it is a man, it is a man!"

I said, "You got that part right, buddy. I don't think I'm going to make it down off the hill. Will you tell some people..." I was gonna give him my last will and testament right there. There's blood all over the place and blood's comin' out of my legs. I was just a mess.

So they said, "Oh, yeah. You can make it. We'll take you down to Troy."

I said, "I don't want to go to Troy!"

Five miles away, near my camp there's a water truck (used for watering the roads), and it has a really big time CB. Not only that, there's a paved road all the way into Bonner's Ferry. We could call on the CB and scoot right into Bonner's Ferry. So we had an argument, but I wasn't in much condition to argue. And Cymbaluk said, "We'll get you down off the hill. You're gonna make it."

I said, "Okay."

I asked him," In the process then, how we gonna stop this leg from bleeding? You got any rope?"

Cymbaluk says, "Yeah, we got some rope. Bowman goes to the truck, cuts a chunk off and ties my shattered leg off, making a tourniquet out of the rope.

I said, "Okay, now my left one. I don't think we can do much about it right now."

The driver Bowman says, "Ah, yeah we can," and rips off his shirt and used it as a compress.

They picked me up, put me in the back of the truck and down the road we went lickety split. Cymbaluk was back there with me. He was holding me and talking to me all the time, "Jesus Christ, I'm sorry. I thought you were a bear. I thought you were a bear. I had no idea."

By the time we got into Troy it was pitch black. We stopped where the driver saw somebody that he knew. I assumed it was the Silver Spur, a restaurant-bar. I heard Bowman yell, "Hey, we've got a gunshot wound in the back. Get in and call."

We ended up at the ambulance station downtown. They patched me up as best they could in the back of the pickup and asked me if I could walk. I was still conscious and said, "Oh, yeah. I can walk." (I've got one leg shot off and one broken; and I got up and, assisted by ambulance people, walked to the ambulance).They had removed the tourniquets and replaced them with air splints.

The helicopter from Sacred Heart in Spokane, Washington, was delayed a little bit, so the paramedics thought maybe what they ought to do was run me to Libby. At the Libby hospital, the medical staff did some basic first aid and asked me what my blood type was.

I had no pain in my legs nor my back—they were numb—until they got me to the hospital in Libby. Then people started prodding and poking me. I was surrounded by doctors and assistants. They were looking for a vein for an I.V. and trying to get my blood pressure. The doctor taking my blood pressure said, "This guy isn't gonna make it. I've got blood pressure 10 over 30."

I was talking to another doctor who told me to scream if it hurt. "You're damned right it hurts!" I screamed. It was something else.

By now I was experiencing major pain from the air splint on my right leg. All the pressure stopped at my groin. None of my injuries hurt, but my leg at the top of the splint was killing me. I told them, "Come on, man, you want to take this thing off!"

I screamed and hollered at people for a while. One lady said, "The helicopter's coming for you." I'd never been wounded, never been in a helicopter, never flown, nothing. So I told her that I wasn't really too keen on flying to Spokane. She told me I was in no shape to walk.

She must have been embarrassed because after she that, she said, "I'm sorry."

I started laughing and swung at the oxygen mask they were trying to put on me. I said,"Get it away from me. I want to talk." I kept swinging at it. I've got one broken leg; one leg's blown off; one damned arm I can't even move. I've only got one arm to swing with.

I was screaming and hollering. I didn't care what they thought. I was claustrophobic. I was hyper-ventilating. I was in shock. The whole nine yards. All I knew was that I didn't want that oxygen mask on me. I knew if they put that on my face, I was gonna die. I yelled, "Get it away from me!" I was pretty wild.

The nurse said, "How about if I just put it there for a couple of seconds; and I won't strap it to your face?"

I said, "That'd be cool."

The helicopter picked me up, and I'm kind of fighting this flying. I'm frightened. Finally I relented thinking, "Oh, shit, if I made it this far, I must be able to make it the rest of the way."

They wouldn't let me go to sleep. I kept telling them if I could only close my eyes and take a little nap...but they kept jostling me to keep me awake. It was about seventy-five minutes by helicopter to Sacred Heart.

They wheeled me in and started doing the same stuff they'd done at Libby. They were going to do blood type. And they wanted to know what happened. I got tired of telling people what happened. It seemed like all 4,138 employees asked me the same question.

First off, a doctor tried to take my thoughts away from my leg wounds. He's going, "You've got a blood vessel in your shoulder just about ready to go."

The bullet missed that major artery by 3/16ths of an inch but the shock coagulated the blood. The impact of the bullet missed the main artery going down into the right arm—it produced a blood clot that shut everything off, resulting in insignificant blood loss compared to what I lost in my legs. That's the reason I didn't bleed to death. Three sixteenths of an inch more and kiss it goodbye. I wouldn't be here.

They finally put me under. Eighteen hours later I awoke and was pretty immobile. My left leg was in a cast from my groin to my toes. My right one was, obviously, not even a leg—they'd chopped it off. I couldn't move my leg, and I could barely use my left hand.

My wife and I were estranged at the time. When I became conscious in intensive care and opened my eyes, there's my wife and my best friend, Pat. That was pretty wild. Pat smoked, and I just kind of looked up, reached out with one hand, grabbed her hand and started sniffing it for the tobacco. They figured if I wanted a cigarette, I was going to make it.

After two days they decided they couldn't do anything more for me in intensive care, so they moved me to another floor. I got telephone calls from sharks, lots of attorneys, television producers, newspaper and magazine people.

I did agree to do an interview with People Magazine (September 30, 1991) because most of the press coverage was totally inaccurate. I wanted the story told accurately for people to know what was going on. The photographer and the writer came to Sacred Heart even before the medical staff operated on my left leg a second time to insert pins. The article was pretty accurate; I insisted on that.

That article and the constant barrage of questions from everybody helped me to deal with my accident; but being a psychologist helped me too.

It was like people were forcing me to deal with it, like every nurse that came in wanted to know about it. Charge nurses were the ones who wanted to take care of me. Always the top person on staff. You wonder who was my doctor on the rehab? It was the director of rehab. Who was my physical therapist? The director of physical therapy. People treated me with kid gloves. And I'm going, "Okay, this is cool."

A week later they put some pins in my left leg to stabilize my femur. Then I started getting phantom pains big time in my amputated right leg. I had to go on some strange medication. After the first month in the hospital I could move around a little bit. By the time they could actually weigh me I weighed 137 1/2 pounds. I'm 6' 1 1/2" and weighed 160 pounds before the accident.

The second month in the hospital I spent in rehabilitation and got a prosthesis. Learning to walk with a prosthetic device is hard when two joints are involved. You have to account for both the ankle and the knee joints, so it's more difficult than allowing for just the ankle joint. I hiked around and learned to walk on it really well I thought. About the first of November, when I'd been there a couple of days less than two months, they kicked me out of the hospital, said, "There's no reason for you to be here anymore."

When I left the hospital, I didn't go back to my mobile home. One of my friends had a month's business in California and Arizona. He asked me to stay in his house. As it turned out, he wasn't gone for a month—he was gone four months. So I spent the winter care taking his country house between Troy, Montana, and Idaho.

Of course I was not in the best of shape when I got out. I was really under weight. I could eat prodigious amounts of food, and it didn't make any difference—I never gained a pound until March, and then I put on twenty pounds in the next few months.

I could walk fairly well with my prosthesis and a cane when I left the hospital. I was a little hesitant of snow and ice, but at least I could get around, and I didn't fall too much.

I still have pain, but it's intermittent. I get some really bad days where I get probably five hundred jolts a day. Sometimes it feels like about two thousand volts of electricity hit me down there in the foot that I don't even have. And it'll go right to my big toe. Sometimes I'll be sitting here and people watch as I jerk with pain. They go, "Whoa, you must have had another one of them little zingers."

And I go, "Boy, did I ever."

To date my financial losses including medical bills, lost wages and earning capacity are at least $150,000. I had seed orders of approximately $100,000 last year. Needless to say I didn't get too many of them. I had some seeds harvested before the accident, but they went to waste because I wasn't around to take care of them.

I'm not a veteran, didn't belong to the National Rifle Association and had no insurance. Fortunately the social workers and financial advisors at Sacred Heart talked me right through that, and we got lots of that stuff covered through public assistance.

I moved to Troy the first of April and immediately started going into the woods collecting seeds and mushrooms. I was still getting letters and calls (eight months after the accident) from people who had read or heard about me. People from veterans' hospitals read the thing in People Magazine and wrote me wanting to know how I could be so positive, resilient and non-combative.

They wrote, "I was sitting here feeling sorry for myself; and I guess all you want to do is go back to living."

And I'm goin', "Yeah, I see the alternative is no fun, man."

I received marriage proposals. I got some of the most bizarre requests you'd ever want to read...people wanted to take care of me the rest of my life. Hundreds, hundreds, hundreds of letters. People even sent money. It was pretty strange.

Several attorneys called me wanting to take my case. The attorneys that I talked to at any length understood me when

I said, "I think it's more important for me to get on with the business of living than it is for me to drag this thing out."

Besides here's what happens in a court of law. I can sue the guy. Yeah, I'm gonna win. It's a given. So if he has an attorney worth his salt (and he did), the attorney will tell him, "The day that judgment is against you, file bankruptcy...or in the process you put all this stuff in your wife's name or your parents' name." The guy who shot me was worth a few bucks plus his insurance.

I went to Libby and gave a deposition to Cymbaluk's attorney. He said, "Weren't you a little alarmed when you saw two guys standing outside the truck with guns pointed at you?"

I looked him right square in the eye and said, "You tell me they were standing outside. I looked! They weren't outside the truck. Them s--- a b-----s shot me out the window because they didn't have their doors open. They didn't open the door on that truck until they got to me."

I could read his mind, "Oh, oh. I don't want this guy on the stand."

I asked the attorney about Cymbaluk's "it is a man" comment (when the hunters approached me in the truck), and he said, "There is some debate. As they got closer to you, they realized that perhaps it didn't quite look like a bear after all."

I did settle with Cymbaluk's insurance company, homeowner's policy of all things. And I was satisfied with that. Most of my medical was covered. I've got just a couple of odd bills that are floating around yet from that, nothing really significant. I've got two, maybe three thousand dollars something like that out of around $75,000 in medical bills.

The settlement with Cymbulak, the guy who shot me, gives me enough money to live on for many, many years. I mean not high on the hog. I can't eat steaks every night, but then I'm not a steak man anyway. They pay me for the next fifteen, twenty years through his insurance company. (As a matter of fact I need to get down to the post office right now cause there's a check for the first of November.)

Bowman's insurance company thought there was a little fault there, and they were getting a little worried because I wasn't in any hurry to sign a release. They dangled a carrot and I took it. I started this business officially so I could buy a couple of reliable vehicles and some reliable cleaning equipment. I sunk more than $15,000 into the seed business.

I guess I don't really bear those people any animosity, but what I would really like to see is for them never to hunt again. I think that shooting someone in a similar situation is inexcusable. The law in Montana reads such that Cymbulak got penalized to the full extent of the law.

He got fined a thousand dollars and had his hunting privileges taken away for two years. I don't think that's fair. I think two years is a crock—go rob a bank or shoot a moose. Shoot a grizzly bear—they take away your birthday. And shoot me? And it cost you a thousand dollars? And you can't hunt for two years?

As far as giving suggestions to others, my experience with scopes is that they collect light, they don't disperse it. Had I been hunting with open sights, I would not have shot. Both these guys had scopes.

Had I known I was the target, I would have made a lot of noise and let the hunters know I was a man. My suggestion to hunters is that they always make sure what's behind their target; and always know what you're shooting at.

Satchel Paige said, "Never look back because whatever's chasing you might be catching up." Although I'm not a Christian, I try to live a reasonably moral life—makes me feel better. "Vengeance is mine saith the Lord." I'll let Him deal with that because I'm pretty busy with the important things in life.

Sometimes my lack of mobility makes for frustrating days. I can no longer gather seeds wherever I want to, and it takes a long time to get the ones I can get to.

Fortunately, I do have other skills that provide me relief from that frustration. I like marketing (you have to not only collect and clean seeds, but you also have to sell them), teaching (here's the most efficacious way to collect those fruits, etc.) and writing (have to do catalogs, collector's guidelines and day to day business correspondence).

Some advantages of being "stove up" (which may give you an inkling of how I cope):

People don't ask me to help them move anymore.

I only have to cut five toenails.

I don't have to change my right sock.

I save water bathing.

So often our plans go awry. On September 7, 1991, on Southside Road near Troy, Montana, two paths crossed. One party was hunting wild game. One was picking huckleberries. The hunters did not get their game; the berry picker did not get his berries. Neither party knew about the other. But within minutes circumstances changed the men's plans. And their lives will never be the same.

Source: *Swallowed Alive*

Gobbled up by the Inlet

"At one point a particularly strong wind gust snapped his aluminum boom at a joint, breaking it."

Wind surfing caught a wave in Anchorage, Alaska, in the 1980's. When the glaciers carved out the region's valleys, Turnagain Arm was born. The Arm stretches southeast of Anchorage 35miles to the Twenty Mile and Placer rivers. The Arm varies in width from five miles to over a dozen. The major windsurfing area encompasses over 75 square miles of water.

Big winds funneling through combined with the Arm's large body of water and easy accessibility to Anchorage launched wind surfing and sail boarders. The surf was up, and the rush was on. Those in the search prayed for a windy day and congregated at their Church of the Windy Waves. It was great sport.

Their playground was an easy thirty-minute drive from nearly anywhere in the Anchorage bowl. On windy days passing drivers enjoyed the multitude of wind surfers plying the waters. Multi-colored sails attached to masts and booms zipped over the gray-brown, wind-swept waves as a gaggle of dry suit clad surfers cavorted and played. It was common to see a sailboard and rider bust a wave and sky ten to fifteen feet off the sizzling surf.

In the late 1980's one of the leaders of the pack suffered an experience that affected the entire body of wind surfers.

It was Saturday, August 6, 1988, a decent day for wind surfing. A dozen miles southeast of Anchorage sailboarders bounced over Turnagain Arm's waters between Potter weigh station and Beluga Point. The gusty winds created the choppy water the participants loved.

Off Beluga Point a dozen sailboarders rode the waves. The tide was relatively weak and the water was at its normal 57-degree temperature in upper Cook Inlet according to U.S. Coast Guard.

Experienced sailor Patrick Hallin was among the group. The 29-year-old Anchorageite was one of most experienced surfers present. He was well equipped and wore a neoprene dry suit and boots, hood and gloves.

Although he was further out than the other sailors, he rode his board within a few hundred yards of them. At one point a particularly strong wind gust snapped his aluminum boom at a joint, breaking it.

Hallin disconnected the boom, mast and sail and gave them to another boarder to tow to shore. Meanwhile he lay on his belly on his 8-foot Fiberglas sailboard and began paddling by hand the few miles to shore. He was a strong swimmer and anticipated no problems. Patrick had a reputation for competence and was the kind of guy you'd want along if you were in trouble.

At 6:00 PM he was a mile off shore. When he failed to appear, fellow sailors grew concerned. He was last seen headed for Beluga Point at 6:30 PM. Boarders spread out on their sailboards and skipped over the waves searching for him.

An hour of serious searching resulted in nothing. When they failed to find him, one went to shore to notify the Alaska State Troopers.

A rescue helicopter and small fire department boat were dispatched to the area and their personnel searched until dark (which would have been around 10 PM at that time of year). They found nothing.

Speculation was that the outgoing tide had sucked Patrick out into Cook Inlet.

Friends and searchers hoped he was on his board or had been able to reach shore somewhere along the Arm. They expected a greater search effort the next day.

On Sunday the U.S. Coast Guard cutter *Sweetbriar* joined the search. Two Coast Guard choppers and several private fixed wing aircraft crisscrossed the Inlet from Point Mac Kenzie west of Anchorage and the drilling rigs on the west side of the Inlet. They found no sign of the missing man.

Twenty-four hours later friends continued to hope that Patrick was alive on his board or stranded on shore. Some searched the shoreline along the highway. Other friends of Patrick's walked the roadless shoreline on the south side of the Arm from Hope to Gull Rock and beyond, over six miles.

The ground searchers found no footprints or any sign of Hallin. Later in the day his florescent hot pink, green and yellow board was found floating within 75 feet of the beach near Point Possession,15 miles west of Hallin's last reported whereabouts. No other trace of him was found.

By the end of the evening Sunday the Coast Guard called off its search. The Troopers, on the other hand, decided to consult the Hallin family before they made their final decision to call off their search.

On Monday planes flown by the Alaska State Troopers, Civil Air Patrol and friends found no sign of Hallin. If he had been on shore near the location of his surfboard, searchers would have found him.

On Tuesday efforts to locate the missing man were concentrated on the mudflats. But all efforts ended in failure.

It wasn't until almost a month later, Thursday, September 1, that part of the mystery unraveled. An oil production worker, Mike Petrov, was working on the Dillon Platform ten miles north of Kenai. It was about 5:00 PM when Mike, working 80 feet above the water's surface on an Amoco Production Company oil platform, saw something floating north beneath the platform. He thought the incoming tide was carrying an airplane pilot wearing a flight suit. Mike tossed a life preserver to the body and radioed the ERA Aviation helicopter.

Marathon had a vessel in the area which motored to the site

a mile north of the platform and seven miles off shore. The vessel's personnel picked up the body, clad in a blue-black dry suit.

Troopers later identified the body as that of the missing man. Patrick Hallin had been found

EPILOGUE

What happened to Patrick from the time he was last seen paddling offshore until his body was found? While Patrick paddled toward shore, did he become too physically exhausted to complete his task? Was he knocked off his board by the wind or a wave? Was the tide too strong to overcome? Did he suffer hypothermia? Is it possible he got sick or blacked out? Maybe he had cramps which incapacitated him? Or did something like a log hit him, knocking him off his board or knocking him out?

It doesn't appear we'll ever know the answers to these questions. But there is every reason to learn from this tragedy and to hope that Patrick's loss will not have been in vain.

People in the community expressed concern and suggested that stronger measures be put in place to enhance the safety of other sailboarders. Sgt. Bill Farber, spokesperson for the Alaska State Troopers, said Hallin lacked a life jacket and a tether.

Gary King is a sailboard enthusiast and owner of Gary King's Sporting Goods. He came to the defense of sailors' choice when it comes to life preservers and tethers. He said that most sail boarders do not usually wear life jackets because they're bulky and retard movement. The neoprene float dry suits they wear provide flotation but not as much as a life vest. Tethering restricts the rider and can cause problems for the sailors.

However a growing number of boarders agreed that in a situation where one has only the board, tethering is a good safety precaution because a wave can wash a sailor off his board or turn it over and separate him from it. It is common then for the wind to push the lighter more buoyant board away from the pursuing sailor faster than he can swim to it (consequently a tether would keep the board within reach).

Perhaps one of the best pieces of advice is for people to use the buddy system and sail with a partner, constantly checking on each other and never leaving your partner.

One precautionary measure used for a while was strobe lights. But most sailboarders felt they were an unnecessary piece of equipment and abandoned them about the time the accident occurred. People theorized Patrick would have been rescued if he'd had a strobe. But what if he was too weak or sick to activate it or to keep it visible to searchers?

Hopefully local sailboarders will continue to expand their safety knowledge and use the buddy system to provide safe return for all.

Source: *Swallowed Alive*

Do Kids Matter?

One of the most significant writings I ever read was "I Taught Them All." It helped me focus on what was important about school and working with kids. I hope that *The B.G.* captures the fact that kids are important, need to our love and protection.

"I Taught Them All"

I have taught in high school for ten years. During that time I have given assignments, among others, to a murderer, a pugilist, a thief and an imbecile. The murderer was a quiet little boy who sat on the front seat and regarded me with pale blue eyes; the pugilist lounged by the window and let loose at intervals in a raucous laugh that startled even the geraniums; the thief was a gay-hearted Lothario with a song on his lips; and the imbecile, a shifty-eyed little animal seeking shadows.

The murderer awaits death in the state-penitentiary; the pugilist lost an eye in a brawl; the thief, by standing on tiptoe can see the window of my room from the county jail; and the once gentle eyed little moron beats his head against a padded wall in the state asylum. All these pupils once sat in my room, sat and looked at me gravely across worn brown desks. I must have been a great help to those pupils…I taught them the rhyming scheme of the Elizabethan sonnet and how to diagram a complex sentence.

Naomi White, November 1943

Source: *The B.G.*

Aunt To The Rescue

What's wrong with this picture? While you're cogitating, I'll provide more food for thought.

This story illustrates the importance of adult awareness to the dangers of predatory animals and the need for an appropriate bear stopper.

Brooklyn, Charles and Cleo Henslee played in their Porthill, Idaho, backyard.

Their babysitting aunt was nearby. The twin boys were a year younger than their 3-year-old sister Brooklyn. Amidst the play, auntie was alerted when Brooklyn suddenly shouted, "Bear! Bear!"

When their aunt looked up and saw a black bear running into the yard from the adjoining woods, she grabbed the children and hightailed it for the house. Aunt, niece and nephews reached the sliding glass door just ahead of the 422-pound bear. Slamming the door behind them, auntie turned to see the bear pounding at the door, damaging the screen door and window frame.

Securing the children in a back bedroom, she grabbed a 7 mm rifle, loaded it and returned to the glass door. Momentarily distracted, the bear looked down.

Auntie quickly slid the door open a foot and with the rifle at waist level fired two rounds into the bear, only three feet distant. The animal dropped dead on the step.

Officials passed the attack off as human error—in their minds some food attractant caused the bear to charge! (Source: "Area babysitter kills black bear," Posted: Thursday, Oct 12, 2006, By ROBERT JAMES, Hagadone News Network, BonnerCountyDailyBee.com, Sandpoint, Idaho)

Here we have another prime example of blaming man. It's

always his fault.

The *BonnerCountyDailyBee.com* web site permitted me to include some of their blogged comments in return for crediting them. You might be surprised by some of the comments that I selected (Author's comment: FYI, I did not select all so some responses to unselected posts should be obvious). The following (verbatim) posts illustrate the people's extreme philosophies.

Nancy, October 12, 2006 8:20 P.M.: "For once an intelligent babysitter! She's hired!"

Dave A., October 12, 2006 8:44 P.M.: "If the bear was attracted to smells from a barbecue grill on the back porch, why did it make such an early attempt on the house? A black bear is more predatory than a grizzly, probably only second to a mountain lion."

Chuck, October 13, 2006 12:39 P.M.: "Did officers talk to the lady to find out if the gun used in the killing of the bear was under lock and key so the small children could not get it? Seems to me that with a pair of twins & 3 year old in and around the house the gun would be secured and the ammunition put up…this all happened so quickly that the bear stood as much chance as getting shot as the children finding easy access to the gun and ammo. I wonder what possible harm could happen to those 3 little children if that gun is not secured? Think about it."

Dynahog, October 13, 2006 3:11 P.M.: "That's about the dumbest thing I ever heard. The family needs counciling on what to do if you sight a bear near the house…My guess is that the "mother" probably started screaming (that caught the bear's attention), and then picking up the kids ran to the house. Too late, the bear was challenged and went for them… NEVER EVER RUN FROM A BEAR. That is the sign of you challenging the bear. NEVER EVER LOOK AT A BEAR IF HE'S APPROACHING AT CLOSE DISTANCE… ALSO GET A STRONGER / TALLER FENCE. Glass sliding doors? Not a very safe house to be in."

Mr Noble, October 13, 2006 3:17 P.M.: "MOVE YOUR a hole

OUT OF THE BEAR'S BACKYARD"

BT, October 13, 2006 10:41 P.M.: "I know a guy that lost a kid to a bear. Enough of the armchair-bear lovers. You should have grabbed some pots and pans my keester. City-fied crackheads! I bet the dumb half of the posters here don't even know where food comes from. Where does the grocery store get it? If you live in the city, please don't try to theorize how folks should live outside cities!!"

Herman from Texas, October 14, 2006 2:23 A.M.: "This is what has happened to our safety when moronic, know-nothing, condo dwelling animal rights A-Holes are allowed to tell people they can no longer threaten animals. From joggers and bikers being killed and eaten by big cats and bears chasing kids for an afternoon meal these predators are no longer afraid of people... and that's dangerous. Years ago just the smell of humans was enough to keep a broad border between us and them, now however, because of idiots who know little to nothing about survival around animals...like the moron that stated you should NOT run or look at the very thing that is about to eat you...guns have become necessary to preserve life. Doesn't that make the animal rights idiot responsible for the death of this hungry animal??? LOL"

Chris, October 14, 2006 6:01 A.M.: "You can read these comments and see which liberal nut jobs value a bear more than human life. That bear needed to die and I am glad this brave woman killed it before it could maul her or worse, one of the children. "

Gronad, October 14, 2006 6:23 A.M.: "Babysitters - 1 Bears - 0"

eddd7, October 14, 2006 6:58 A.M.: "That's it Dynahog...... blame the children!

"Paul".....yeah, with a 422 pound bear trying to get through the slider, the first thing I'd go for is the pots and pans. And, as for Mr. Noble".....what animals lived where you lived, before YOU lived there? None? Jeeeeesh. Where do we get these people??"

Lawrence Robinson, October 14, 2006 7:11 A.M.: "A bear came charging out of the woods, hell bent on mayhem, because there was a barbeque on the back porch? How bloody stupid do these government types think we are? Why didn't the bear stop and give some attention to the barbeque then? Those fuzzy little bears. Ya just gotta love our government officials!"

Scott wrote on October 14, 2006 7:43 A.M.: "Okay, are there really agressive brown Bears where this happened? I've never heard of a bear that was unprovoked chasing people. They're generally pretty timid creatures. These boneheads have been watching too many movies. Did the stupid babysitter think that it was going to break in through the sliding glass door and eat them? I say that her story doesn't make sense." (Author's comment: Yo, Scotty. Read herein about Lisa Dunbar, the mother who tried to save her son from a black that came through the opened sliding door for her!)

Topekan, October 14, 2006 8:29 A.M.: "Dynahog says it's the family's fault that they hadn't taken Bruin Defense 101? As far as needing counciling goes, that's "about the dumbest thing I've ever heard." I suppose Dynahog would have preferred that the bear had enjoyed a four course repast of homo sapiens and then gone back to the wild. Animal rights activists are the ones who need counseling."

Smoki in Washington, October 14, 2006 9:47 A.M.: "Good for her. I hate to hear of animals shot because of people's stupidity, but in this case, she was right on target in more ways than one. And for the comment about locking guns up - my daughter was taught at age 2 what a gun would do, has had her own rifle (a 22) since age 4. Don't lock up the guns, educate the kids. A locked up rifle would have gotten someone killed that day."

Tom, October 14, 2006 9:47 A.M.: "As I live in bear country, a full grown bear on two legs, pounding on your sliding glass door with small children and women inside is a serious threat. Only self-proclaimed "idiots" would advocate rattling a few pots and pans (yes, make the bear mad and maybe it might just knock the door completely down and enjoy a smorgasbord of whatever it wants), or worrying about whether or not anyone had a "bear tag", or trying to run away from the bear in the first place with little children in your arms (sometimes running is the only option, especially when you have safe cover nearby). Then there are those who think we should all move out of bear territory. These are the same ones whose knowledge has completely abandoned them when it comes to understanding that, except for the deserts, the whole country was bear territory before civilization moved in. So retreat for the sake of "bear territory" means for civilization to move to the tallest mountains or the desert. Such knowledge and perfect wisdom—ain't the kind the women used. Theirs was a good dose of common sense—and the desire to live."

Nancy Woods, October 14, 2006 10:16 A.M.: "Thank God the babysitter kept her cool and did the right thing! Its sad to say but Greg Johnson's response is all too common.....trying to defend and make excuses for the bear...these kinds of comments from an official might cause someone else to hesitate just a little too long before defending themselves and loose their life."

Gary In Sacramento, October 14, 2006 11:47 A.M.: "98% of the people think like normal. Then here comes the Liberal Tree Huggers with all of their stupid garbage about how "we the people" are the problem. Give me a break. I love animals as much as anyone BUT when the animal is out of control and crosses the line, they have to be controlled and the emergency of the moment determines the outcome."

Rae wrote on October 14, 2006 1:12 P.M.: "This is what happens when morons who live in bear country don't properly secure food sources. Poor bear." (Author's comment: Rae, I refer you to Lisa Dunbar—no mention of food here, and she lost her most precious child. Do you have children?)

Gene Gray, October 14, 2006 2:22 P.M.: "I am 89 years old........grew up in North woods of Wisconsin and now live in Southern California. I have hiked and hunted most of my life-until 5 years ago. I recommend all animals dangerous to humans-bear, mountain lions, and snakes be eliminated." (Author's comment: thin the herd!)

Mike Kuhn wrote on October 14, 2006 8:30 P.M.: "What does it matter if she had a bear hunting permit? Would she have been CHARGED had she not had one? I suppose she would have been CHARGED had she not, from the gyst of this story. In the first sentence, eighth paragraph, the article mentioned that she had a "bear tag". I suppose that means that had she not had a government permit, that CHARGES would be PENDING. I'm surprised that other CHARGES weren't brought, such as shooting near an occupied dwelling (there were CHILDREN inside, for pity's sake!), animal cruelty, and endangering the welfare of an animal. Add to that endangering the welfare of a child (by virtue of having a firearm in the house), which would be three CHARGES, since there were three kids. She probably should have been CHARGED with criminal negligence as well, and further CHARGED with reckless endangerment. Following these FELONY CHARGES (all of them, since nothing is a misdemeanor anymore), she should have to attend ANIMAL SENSITIVITY TRAINING…"

alee ess, October 14, 2006 9:30 P.M.:

"This summer there was one bear story every week where black bears were coming into the yards of the LA suburbs (Claremont, Pasadena, etc). I visited my son in Wisconsin and parents in Michigan this summer and am astonished to hear coyotes in their yards every night! This was unheard of just a few years ago. There are also sightings of cougars throughout Michigan. It was disputed by authorities until the cougars started killing horses on farms. Locals have caught animal rights activists releasing coyotes on private property, where they are ruining many farmers in lower Michigan. How many children need to be attacked and killed before people wise up and say ENOUGH ANIMAL RIGHTS BS!"

Joe Siegl, October 15, 2006 5:01 A.M.: "Can't help wonder what one of them Animal lovers would have done if one of them was the Baby sitter or their loved ones would have been attacked? Call Fish and Game while the bear was running away with one of the kids hanging from its Snout?"

Wyoming Skye, October 15, 2006 9:27 A.M.: "In Canada they have taken away the right to bear arms when hiking and working in the woods and only duly licensed government officials can kill a predatory animal. The animals have obviously figured this out because predation on children, hikers, campers, and forest workers has skyrocketed since the law change. This has been shown for grizzlies, black bears and mountain lions who are learning to prey on defenseless people. Nature is the law of the strongest. People without guns are not the strongest. In Wyoming grizzlies will come running now at the sound of a rifle. They have learned it means dead elk. I like to have the wild spaces and the animals but we must be able to protect ourselves around them to gain their respect. The only thing that will really save nature is human birth control. We are overpopulating the earth."

Mountain girl, October 15, 2006 1:46 P.M.: "Banging pots and pans is NOT effective—I tried it, and also some really obnoxious rock music played very loudly, on a 2-year old cub who kept coming to our yard looking for a litter of baby kittens a stray mother had hidden somewhere on our property. The bear was not impressed and did not leave until it was good and ready. All I have to show for my efforts is some mangled pan lids It is a shame that our 300 million population means loss of bear territory, but co-existence doesn't always work and bears ARE dangerous, wild and unpredictable. Tell ya what—you bear lovers out there take up a collection to build a huge bear-proof fence and a few million acres of forest land to enclose the hairy dears in and we'll ALL be happy."

Source: *SAFE with Bears*

Nightmare in the Inlet

The plane's intense white landing light stabbed across the black waters into the nothingness of night. Kaleidoscopic green, red and silver flashes pierced the darkness from the plane's wing and tail strobe lights. The navigation lights on the panel of the Cessna 185 leered at the lone figure standing dazed on the gravel bar. He tried to make some sense of his situation.

The combination of blackness and pulsating, colored lights created an eeriness for Bob Elstad. His red trimmed white Cessna N94178 lay piled at his feet, useless in Turnagain Arm on the outskirts of Anchorage, Alaska. His destination a few thousand yards to the north lay shrouded in fog. Six miles to the east flirting headlights of passing vehicles teased him.

While contemplating his condition and gathering a few survival items from his craft, he reviewed his past few hours and retold his story.

I left Lake Hood, one of Anchorage's float plane bases, around 4 o'clock in the afternoon of October 29, 1979. I headed to my cabin at Lake Creek on the Yentna River, some ninety miles northeast over Cook Inlet and the Big Susitna River. I hauled four sheets of 4x8 foot plywood on what I figured would be my final trip of the winter. As is customary I carried materials between my floats on spreader bars (two horizontal bars that separate the floats). I'd secured the 3/4 inch lumber with motorcycle straps. I also had a couple of blankets and an old jacket as well as a ceramic toilet in the back baggage compartment.

Although a friend volunteered to help me, he never showed up. So, having secured the lumber on the floats, I lifted off Lake Hood and flew out to the cabin. The weather was VFR (pilots flying according to visual flight rules) at the time. Since the river is really low at that time of the year, taxiing up to the cabin was out of the question. I parked at the mouth where Lake Creek dumps into the Yentna. After three exhausting trips with the plywood, struggling three blocks upstream along the beach to the cabin, I started my return flight.

I had about an hour's worth of fuel on board. Normally the one way flight takes twenty-five to thirty minutes, so I wasn't concerned about my fuel supply. I figured I had more than enough fuel to make the trip safely, barring any weather problems.

On my return to Anchorage the weather was turning on me. I passed through a snow squall and continued toward town, cruising at fifteen hundred feet. When I approached Anchorage, I found it socked in--both the entire city and the Port of Anchorage were shrouded in a giant, white cloud. It looked like a silver-gold, mushroom with a bright light under it that just glowed...in an eerie, spooky way.

Aside from the cloud it was a moonlit night. But anything in or around Anchorage was zero-zero visibility.

Hood Lake was closed so I circled around for a while. If I'd had three and a half hours of fuel, I would have climbed up ten thousand feet and flown over the mountains to Lake Louise or some place where I could see in the moonlight and land the plane safely. I could have got up on the top and got a directional from the airport or used my compass. But I just didn't have enough fuel to make that flight.

I talked to the Anchorage International Airport tower and they said it was socked in from Kenai to Tyonek, a thirty-five by seventy mile fog bank. They asked me if I wanted to declare an emergency and land on a runway at the airport. I didn't want to mess with the FAA and make that emergency situation. It was my choice to land where I wouldn't have complications. Since my plane was equipped with floats and I could see the Inlet and land safely, I chose to forego a runway landing. The Inlet's waters looked as smooth as glass.

I thought of making a landing down near the Port of Anchorage, but not knowing what was out there, I was afraid that I might run into a barge or ship at anchor.

I circled on the edge of the fog offshore from the Campbell Lake area between there and Indian. I kept looking, thinking I was going to get into Campbell Lake which has no tower. I even dropped into the fog a little bit near Campbell Lake.

Portage Sound was VFR, so I decided since my fuel was getting lower and lower and lower, that I'd better commit to a landing out there. The full moon enabled me to see. I'd touch down and let the rising tide float me to shore. I'd be home free.

I set up for my approach and settled down toward the shimmering waters below. The airplane eased in. Anchorage tower had advised me that the tide was on its way in. I had some fear that the big waves might get me; but there weren't any. The water was as smooth as I've ever seen the Inlet. It looked like another perfect landing.

Suddenly there was a lurch and a rending roar. The plane flipped upside down and tore the tail right off. My left float hit a sand bar I couldn't see. It was a routine landing until I hit the sandbar.

The plane turned over so fast that I didn't even have time to think about it--one second I'm landing, the next I'm hanging upside down in my seatbelt. I was just thankful that I wasn't all busted up so I could still get out of the airplane and do something to help myself.

I got out of the seat belt, opened the door and exited the plane. Even though I wasn't knocked out, the crash threw me for a loop. I felt the back of my head and discovered a long vertical cut. It had opened up so much I thought I might be touching my brains and perhaps I'd die that way.

Evidently the toilet bowl had come flying forward from the baggage area and hit me. The toilet disintegrated like tempered glass. Had the toilet not shattered, the blow may have killed me. I then hit the instrument panel banging my head and cutting myself.

Except for the moonlight and the flashing of the Christmas

colored strobe lights and the landing lights stabbing across the inky waters of the Inlet, it was pitch black.

I could see by the light of the moon. I saw the gravel bar. The big mushroom cloud still hung over Anchorage, like an atomic bomb cloud. As I regained my senses, I noticed the incoming tide lapping at my plane. I needed to head for shore pronto!

I looked into the plane and gathered some survival gear. Of course everything that was on the floor was now on the roof. I put two blankets and an old jacket into a Hefty garbage sack so that I'd have some kind of life device in case I got into water. Hopefully the bag would hold enough air to float me.

With my boot heel I tried to scratch an arrow in the hard gravel bar indicating my direction of travel. But it didn't work.

I could see vehicle headlights on the Seward Highway south of Potter's Marsh, probably six miles away.

I couldn't make a straight shot to the beach because deep, water-filled channels blocked my shortest path to the highway. The gravel bar was several miles long. I started walking towards shore and that, big, foggy cloud.

I was wearing hip boots, cords, a flannel shirt and a light coat. It was between thirty and thirty-six degrees. The wet mud and water intensified the cold, however it wasn't cold to the point that I was freezing to death.

Using the car lights as a reference, I followed the sandbar east toward Potter's Marsh. Turnagainn's main body of water was on my right.

As I walked, I realized the gravel bars were as hard as concrete, like pavement. I couldn't even put a foot print in them. It amazed me.

I had wondered if the Inlet would swallow me up. I've lived here all my life, and most people who crash in the Inlet or get stuck in its mud, never get out of it. From duck hunting and hooligan fishing experiences as a kid, I realized how easy it is to get stuck.

My fear of getting stuck was not real pronounced. I knew my object was to get to shore. I just kept telling myself, "I'm going to get back to see dear old mom."

Then I began to wonder if I'd be able to get to shore before the water engulfed me...the silt would weigh me down...or I wouldn't be able to swim because of the strength of the tide. Getting to shore was my ultimate goal.

I kept walking. Finally I reached the end of the sandbar and encountered my first crossing attempt. I wondered whether or not the water would rise over my hip boots forcing me to swim. That would have gotten me colder and wetter. Could I make it to the next sandbar?

I waded into the water. It rose around my waders but it didn't go over them.

I felt my way along, testing the bottom of the Inlet, carefully placing one foot in front of the other. Fifteen minutes later I walked out of the water onto the next bar.

I continued east paralleling the shoreline until I came to another body of water. It was big enough to land a float plane in, 300 feet wide and miles long. I said to myself, "If I can't make it across, I'll just have to back up, take my clothes off, put them in the Hefty bag and try to swim that couple of blocks of slough there."

As I waded into the ebony water, it rose slowly. It was never more than thirty inches deep. As before the water did not go over the tops of my hip boots. I waded across it to the next bar.

I walked another couple of miles until I was close to the shoreline. I'd crossed two bodies of water without having to swim.

I got to the shoreline and encountered the difficulty of the mud banks which were too high to see over. I thought I'd be safer on top of the banks, so I started up. I ran into big, crevasse-like rivulets. The mud was slick and jello-like; and I kept falling. I wallowed in the gray muck. I fell and regained my footing so many times I lost count. I also discovered it was like quicksand.

The going was easier on the gravel bars below than on the slick slop above. The bottom was hard, gravel covered by four or five inches of water.

Finally I managed to find my way through the goo and get to shore. I don't know what someone else does in a near death situation where the Inlet's chasing his butt, but I told myself, "I love my mother and all my friends. I will make it back to see them all." That's what I kept telling myself. For some reason that's what kept me plugging away.

It took me close to three hours to reach the highway after I left the plane. I must have looked like some hideous monster--I was caked with mud and blood.

I hit shore near the shooting range building by Rabbit Creek Road. I saw a light in there. I wanted to get help, but I was afraid that somebody might shoot me since I looked like some kind of freak. I was a scary looking human being--all cut up and covered with blood and mud, red and gray from head to foot.

I passed the building, got to the highway a hundred yards beyond and tried to hitch a ride. I could see people approaching. Drivers looked at me and veered around me. It was as if they were thinking, "I'm not picking up this creature."

I said to myself, "What do I have to do to get some help here?" I was beat. When no one stopped for me, I gave up in frustration and walked uphill toward Anchorage.

Then I saw a vehicle sitting on the shoulder of the road. I approached the driver a little nervously...I didn't want him to think I was some kind of peeping Tom and shoot me.

The driver got out of the car. I said, "Hey, Mister, could you help me? I just wrecked my airplane in the Inlet."

He was a newspaper reporter looking for the downed pilot! He'd come out to Potter's Marsh on a hunch.

We started for Providence Hospital in Anchorage. Along the way, I said, "Hey, buddy, why don't we stop and get a beer? I need to get a cold beer, wash this mud down." He didn't stop for a drink; I think he thought I was going to die in his car. I had to show him how to get to the emergency room.

When I got to the hospital, I saw the fright on peoples' faces. The first thing I wanted to see was what I looked like. I knew it was like something out of a horror movie. I discovered they couldn't have dressed me up any wilder.

When the medical personnel started examining me, they couldn't understand why I wasn't suffering from hypothermia. The fact that I hadn't gotten my body totally immersed in water was what kept me from getting colder and going hypothermic.

They wanted to keep me overnight. But I talked them out of it. I told them, "I'm okay." They took seventeen stitches to sew my head up and released me.

Shortly after I got to the hospital a dear friend of mine, Pete Potter, showed up with his wife Jane. It was really nice to see somebody that I knew. They lived on Campbell Lake, and he had been listening to my entire radio conversation through his scanner as I circled Anchorage. Knowing and caring for me he actually went down the highway looking for me.

Pete came over to me and said, "Bob, I tried to get a search party organized for you. I drove the highway for hours looking to see if I could find you out there."

I was grateful that he thought of all that. Nobody else did. He had tried to get a boat to go out at the Port of Anchorage, but the weather was sour. They just didn't put together a search. I assume they figured a downed pilot in the Inlet was a gonner anyway.

The next morning my buddy Potter and another guy picked me up. We flew over the Inlet looking for the plane, and we found it swirling around in the receding tide. We hired a chopper to go out to pick it up.

An old friend of mine, Kip Kippingham, who retrieved a lot of bush planes, told me what I would have to do to get the plane out. He said he didn't think that I'd be able to salvage anything but the engine and the floats. The silt gets into the wings and the plane is so heavy that if you try to lift it with the chopper, the pressure pulls the wings off the airplane.

The wind kicked up to sixty to seventy knots, and they had to wait for the winds to die down. After the third tide the winds abated, and we went back out. But the plane was gone. The tide took it out to sea.

My loss was $75,000. I had put the plane up for the winter and had just cancelled my insurance coverage the week before. In the interim I decided I needed four sheets of plywood at the cabin. It would be easier to take it on the airplane. I rationalized, "One little last flight isn't going to hurt anything."

Source: *Danger Stalks the Land*

Post Trial of Jesus

Pilate surrendered the Nazarene to the mob and handed the Deliverer to his soldiers. They saw a great joke in this provincial Jew claiming to be king. Not only had he been subjected to a mock trial and falsely accused, but also he'd just endured a shameless flogging. They could hardly wait to get hold of him and to further ridicule him. They would have their chance, if only the Rabbi would survive until Skull Hill.

Turns out the Nazarene would face execution with two others. Now he and his two condemned fellows maneuvered down the marble steps and onto the cobblestone courtyard. All three began their final journey to their execution. Each of the condemned men was accompanied by five executioners, dispatched at the front and rear. The procession moved slowly along the Via Dolorosa, the Way of Sorrows. A centurion led the group.

Carrying his own cross to the execution site signified to the city that the condemned no longer had anything to do with them.

As I followed along with the crowd behind the soldiers, I heard women wailing and lamenting the Deliverer. I found myself wondering about Gaius and how this turn of events might affect him.

I observed one woman offer the Prophet a cloth to wipe his face. But the Centurion pushed her away. Other onlookers made similar offers, only to be rebuffed.

Leaving the courtyard of Pilate's palace the group moved toward the Gennath Gate. Because of the Passover celebration Jerusalem streets bulged with thousands of locals as well as visitors from every corner of the world.

On either side of the street merchant tables and stalls

beckoned consumers. Vendors sold whatever the customer wanted—dates, figs, water, roast lamb, olive oil. The street was alive with people. Their cacophony of activity arose—some stooped with age, children playing whose shrill voices reverberated off buildings, beggars tapping their sticks on the cobblestones, merchants carrying baskets of vegetables or lemons or almonds, others with casks of wine.

The processional bore along toward Golgotha, the Place of the Skull, the place of hanging where the Jewish elders anticipated with joy the pretend Messiah's death. Golgotha's rocky hill northwest of Jerusalem lay a lifetime away if you bore a crossbeam upon your battered back—650 yards of brutal agony, every step riddled with ribald scoffers and accusers as well as sympathizers. Six-hundred-fifty yards from the flogging at fortress Antonia to the place of death.

Along the entire route the crowd's wicked voices rose as one. Their passions united. But momentarily the crowd noticed a lifeless tree. Upon careful inspection they noticed at its base the body of Judas. At his own hanging his body weight had broken the rope around his neck and he had fallen to the ground, a mangled body. Dogs now devoured it.

The Nazarene struggled over the cobblestones, staggering under its weight of the crossbeam. His back one huge, open wound. It would have taken most of his energy in that condition just to walk, yet he struggled onward with this shouldered burden.

Although I've witnessed many floggings, I did not see him scourged. I saw him with his crossbeam. I followed him as closely as possible, observing the incredible injuries inflicted upon the Nazarene. He was beaten beyond belief. He was mutilated. He left a trail of blood. He was scourged as badly as any man I've seen who lived. I found it amazing that he could even walk, much less carry the 110-pound beam.

From every quarter came taunts. Soldiers and mob alike shouted abuse and struck out at the Nazarene.

Some whom he'd healed or helped trailed at a distance, powerless to help. Some of those broke out into tears; others mourned.

Weeping women stepped forward but he told them not to cry for him. I recalled what he'd said to women hinting of the future destruction of Jerusalem, "Daughters of Jerusalem, don't weep for me. Weep rather for yourselves and for your children. Look, the days are coming when the people will say, 'Happy are those who are barren and the womb's that have never borne, the breasts that have never suckled.' Then they will say to the mountains, 'Fall on us!' and to the hills, 'Cover us!' For if men do these things to a green tree, what will happen to a withered, dry one." And I wondered exactly what he had meant.

His gruesome form looked barely human. In spite of His efforts to walk erect, the weight of the heavy wooden beam, together with the shock produced by copious blood loss, was too much. Exhausted and at the end of his strength, he stumbled and fell, the cross falling from his grasp. He lay there in his own blood and sweat, the crowd jeering, mocking and laughing. Some spit on him. Others chanted for him to get up. Some made fun, asking him how it was that the two thieves could carry their burden but he couldn't, challenging him to get up.

For the first time I tried to analyze the intricacies of the execution process. I thoughtfully wondered about the indescribable pain of the flagrum. I found my mind racing ahead to the hanging and wondering about the spikes…jabbing into and through flesh and muscle. And what about the nerves and ligaments of the arms and feet? What would it feel like to have metal pounded through your extremities…plastering you to a hunk of wood?

Watching the Nazarene struggle with the post—covered in his oozing blood and gore and with flesh hanging from his back—I'm forced to wonder. It's my fortune, or perhaps misfortune, to monitor the activities of this Jew. It is not my duty to defend him. However something is terribly upside down here.

Based on the beating he endured, he should be dead. How could this injustice have occurred? We have an innocent man dying for nothing—nothing that he did and with nothing to be gained from his death. What's to be gained by his accusers? Why should his death matter to me? In light of the Jewish Tanakh, I am living in what must be the very decisive time of the Holy One, born in Bethlehem, come to mankind. Can it be much clearer?

Yes, he's a Jew. And I'm a Roman. Still, I'm a man. I know courage. I know honor. I know loyalty. And I know injustice. As a Roman patriot I know a real man when I see one.

I'd seen him stumble a couple of times. But this time when he fell, he couldn't rise. His damaged muscles had been pushed beyond their endurance, his injuries crippling him. He lay there momentarily. He did not whimper. He did not seek assistance. He just lay there.

The Roman Centurion in charge, eager to get on with the hanging, hawk-like, scanned the masses of people on either side and noticed a great, burly black man. With leather banned wrist the Centurion thrust his arm, pointed an index finger at the stalwart North African onlooker and commanded, "You. Pick up this crossbeam and carry it for the King."

The man, a Cyrenian named Simon, moved forward. Simon had heard of the Messiah. Although his sons Alexander and Rufus believed in the Nazarene, he did not. Simon hefted the transom onto his shoulders and followed the Centurion. The Galilean somehow arose and struggled on behind, still bleeding and sweating the cold, clammy sweat of shock.

Source: *Brachan*

Larry Kaniut

Motorcycle and Bear
Battered biker has a bear tale to tell

HELMET SAVES LIFE: Pelvis broken, new motorcycle destroyed. By ZAZ HOLLANDER, *Anchorage Daily News*, August 10th, 2005

WASILLA -- The bear was at a dead run downhill toward the Old Glenn Highway when Garrett Edgmon came around a bend on his new Kawasaki motorcycle.

Edgmon barely caught a glimpse of the reddish-brown fur coming headlong at him out of the corner of his eye as he drove south at about 45 or 50 mph.

Then the bruin's ribs slammed into his front wheel, sending the bike hurtling across the pavement.

"Bears ain't exactly soft," Edgmon said by phone from Anchorage on Tuesday afternoon. "Trust me, they're not. It hit me pretty hard."

The commercial fisherman from Dillingham ended up with a broken pelvis, numerous bumps and bruises -- and a heck of a story to tell.

As man and bear locked eyes, Edgmon didn't think he would see his 41st birthday next month. Then he was thrown onto the bear's head and neck. The two skidded together for a little ways on the highway, about two miles from where the Old Glenn leaves the northbound Glenn Highway.

Edgmon felt his head bounce. He heard his helmet shatter.

Meanwhile, Palmer resident Scott Hanson came up in his red pickup and pulled over. Hanson later told Alaska state troopers the bear did a flip and then disappeared under a guardrail.

Edgmon only remembers getting up, shocked and in a great

deal of pain, and trying to drag off the road the 750-pound 1200cc Kawasaki Voyager he bought last month.

Hanson called 911.

Edgmon was treated at Valley Hospital. The full-face helmet he wore saved his life, he said. "If I didn't have a helmet on, I would have been dead."

Edgmon is staying in the city with his wife as she undergoes cancer treatment. He said his bike was insured. But he doesn't plan to get on another motorcycle any time soon.

Doctors told him he'll need a walker to get around for the next two months, effectively through the fall fishing season.

State biologist Gino Del Frate said he knew of no plans to track down the bear, described by Hanson as a young brown.

Trooper Mitch Lewis said he scanned the slopes above the highway with a scope on Monday but saw nothing. It's unlikely the bear wandered off and died, Lewis said.

But Edgmon figures the critter must be badly hurt.

"If not, he is one miracle bear," he said.

Source: *What's Bruin?*

What If?

Thousands of stampedes headed for the Throndiuk River in Canada's Yukon Territory in the late 1890s. That was its geographic name before the newsmen got hold of it, changing the Indian word meaning "hammer water" into Klondike. The locale was a place of trapping salmon by way of hammering wood posts into the streambed. The Klondike discovery was made and the rush was on.

Some years later Harry Boyden followed his predecessors to the gold fields near Dawson City, arriving in 1908. Four years after that he joined gold stampeders flocking to Chisana in the Wrangel-St. Elias country, a couple of hundred miles south of Dawson City. Harry prospected and freighted cargo in the White River-Nabesna area before moving to McCarthy in 1936.

He later returned to the Chisana area where he ran a trading post at Nabesna until 1957. He then built a cabin at Chistochina Flats and resided there until his death in March 1968. During the last thirty years of his life Harry gained fame as a guide. The same legendary Alaska guide tells this story.

It didn't look good. It never does when a man goes solo into the wilderness and is caught out, back of beyond with little food and gear, especially when the weather is well below zero. It was 1925, and the trekker was in a pickle. He was deep in the White River country near the Alaska-Yukon border, a savage and unforgiving land. Only by piecing together the evidence he left—scrawled notes, equipment, clothing, tracks and his own remains would the survivors be able to guess at what happened on his journey.

He was in the Wrangell Mountains. Thoughts of what if plagued him. What if I'd brought more gear? More food? An extra horse? What if I'd come two weeks earlier? Looking off into the black of night, his tiny fire brought some solace. He sipped weak tea and planned the next 24-hours.

While wet snow pelted his rain pants and slicker, he cursed the white stuff which was already a foot deep. He'd been in more jams than he cared to remember and knew he'd find a way out of this one. His journey had been compounded by the dead horse, lack of food and now the snow.

He'd ridden horseback into the mountains, but the horse had wandered off one night. For several days he'd searched for it, finding no sign of the animal. Then he saw a flock of ravens circling down river a couple of miles. He went to investigate and found his horse at the base of a cut bank. It looked like the horse had dropped from the 50-foot bluff and broken its neck. The discovery was disappointing, but it was not a cause for great concern. Just one that demanded a change in strategy.

The man turned and headed for camp, noticing the southern sky beyond blotted out by gray snow clouds. It was only October 10 and somewhat early for snow. It probably won't stay, he thought.

He pressed on, tried not to think about the necessity of getting out and the problem it posed. He was some fifty miles from his cabin. To reach it he'd have to climb to higher elevation in order to cross the mountain pass which would have at least twice the snow on the ground as his river camp

He knew that crossing two to three feet of snow would be extremely difficult without snowshoes—without webs he'd be nearly helpless.

Another factor to consider was the probable temperature drop of 30 to 40-below. Momentarily he thought about staying, hoping that someone would come looking for him in this desolate country. But he knew better. Who would come out here this time of year? There is absolutely no reason for anyone to come here now.

He was positive that no man lived in the valley. He'd seen no one in his recent search nor any signs of human activity, and he knew no Indians resided here. Trapping season was three weeks away. He knew he had to make a move soon or it might be too late.

His situation demanded a survival strategy. He knew the necessity of remaining calm and assessing his situation.

I'm a gamer. I can do it. I've been in other jams and worked my way out. More food, warm clothes and snowshoes would make it easier, but I'll have to make do with what I've got.

He knew the first ten miles through timber would be the easiest and that the next thirty in the barren plateaus east of him would be the toughest to negotiate. Those rolling hills will be covered with two to three feet of snow. There won't even be a twig for building a fire.

He also knew that the wind following the storm would come howling out of the north, cutting through clothing like a sandblaster. To be caught out poorly clothed in below-zero weather in screeching winds would be like committing suicide… slowly.

He turned in, knowing that the trip was unavoidable. He lay cozy in his sleeping bag. And he cursed himself for making an impulsive decision and preparing so poorly. At home he'd be snug and warm and his sixteen horses would be feeding near his cabin in the meadows. He was angry that he hadn't brought a spare cayuse.

He hadn't intended his trip to turn out the way it had. Originally he'd planned to scout new game country for four, maybe five days, push ahead for new territory. But it seemed that every new valley and distant ridge was more tantalizing than the last, and he kept traveling deeper into the mountains…eventually losing his horse.

When he awakened the next morning, he roused out of his sleeping bag. Eighteen inches of snow had accumulated overnight. He prepared some of the last of the tea he'd hoarded, boiled a few strips of dried moose meat and chomped a piece of pilot bread. It wasn't much but it was better than nothing.

He dug into a saddle bag and extracted seventeen shells for his .22 single-shot rifle, thinking he might get a crack at the moose which had left the tracks he'd seen while searching for his horse.

Leaving camp with his rifle and skinning knife, he headed for the horse carcass, planning to extract what he could for his sustenance over the next several days. During the night the stomach had been torn open and part of the entrails eaten by a wolverine. Ravens had picked a large hole in one ham.

The frozen flesh compounded the use of the sharp knife, however he carved off fifteen pounds. The horse had put in a long season in the mountains and was lacking fat, but the man sliced off as much as he thought he'd need, knowing it was necessary to provide body heat in the days ahead.

When he returned to camp, he prepared a cup of tea, ate from his dwindling supply of moose meat then cut four 8-foot green willows from which to fashion snowshoes.

He spent the next morning finalizing his snowshoes with rawhide strips of horse hide. Then he placed them near the fire to shrink-dry them. Next he took the saddle blanket and constructed a backpack. Then he made a sling for the .22 rifle.

The following morning he placed his saddle in a tree where it would be safe from rodents and rabbits. Better carry the snowshoes through the timber so they won't get damaged. I can put them on when I leave timberline. He shouldered his pack, grabbed his rifle and set out on his journey over the mountains.

Exhausted near dark, he reached the edge of the timber. Not as good as I'd hoped, but it'll have to do. He selected a large spruce, dropped his gear at its foot and broke off dry branches below its overhanging limbs. He scrounged enough dry firewood in the area to build a large fire. This will be the last heat I feel till I get through the pass and over the barrens. Might as well enjoy it as much as possible.

The temperature plummeted during the day, and he knew he'd feel its effect this night. When the northern lights twinkled and hissed overhead, it was laughter-like, mocking and leering down at him. Almost a live thing making fun of my stupidity. He was angry with his situation. Again, it caused him to question his lack of preparation.

He shivered through the night, rebuilding the fire before daylight. It hit 25-below overnight, all the reason to cherish his last piece of moose meat that he boiled with a hunk of horse fat. He savored the meat with his last piece of pilot bread.

Finishing his meal, he gathered up his pack, rifle and webs and struck out for the open country beyond. He struggled onward through the crotch deep snow, fighting exhaustion and the tangled alder thickets. With two hours to go until nightfall, exhaustion again embraced him as he topped the last ridge and looked out across the bleak, snow filled land known as the barrens. Snow three feet deep leered at him over thirty miles of rolling hills on the plateau. The white stuff, untracked by another human, lay before him, both beckoning and mocking.

He guessed it was 35 to 40-below as his nose hairs and beard frosted over. But he had chosen his path. He tied on his snowshoes and trudged onward.

As he labored along, the webs lacking the usual upturned front caught a lot of snow. It was a grueling trek, each step sinking nose-ward on a snowshoe and exacting a tremendous amount of energy to bring the tip above the snow for the next step.

He guessed that he'd covered two miles in the final two hours before darkness engulfed him. He selected a gully to get out of any potential wind and scraped out a depression with his snowshoe. He spread his sleeping bag in the dip and covered it with the piece of canvas then placed a foot of snow on it for insulation. The canvas would keep any melted snow from him.

Planning ahead, he carried a hunk of horse meat into his bag with him, hoping it would thaw during the night next to his body. But such was not the case. When he awoke the meat was still half frozen.

He gnawed on the meat a while before setting out into the waist deep snow. He traveled this way for two days. Then he repeated the mundane process: right foot step, sink, lift the front of the left web from the snow and step with it while the right snowshoe sank; lift the front from the snow on the right snowshoe and shake it off before stepping again. Onward without end.

Two days and two nights witnessed the same activity...stop for the night, scrape snow to form a depression on the ground, spread his sleeping bag and canvas, cover them with snow, arise in the morning, gnaw more raw frozen horse meat and attack the day.

By nightfall of the second day he knew the frost was penetrating his extremities. Can't keep my hands warm. Think they're freezing along with my face. Must be about 45-below. Adding to his troubles, a frigid wind out of the north cut like a knife.

The rifle was extra weight. That night he thought about jettisoning it but he reasoned that it could bag ptarmigan or a caribou should he get the chance. It was a tough decision. The weapon could save his life.

The wind woke him the third night. Wind driven snow scoured the landscape. Like a high powered sand blaster, ice particles blistered the barrens and everything in their path. There was no let up. His situation gripped him with fear. What if I'm buried by the drifting snow? All night he listened. And the snow in his depression built up.

At daylight he dug his way out, hearing the howling wind the whole while. Once clear of the snow, the icy hand of death pummeled him from every side. Visibility limited him to a handful of yards. The bitter wind and blowing snow, combined with the 45-below temperature, drove him back to his nest. Gripped by fear and hopelessness, he knew that he was hamstrung by the elements. No land marks. Will have to stay here till I can see. Maybe the wind will let up soon.

He lay in his nest gnawing on the frozen meat and wondering and hoping. How long will the 10-pounds of meat last? How much longer will the wind pin me down? If I stay warm and conserve my strength, I may get out.

One day turned interminably into the next until a week had passed. He left his cocoon only to grab another hunk of frozen meat or to relieve himself.

For seven days the wind prevailed. She played a cruel joke on him.

When he awoke on the morning of the eighth day, he arose to silence. The wind stopped. He struggled from his sleeping bag and gazed upon the sun. For as far as he could see a frigid, white world loomed to the horizon. Ridges poked up all around, but the gullies were choked with snow drifts, some as deep as 20-feet.

At that point he cooked his goose.

Though reasoning may have been beyond his capabilities, he thought of a solution. My meat supply is nearly gone. If the wind starts again, I'm dead. Back at the river I can have wood, a fire and heat. I can get more horse meat. I might find that moose or get some rabbits. Maybe I can make a better pair of snowshoes and walk out.

This proved by far his most trying wilderness test. A tough customer, he hated to admit defeat but the cold, the wind and the snow had whipped him. He accepted it and chose to re-group and to try again. He turned back.

After three grueling days he reached his river campsite. He immediately made for the horse carcass expecting to find meat. But a wolverine and a pack of wolves had beaten him to it. They'd left nothing but some bone fragments, hooves with the shoes on, the skull plate and strips of hide. Not even enough here for a thick broth.

Over the next week he hunted hard for the moose, but failed to find it…or any other creature.

Although protected from the wind by the forest, the cold and hunger brought him closer to death's door each day. Starvation sapped his strength.

Late November found him checking rabbit snares. That's when tragedy struck. Thin ice and the cold teamed up to destroy him. While crossing ice he plunged through into the water below and got drenched to his crotch. From the time he freed himself from the frigid water and reached his camp, his hands and feet were frozen.

Death stalked him now as never before. He shivered the night away trying to get warm in his sleeping bag next to the dying fire. Camp bound because he could not walk, he watched his hands blacken then turn gangrenous. I can't walk, hunt, collect wood or eat. How long till the Grim Reaper calls my number?

By day he watched the gangrene get worse. He wasted away, becoming weaker with each sunrise. By night he languished in his sleeping bag, shivering and agonizing because of the physical pain. Who could know the depths of his despair?

Slowly but surely, starvation pinched his spine. December witnessed his hopelessness. And Old Man Death knocked on his door, welcoming him with open arms.

And surely the if onlys must have plagued him to the bitter end.

Source: *Danger Stalks the Land*

Who Said Zoo Bears Are Tame?

By Robin Paul and Larry Kaniut

"...this massive bear coming toward me...was like King Kong..."

It's not every day that a zoo bear takes a bite out of a visitor. But it happened on Friday July 30, 1994. Kathryn Warburton, a 29-year-old dental worker from Sydney, Australia, had planned a vacation in the United States and was having the time of her life. She had arrived in the Last Frontier and wanted to experience as much of Alaska as she could before returning to her native Australia. This spunky blonde embodied the adventurous spirit of our neighbors Down Under

Several events led to our learning about Kathryn Warburton and her encounter with Alaska's favorite bear. Heidi Baer, our next door neighbor, was getting married. Heidi's uncle Gary Paul had brought his family to town for the occasion. In the face of all the preparations Gary and his wife Robin took their sons to the Anchorage Zoo.

One of the zoo's favorite attractions is the polar bear Binky. Binky is the 20-year-old male bear that was brought from the Beaufort Sea after his mother was shot in 1974. When Binky was tiny, zoo workers played with him and rubbed his stomach. But since he has grown in size, age and cantankerousness, no one goes into his cage any more. Binky bit off a worker's finger around 1980 and is one of more aggressive animals at the zoo. But today Binky lazed in his lair.

Gary and Robin Paul approached the polar bear area. Meanwhile Kathryn decided to move closer to Binky's cage for a close up picture. That's when the excitement began.

We learned about Kathy and Binky when the Pauls returned to the Baers. I asked Gary if he'd be willing to comment on their experience. Robin mailed me a summary which she called "Binky the Bear and the Paul Family." Most of her text follows.

In late July of 1994 Gary and Robin Paul and their three young sons, Garrett age 9, Austin age 7 and Carson age 3, flew to Anchorage from their home in Juneau to attend the wedding of Gary's niece Heidi Baer. The weather was sunny, the day was young and we decided to go to the Anchorage Zoo. Our boys had never been to a zoo and were excited as the five of us headed off.

The zoo wasn't too crowded that morning and we wandered around leisurely. As we went up toward the polar bear area, there was a great viewing area of the polar bears and we stopped and talked about the bear lying near the fence. Binky lay about twenty feet from the tall pipe-style fence near the shallow drainage ditch, his platter-sized paws facing us. We talked about how huge his feet were and about the fact that even if he looked fat and lazy, all bears have 4-wheel drive and can move fast.

As we continued up the path, a motion off to our left caught our attention. We were shocked to see a young blonde-haired woman about to straddle the low fence near the front of the area where Binky was lying. She had apparently looked around and seeing no one, had decided to go down close to the bear for a close-up picture. She had already climbed over the first low fence by the path and had gone approximately twenty feet down the grass slope to the second fence near the bear cage.

There were no warning signs on the pipe fence that rose twenty feet vertically with one foot spaces between the bars. It appeared she was safe from the king of the Arctic.

She was facing our direction, head down, and was lifting her right leg over the fence. Gary was about to yell at her to get away, but instead he ended up yelling, "Look out!" It was too late.

In an instant, Binky was up. Lightning-like the 850-pound

boar rushed to the perimeter of his pen, extended his neck through the bars and grabbed her with his teeth. Faster than it can be told, Binky jerked his neck back and dragged Kathy toward the high bars. Binky pinned her to a bar with a paw and chewed and pawed her leg into his cage.

With his huge mouth he bit into the soft part of her waist between her ribs and her hip bones on her left side. His bite was massive and looked as if he compressed that area of her body down to a three-inch girth.

We were the only ones there to witness the bear's action. Gary and I looked around to find something to throw at the bear. There was nothing. Gary told the girl not to fight the bear because it would make the bear madder. The boys were sobbing. I was frantically looking around for help. Gary stayed near the girl while I ran back down the path toward the elephants' area yelling for help.

Mass confusion reigned. People started running up the hill to help. The first zoo employee to get there, Kevin Pickel who took no thought for his own safety, jumped the first fence by the path, ran across the grass and grabbed the girl. He had nothing to use against the bear—no one did. He threw his radio (a walkie talkie that some zoo attendants carry) at the bear's head, and it bounced off into the cage. Binky wasn't about to loosen his grip on the girl's waist. Kathryn tried to push off from the pen and away from Binky with her right foot, but her efforts were futile.

Another employee, Shane Larson, ran for help and to call an ambulance. By then other visitors to the zoo (about five or six feet from her) screamed and tried to pull her away. It was a painful tug-of-war that at times suspended her in the air. A firefighter from Dillingham, Alaska, and another man joined in the effort to free Kathryn. Other people stood in the background, awestruck.

Gary tried to break off a board from the fence, and finally broke off a branch from a tree and handed it to the people down by the girl. Other people helped break off branches too and rained huge blows on Binky's head. Finally, as they beat on the bear and pulled on the girl, Binky's grip moved down to her hip, then her thigh (she was wearing shorts and you could see the bites in her leg), then toward her knee, down to her calf, and finally to her foot.

A huge tug of war was going on with the girl. Finally Binky clasped her tennis shoe which came off; and they pulled her free and out of his reach. During the entire time, Ms. Warburton, really didn't make any loud cries or screams. Perhaps the shock and the force of the bear's jaws prevented her from doing so or perhaps she realized that doing so would further irritate the bear.

They attended to her on the grass as the crowd, still in shock, cried. After I had run down the hill for help and then ran back to the area, my attention turned toward our sons who had been left alone watching in horror. I moved them behind some people where they couldn't see Gairett, the oldest was hysterical...at his age he knew and fully understood what was happening. Austin and Carson were crying and shaking.

After the rescuers got Kathryn on a stretcher and we felt we had done all we could do, we quietly but swiftly, moved away from the area, still in shock. We thought we could look at more animals and regain our composure. We moved up the path to the next area where the animals were all ears and eyes and obviously agitated and attracted by the smell of blood. After we saw three large brown bears standing on their hind legs, looking over the high fence with anticipation, we decided to leave the zoo. Moving toward the exit, I overheard a mother tell her child, "Let's go see the bears."

I blurted out, "You can't go down there, they've closed the area." This intrusion was met with a snotty look as the mother scooted her child toward the path down toward the bears.

We returned to our mini van, climbed in, and drove off with no direction in mind, each reliving the event. We didn't want to talk to anyone and ended up at Arctic Valley where we got out for a little walk. Finally we got back in the car and stopped at

Carr's in Eagle River for some deli food. No one though, had much of an appetite.

We went back to the Baer's house and related our story. I was concerned that since we were the only ones to truly witness the attack, we should let the zoo manager know in the event they needed information. We called and talked with Sammye Seawell, the zoo director, leaving our number.

The boys were fairly subdued for a day or so. Garrett couldn't sleep that first night. Gary and I relived the scene over and over in our minds. The boys were intently listened to any update on Kathryn's status. For their own peace of mind I guess they needed to know she was going to be OK.

I called the hospital, talked to the floor nursing supervisor, left my name (in the event Ms. Warburton needed to talk with us) and explained her reason for knowing how that Kathryn was doing. The nurse told me to tell the boys that Ms. Warburton was doing OK. The boys felt better after this and didn't seem as much on edge.

After our family returned to Juneau, things seemed OK. We talked about the incident. The boys couldn't understand why that lady went so close to the bear. They firmly believed that the lady was wrong and that nothing should happen to Binky because it wasn't his fault since he was just being a bear. They drew numerous pictures of Binky with signs saying Member, Binky Fan Club.

The most obvious lasting impression on the boys, especially little Carson, was that they were very cautious at the Paul cabin. Carson would not go outside without his mother or father for many months. After a year went by, Carson was observed staring out the window of his home in Juneau. When his father asked him what he was thinking about, he replied, "Are there bears in those woods?" When his Dad said yes, Carson asked if they were going to coe in and get him. He was told no, and looked relieved to know that they didn't want to come into a house anyway.

Looking back now the incident reminds us of a dog with his prized catch. We know that if Kathryn hadn't been bit on her side and hadn't been in that horizontal position, Binky could have pulled her right into his cage area. Besides her position the other thing that saved her was that the bars of the cage didn't give Binky room to jerk her from side to side. His massive head was tightly wedged between the two bars and he was able to just hold on.

AFTERWARD

Kathryn was rushed to the hospital and treated for a broken leg, lacerations, punctures and infection. Her bite injuries were up to 6 inches deep. Her recovery was routine except for the public's response and the concern for infection.

A major concern with ursine bites is infection. Such injuries demand constant monitoring. The treatment she received at Providence Hospital in Anchorage may not be duplicated in Australia since they have no bear maulings and no infectious bear bacteria. (see APPENDIX 8 for infection information.) Not the least of Kathryn's concerns is that she has no medical insurance to cover her mounting medical costs.

Kathryn and Binky received world-wide media attention, propelling Binky further toward cult-hero status. He had returned to normal within an hour (but in July 1995 Binky and his pen mate Nuka died). A public outcry followed Kathryn's episode with Binky, and people's emotions ran the gamut. Some wanted Kathryn to be put into Binky's cage; others wanted Binky put to sleep.

Kathryn said that Binky, "...just sort of came up from nowhere...I couldn't believe this massive bear coming toward me. It was like King Kong, you know?" She admitted, "Looking back, it was the dumbest thing I've ever done in my life. It didn't occur to me it was vicious. I've been told it had been there since it was a cub and I thought it was quite tame."

Larry Kaniut

Life after Binky found Kathryn on the mend and thankful to be alive.

Source: *Some Bears Kill*

Five Men

Straining to see through the smoking sleet slicing his visor, flight engineer Fred Kalt, tries to make out a crouching figure in the chopper's rescue basket. He can't move the basket. Then he hears over his headset, "Someone's hanging on the basket!"

Moments, as in nano-seconds, later the basket clinger is gone. Down, down, down. One hundred and three feet into the smoking surf.

Meanwhile the sound of steel on the deck reminds the rescuers that a man lies in the basket—his beard festooned with icicles...his cheeks look like ice. The rescuers strip Bob Doyle of his survival suit and wrap him in a thermal bag. He's been in the 38-degree water nearly eight hours...with four others who'd hit the water when their ship sank.

*   *   *

Mission minded, two groups of men set out...one for fish, the other for men. Five men ended up in the water; five men flew in search of them. The Coast Guard men were trained to save lives.

If ever man met mountain, it was on the Fairweather Grounds in the Gulf of Alaska. The date was Friday, January 30, 1998. Five men aboard the *La Conte* launched from Sitka to long line 150 miles to the north. The 77-foot long, 66 ton ship, built in 1919, was outfitted with the latest in electronic gear. Mark Morley, skipper, and deckhands Mike Decapua, Robert Doyle, William Mork and Hanlon pushed into the Gulf of Alaska aboard the *La Conte*.

Who would have guessed they'd be blasted by a storm of immense proportions? Who would have known those five would abandon ship and struggle in the frigid water, a cataclysmic struggle for survival? Who would have guessed that five other men met the "mountain" and scaled the "rescue peak"?

*   *   *

La Conte wallowed through the water, grunting up a wave, falling off and slamming into a trough. Often, unable to climb the hundred-foot wave—twice as high as the vessel, she merely punched her way through the wall of water. The wind chill registered 18 degrees below zero and spray froze the moment airborne. The ship crawled toward safety, the nearest landfall 80 miles east. Severe wind gusts pummeled the ship, riddling mixed hail or sleet, hamstringing her progress. In six hours she managed a mere three miles.

Fighting to maintain his footing at the wheel, Mark Morley struggled to see through the half inch Lexan window, sheeted with ice. The pounding seas and temperature turned the rigging and the mast ghostly white. The ship took a shellacking. The darkness of night embraced the ship. It didn't look good.

Both sump pumps had shorted out. Water flowed both outside and inside the vessel. Previously the bilge had pumped twenty-two hundred gallons an hour. Now…ZERO.

A rogue wave slammed into the ship. The *La Conte* floundered. From the doorway deckhand Decapua warned skipper Morley that they were taking on water. Below deck Bob Doyle was tossed about in shin deep frigid water before being slammed into a bulkhead.

Joined by Mork and Hanon, Decapua arrived and began bailing water with Doyle. Their bucket brigade was futile. Water was thigh deep. Then chest deep. The engine was silent. The *La Conte* lay dead in the water.

Morley appeared at the hatch, saw the men neck deep in water and shouted, "Get outta there. We're going down!"

Men pulled on survival suits and prepared to abandon ship. Morley called a MAYDAY on his VHF radio. He heard nothing but static. He grabbed his EPIRB—a transmitter that emits a satellite signal—and scrambled onto deck. A mountain of water rose above the stern, momentarily hung there, then smashed the wheelhouse, blowing out the windows...shotgun loud.

Amidst the screaming bedlam and with plates and canned food falling onto the men below, Morley instructed them to rope their waists and to connect themselves together onto a three-quarter inch rope. The raft they desperately needed was NOT onboard. The human chain clawed its way up the deck and each man crawled over the railing.

Above...the roar of the wind, blowing hail like mini-guided missiles, blasting their bodies. Below...a seething ocean, disguised as a dark hole. They didn't know if they'd drop fifteen feet...or a hundred. If they'd be swallowed by the sea by drowning or by hypothermia. They had no choice.

In spite of the fact that they could be smashed against the ship's hull or drop a hundred feet, Morely shouted, "We go in together. On three!" At Morley's "three!" they hurled themselves into the frothing, black void.

Their hope of rescue was on par with Mighty Casey after three strikes in Mudville. Or you might say, similar to Larry Bird's missing a game winning hoop at the buzzer of a crucial game... not so good.

*   *   *

William Monk felt the cold, tightening like pliers on his temples. Thump, thump, thump...he heard the rhythmic sound of his heartbeat. Falling forever into the darkness. Then he rose from the water depths, bursting through the surface, gasping air...and then...down again.

The second time he reached the surface. He kicked his legs before realizing his survival suit was inflating. He knew he wouldn't drown.

The first thing he noticed was the red and white strobe light on the EPIRB. Then he recognized swirling ice, floating bird carcasses, pieces of wood, a buoy and...several hundred yards in the distance, the *La Conte*. He saw only the hull, pummeled by the sea. It disappeared behind a swell. When the wave passed, the ship was gone.

Within moments, his shipmates popped to the surface, heads only a few feet away: Hanlon, Morley, then Decapua and Doyle. Seemed like ice and hail replaced the air, challenging their ability to breathe. A thundering, rumbling wind compounded their efforts to communicate, forcing them to shout to be heard.

A man's chances of surviving five hours in those waters were about 50/50.

*   *   *

Two U. S. Coast Guard Jay Hawk helicopters responded to the EPIRB and headed for the five men in the water. The first chopper flew into the maw of horrendous winds. They suffered mechanical problems; their co-pilot was dizzy and vomiting; the flight mechanic shook from exhaustion and vertigo; they had lost communication and with dwindling fuel on board, aborted their mission. The chopper returned to base.

The second chopper cruised to the Fairweather Grounds and searched for the five fishermen. Fighting winds that allowed the bird to travel a half mile in twenty-five minutes, they continued. At length the rescuers spotted the EPIRB and five survivors clinging to a fishing float around the EPIRB. Five flares jettisoned from the chopper toward the water. The rescue basket slammed around in the wind, unable to reach the water. The flares died out. Nearly five hours earlier the *La Conte* vanished. The chopper must return to base. They left the men in the water.

Even though the Coast Guard classified this as a high risk mission—survivors are close to perishing in desperate straits and rescuers flying into a life threatening situation, a third chopper launched to attempt rescue. Pilot Lt. Stephen Torpey, co-pilot Lt. Cmdr. Theodore La Feuvre, rescue swimmer Michael Fish, flight mechanic Harold Lee Honnold and flight engineer Fred Kalt forged into the night and the totally wailing weather. They did their jobs, never dreaming that their mission would become a classic story heralding heroism and talked about forever throughout academy classes and airbases. It could be a game changer for each man involved, whether in the air or in the water.

In addition to their training, they carried an extra flight mechanic, chemical glow sticks enabling the survivors to see the rescue basket in the dark, 26 special flares that burn for 50 minutes and an additional 700 pounds of extra fuel.

They reached the scene. Torpey and Le Feuvre fought headwinds, blurred dials and nausea while approaching the area of the missing men. Crouching by the jump door and shouting altitudes Kalt and Honnold assessed their roller coaster ride as nightmarish.

Kalt spotted what appeared to be reflective tape on waving arms. He dropped nine flares which hit the water and burst into white light. He lowered the rescue basket which landed in a trough several hundred yards downwind from the men. He continued to hoist and the basket, failing to get it closer to the survivors. Meantime Honnold shouted directions to the pilots.

Even though rescue jumper Fish volunteered to jump into the ocean, Torpey refused to allow him to do so.

As Kalt dropped more flares, the craft was hammered by a severe blast of wind and blown a quarter mile backward and into a trough. Honnold, Kalt and Fish screamed "UP!" to apprise the pilot of the danger of being hit by a wave which would likely be fatal for the crew. A rising wave rolled up to meet them...and they barely out climbed it. It took twenty minutes to return to the survivors as Torpey dragged the basket within five yards, close enough for them to reach it.

Honnold spotted a man swimming for the basket and flopping into it. He shouted "Survivor in the basket" and Kraft hit the hoist lever to bring it up. Spinning and bouncing for ten seconds the basket reached the door and a William Mork rolled out, curling into a fetal position on the floor. Fish slid a thermal sack around him while the basket dropped for another man. When the basket hit the water and a man climbed into it, Kalt raised it. It bounced like a Yo-Yo and seemed to be stuck. Then the chopper guys realized there's a man in the basket and another hanging from it. Before they pulled the one in the basket into the chopper, the other man dropped from sight.

The helicopter crew has been airborne three hours. They're dehydrated and dizzy with vertigo. The three rescued men are hypothermic. With serious fuel problems added to the stress of the past three hours the chopper heads for Yakutat, closer than their base in Sitka. Two men from the sunken *La Conte* are still in the water. Awaiting rescue. Hoping.

Next morning two Coast Guard C-130 planes based in Kodiak and a chopper from Sitka criss-cross the water of Fairweather Grounds. At 3:30 PM the chopper wrests a body from the water. It's Mark Morley, skipper of the *La Conte*.

The assumption is that the missing David Hanlon will be found within a week. The search cost $678,545 before being called off February 4th. Six months crawled by before David Hanlon's remains were found.

The crewmen from the *La Conte*—William Mork, Mike Decapua and Robert Doyle recovered. They still fish the high seas. The chopper crew—Lt. Stephen Torpey, Lt. Cmdr. Theodore La Feuvre, rescue swimmer Michael Fish, flight mechanic Harold Lee Honnold and flight engineer Fred Kalt— were awarded the Distinguished Flying Cross, highest aviation honor given in peacetime.

Source: *Swallowed Alive*

In Search of a Record

In late March 1996 I went to Back Country archery on Arctic Spur Road in Anchorage to talk with archer Bill Cypher about adjusting a compound bow a friend had loaned me. I noticed a photocopy of a hunter with a brown bear in an 8x10 frame on a coffee table. On closer inspection of the photo I was stunned to discover a bear the size of no bear I'd ever heard of. I was amazed when I read about this bear and its monstrous dimensions:

Darrell Thompson shot this bear near Port Heiden, Alaska, in the spring of 1954 with one shot in the chest from a .375 H & H. Thompson took the hide to biologists at the Fish & Game Department in King Salmon, Alaska, and they determined the following statistics from the nature of the hide:

Estimated weight	2,200 pounds
Estimated age	35 years
Hide squared	nearly 14 feet
Ear tip to ear tip	25 inches
Front paw	13 inches across

Skull scored at 34 9/16 inches—not entered into any record book.

The official record for the largest brown-bear skull is under thirty-one inches.

I asked Bill if I could get a copy of the picture and use it in my upcoming book. He said he'd check with his friend Scott. A week later I stopped back and Scott Pierce had given Bill the okay to use the picture. Bill loaned me the photo; I took it to a print shop and got a hundred made before returning it to Bill with eighty extra copies.

The more I looked at that picture, the more curious I became. I wanted to learn about the hunt and was particularly interested in documenting these statistics. I decided to check with the Alaska Department of Fish and Game.

I drove to ADF&G to see my friend Rod Perry, Wildlife Tech. I asked Rod if their records might list Thompson's bear. Rod said the department didn't start affixing official seals to legally shot bears until 1960, so there was probably no official record of its size. Rod knew Dean Thompson, the son of the man who shot it. I made a note of Rod's disclosure and decided to give Dean a call after I contacted ADF&G's retired bear man Lee Miller.

Dean told me that Darrell lived in Anchorage, so I immediately called him. On 10 May 1996 I drove to his home near West Chester Lagoon. I spent a delightful afternoon with him. From the moment I met him I noticed his model airplanes. Hanging from his ceiling were two remote control planes he'd built, one a Norseman and the other a Piper 14. He said that the PA-14 had a 10-foot wingspan and a 6-foot fuselage, a 5 horsepower engine, and was modeled after his own N5184H. It cost $5,000 to build, and it took over five years.

He told me that prior to his ferrying B-29s from Hoffitt Field to Eielson in 1942 he had hunted deer and elk extensively in the Flathead country of Kalispell, Montana.

Then he told me the story of his 1954 bear hunt near Port Heiden. He took his client Hugh O'Dower, a millionaire building contractor from Kansas City, Missouri, to a favorite spot on the Uganik River at Alaska Peninsula's Wide Bay.

They stalked within a hundred yards of the bear when the hunter dropped it. After congratulations and pictures Darrell enlisted the help of Johnny and Virgil Christiansen to move the hide to Darrell's bush plane. They estimated the hide weighted 300 pounds.

Darrell took the hide and skull to King Salmon. Since no records were kept of the bear's size, the only documentation is Darrell's picture and his testimony. Fish and Game experts told me that shooting a 14-foot brown bear was equivalent to bagging a 100-inch bull moose or a double-curl Dall ram. Nevertheless I wanted to pursue Darrell's record.

Since the remaining means of documentation lay in measuring the mount, I wondered what had become of it. Darrell told me that a taxidermist in Whitefish, Montana, mounted the bear life-size with the skull inside the mount. It was shipped to Hugh O'Dower's home in Kansas City, Missouri, where it had since been placed in the Museum of Natural History in Kansas City, Missouri.

I called the museum and spoke with Julie Matson on 24 May 1996, requesting her assistance in measuring the bear. I asked her to measure the front paw width, the length from nose to tail, and the width from the left paw over the shoulders to the right paw. I knew that if her measurements were near 13 inches on the front paw, it was likely Darrell's bear and would substantiate his claim. In the same manner a squared measurement of thirteen to fourteen feet would help verify Darrell's claim.

I called Julie again on 12 June 1997, and she told me that "a bear killed by a Kansas City man was moved to another institution." She said she would attempt the measurements on the bear in their museum and would call me with the results. As of 13 June 1997 I have been unable to verify the measurements of Darrell Thomson's record brown bear.

Source: *Some Bears Kill*

A Thousand Stitches

By Stephen Routh

"I kept my arm jammed into his mouth."

What began as a pleasant day of flight-seeing for husband and wife ended in a fist- to-paw donnybrook between a very determined man and a black bear. When the opportunity to speak with Anchorage attorney Stephen Routh, I was grateful to get the facts and pleased that he survived his fist fight with a bear.

To better understand this story you must know that Stephen's Citabria aircraft is a two-seater, with the pilot's seat forward of the passenger's, and the cabin is roughly two feet wide and five feet long.

I was a fairly new float pilot in1980. July 29th was such pretty, sunny day that I invited my wife to go flight-seeing with me. I planned to practice landing and taxiing with my Citabria. We were out cruising around, landing on a few lakes and enjoying the weather.

As the day wore on, the weather began to kick up quite a bit with high, gusty winds. Since my state of piloting skills was somewhat limited, I thought the proper move was to overnight. It was getting late in the day, and I had a tent and camping gear on board. We sought a lake with a nice spot to pitch the tent, where we could have some food and return to Anchorage the next morning.

After flying over a couple of lakes, we found one that looked like a good camping area. The lake had nice high banks with level ground surrounding the beach. It appeared to be an adequate place to tie a float plane down, pitch the tent under the trees out of the weather and spend a nice evening.

I set up for my approach—pulled the carb heat, trimmed

the plane, reduced power and settled safely onto the lake. We taxied to one area where I got out and looked. It was swampy and inappropriate to camp. We taxied to another place and looked that over. It wasn't appropriate either. We taxied to a third place. The bank's height contained the crescendoing noise of the plane's engine as we taxied on step. There's no doubt that any animal within miles would have known that there was an airplane making a lot of noise on this lake.

I nosed the airplane in; then I heeled it around. With power off I turned around so the float heels were up on the shore. I had a twenty-foot rope tied to the rear cleat on one float. I grasped the rope in one hand and walked up the little bank, looking for a spot to camp as well as something to anchor the plane to.

I wasn't particularly concerned about animals. Over the years I've followed all the rules, practiced avoiding animal problems. My outdoor experience is pretty extensive. I've spent a great deal of time fishing. I have good survival skills. I've been in a lot of bear areas and have successfully avoided bears—by making noise and keeping food away.

I looked to the left and didn't see much. I looked to the right. I looked back to the left. Something caught my eye, and I looked back to the right. And right in my face was a bear—just right there. I don't know where he came from, but he was right there. His jaw was a little lower than my chin. It was so startling and so close that I involuntarily screamed. It wasn't the approach I'm used to with bears. Normally man and bear run in opposite directions. But he was within a foot of me standing up on his hind legs, mouth open, nose to nose.

I remember thinking, 'This is great. I'll run down my side of the hill, and he'll run down his side of the hill. We're both scared to death. I'll laugh and joke telling my wife. I'll sit in the airplane and probably shake for a while. Then we'll figure out something to do...maybe sleep in this airplane in the middle of the lake.'

I turned to run back to the airplane, thinking he was going in the other direction. I also figured the lake would be my salvation should the bear pursue. As I turned to get out of there, he grabbed me. The bear's big, hairy arm-like forelegs shot around me literally in a bear hug, chunk. Then I felt him snapping at the back of my head. He was all ovr me. His jaws kept snapping, and I kept moving my head so he couldn't gain purchase on my neck...we were both in a kind of a hunting-survival mode. He was snarling and pummeling me. He bit me, grabbing my skull and hair. I felt the back of my head crunch and tear. He grabbed my lower ear in his teeth. I felt my left ear go...huunk.

At 6-foot 2-inches tall and weighing 195 pounds I was in phenomenal shape, but I was no match for this animal. He stood with his forelegs around my torso, and his back legs were hanging on me or clawing me. He was a little shorter than me. Gauging from the fact that my legs buckled with him on my back and the length of its legs, the bear probably weighed 350 pounds. The power of the animal was just phenomenal. I kept on thinking, This is a black bear; it can't be that strong.

I couldn't support his weight, and I fell. Since we were heading downhill, we tumbled together to the lake. All the while he snarled and bit and snapped. I thought, This is a strange way to die. I was convinced that I wasn't going to make it.

We fought near the shore in ankle-deep water, and I was on my knees most of the time. He was all over me, and I didn't have time to get up. Somehow I got turned toward him; and I was staring him right in the eye. I looked into his eyes and tried to reason with him. Thinking it might calm him down, I said, "You don't want to do this."

There was such incredible fury in that animal's face. That was in every sense a WILD animal. There was no appeal to him—he had his mission; and that was to eat me. That was all he saw. It seemed that he was just incredibly angry.

I had to get something to try to kill him. I felt that one of us wasn't going to leave there, and I began to fight back. I couldn't stop his forlegs from coming around me. He reached around me with both forelegs and raked my back with those claws. I was amazed by the length of the bear's forelegs. I have long arms and pretty wide shoulders (I wear over a size thirty-seven inch shirt).

The bear's outstretched paws went beyond mine. With my arms outstretched I could actually grab him by his wrists, but he still had claws behind them. Even with that leverage and me holding his wrists, I could not stop the arms from coming around; and I'm strong. I could have done that with most people, not many could bring their arms around me if I was holding their wrists from an interior point because I would have had the leverage.

Over and over I felt the claws rip into my sides and back as those powerful paws raked me. I reached into my back pocket hoping I could get my Buck knife. I reasoned that I'd kill that bear. He was so busy attacking he wasn't concerned about being counter attacked. I figured I could jam my knife in his throat, or jam it in his mouth. Since I didn't have my knife, I probed for my comb. My theory was that I was going to take the comb and jam it into his throat and maybe choke him.

But I couldn't stop those arms from coming around, and I couldn't stop that mouth from working on me. And the mouth kept going for my throat. He bit the back of my neck, my hamstrings and all down my spine where he tried to break the spine to disable me. He was a very efficient killing machine.

I decided that the best way to survive would be to give him something to chew on. Finally I decided all I could do was to sacrifice my left arm. I took my left arm, and I jammed it inside his mouth at the forearm (Stephen rolled up his long shirt sleeve and showed me the scar tissue on his left wrist). He kept busy gnawing on that. He tried to move his head to get around my arm so he could come back at my throat; but I kept my arm jammed into his mouth.

While I was being torn apart, my wife was standing and watching from the floats a mere fifteen to twenty feet away. She had no idea what to do and stood there screaming at the top of her lungs.

I had no knife. No comb. I thought I could get a rock from the beach to crush his skull, however the shoreline of the lake was real silty and muddy. It was covered up with organic stuff with no rocks visible. There was an old log where we wrestled in the shallows. The log had old moldy, dead leaves on it. At one point I saw a branch on the log. I ripped it off and slashed the bear in the face with it.

He didn't like me messing with his face. He protected himself more than he was attacking me. I hit him in the eyes with the branch. He dodged my efforts and backed off. That's when the bear noticed my wife and went after her. Joanie climbed into the airplane and managed to close the door. In a couple of jumps the bear was at the heels of the float. The water was shallow, about six inches deep. There was kind of a bench there before it got deeper. The bear jumped onto a float and ran to the cabin where it stood up and clawed at the Plexiglas windows, trying to get at Joanie.

I thought about my chances of survival on shore, knowing I might well bleed to death in the water. On the other hand the cold might stop the bleeding. I decided that my best chance for survival was to get into the water so I headed out into the lake. I think it's a pretty deep lake. I was in water way over my head, probably twenty to thirty feet deep.

I managed to get one hip wader off, but I couldn't remove the other one. I must have been in shock because I've never had a problem in the water. I've been a champion swimmer; but I couldn't get the wader off. I just began kicking out in the water to get away.

The bear clawed on the plane for a while. Then he ran to the end of the float and looked up and down the beach hunting me. All of a sudden he focused on me and immediately entered the water and headed for me.

As much as I had a glimmer of hope before, I figured he's far more equipped than I for this battle. I thought of myself, This is where you're going to die. He swam towards me, mouth open and snarling.

I did something that was real instinctual—I splashed water. I would slip him...lay back in the water and then push water, which would propel me away from him while sending a wave into his mouth. I'd push, and he would cough...aarrffff ...and spit the water out...and snarl around and come up and look and see me. Then I'd do it again. I don't know how long we did that, but I must have poured a ton of water down the bear's throat before he finally gave up and headed back to shore.

I found that I could keep myself up, but I couldn't maneuver too well. I realized that I had serious injuries. I determined, There's no way I'm going back to shore. If I'm gonna die, I might as well die in the water and not be eaten by a bear.

I was shouting at my wife to start the airplane. If she could just get the airplane going and step on a rudder to get to me, I could climb on a float. At least that would be one positive step. She repeatedly pushed the start button... rrraaahhhrrruuuhhhrruuuhhh; and it wouldn't catch. I kept on shouting out, "PUSH IN THE RED BUTTON! PUSH IN THE RED BUTTON!" That's all I could think about, the mixture control (you pull the mixture control out to stop your airplane, cut the engine down. No gas gets to the engine if you don't have the red mixture button in).

Finally she said, "Oh!" Though she'd never flown alone, she'd flown with me enough to know where the mixture button was. She pushed that in, and vroom, the engine came to life. Then Joanie came taxiing out. What a wonderful sight!

I had a real tough time getting onto the float. Joanie had to drape me over the float, and finally I was able to crawl up. My left arm was in bad shape. I saw the bone inside and thought, This is not a good deal here at all. Then I reached the back of my head and felt my ear dangling. I touched the back of my neck and found it was covered with blood.

It was difficult getting inside the airplane. Joanie kind of pushed me and I tumbled in, one leg after the other.

She lifted up my shirt to assess my injuries. Then she put it down and didn't say anything. She thought I was in pretty bad shape. After seeing the look of horror in her eyes I thought, I still might die.

Even though I didn't see the bear after reaching the safety of the plane, I was afraid to go to shore because I thought the bear might come back. I got into the pilot's seat and she helped get the radio on. I wasn't functioning real well; I was really messed up, but I remember I got on the radio and started talking, basically pleading, saying, "Somebody help."

There was a DC-6 flying five miles overhead and it began circling. We couldn't see him but I was talking to him. Rescue Coordination Center sent an Otter out. Everybody was looking but nobody could figure out where I was. I didn't even know the name of the lake; or if I knew it, I had forgotten it at that point because of my condition.

I was such a mass of injuries. There wasn't much anybody could do. Where would you start? I was bleeding all over the place. The bear had shredded my new Levis, causing me to ponder its power (I knew a man couldn't rip Levis material in his hands).

We're sitting in the middle of this lake, and it's getting darker and darker. I knew that after a period of time nobody could land—it's too high sided, and you can't see the water and the beach and land. People kept assuring, "Yeah, we're on the way. We'll be there any minute." But they had no idea where I was. The ELT (Emergency Locator Transmitter) was going, but it was frustrating observing how the systems didn't come together quite right.

My wife had the foresight to pull out the emergency gear which included flares. She shot off a flare followed by another A pilot flew over us and began circling. He came down and landed. Since it was close to the Fourth of July he initially thought this was part of the celebration. But then he thought, Wait a minute. This can't be right.

I was in the back of the airplane and too messed up to even transfer airplanes. He took one look at me and knew that there was trouble. He said, "Can you get into my airplane?" Seeing blood and my condition, he said, "Don't even try."

He decided to taxi my wife and his passenger across the lake to a cabin then return for me. They knocked on the door. An occupant opened the door, looking half asleep and said, "We're on our honeymoon, leave us alone," and slammed the door. They sat outside for awhile, and finally my wife couldn't stand it anymore and said, "I'm not going to stay out here anymore." The folks realized there was an emergency and let them in to spend the night.

Meanwhile the pilot returned, got into my airplane and took off for Anchorage. We landed at Elmendorf. Because it was so late with no lighted landing areas on water, they had cars shining their headlights across the water so he could see to land. From Elmendorf I was taken to Providence Hospital, about seven miles away in east Anchorage.

AFTERWARD:

Our flight-seeing trip was an intended campout. I was in real good physical and mental shape. I had planned to go for a few hours flying and then spend the night somewhere with food and tent and everything would be comfortable.

The mauling seemed to last almost a lifetime. But in reality I think the actual attack took less than ten minutes. Things happened so fast but seemed like they were happening so slow. The first phase was probably over in two to three minutes and the second in the water maybe a minute or two. If it was ten minutes from the time I first saw the bear until I got on the float, I'd be surprised. It seemed like half-an-hour but it must have been much less than that.

I survived the shock; I think going into the cold water was the best thing I could have done. The cold water probably saved me, slowing down the bleeding substantially. If I had been on that lake another hour or two it would have done me in—the loss of blood or hypothermia would have got me.

My injuries included a severely mangled arm, lacerations to my head, neck and legs and a nearly severed ear. My worst wound was to my arm, where I jammed it into the bear's mouth. I got a deep wound infection. It was a real nasty infection that got deep into the arm. They treated it with a machine that circulated water which slowly cooked my arm in an effort to beat the infection. I was on different types of IV antibiotics. Finally one, Keflex, killed the infection. I was told that the next stage of antibiotic would probably cost me my hearing.

My dangling ear was sewn back in place. There are a whole bunch of stitches right in that area where three different areas come together. They did such a fine job in the ER with that people can't even tell my ear was chopped off. I ended up with about a thousand stitches, but if you looked me over you wouldn't know it. I was in the hospital ten days. I was fully insured. To be honest I don't recollect how much treatment was. Five thousand dollars for the hospital bill comes to mind. I signed the forms and the hospital took care of the rest.

I had a .44 magnum pistol at that time. I guess I'd grown careless and I didn't have it with me on the beach. A month ago I shot a good sized black bear on my porch at my cabin at Lake Creek. I dropped him at six feet in the shoulder with my .44 magnum. He ran and went up a tree and fell out. I tracked him by his blood spoor for three miles and never did find him. My confidence in the .44 magnum is really down to zero now, except to shoot yourself to avoid the agony.

I'm a real advocate of fighting back too. I hear people talk about rolling over and playing dead. With this black bear I wouldn't have had to play dead, I would have been dead. I have no doubt that he would have munched on me while I was hiding my head and trying to survive.

I don't think the bear was surprised. In taxiing on that lake anybody would have known that there was a man out there because there's no missing the sound of a float plane taxiing, especially when you have a high sided lake.

I received numerous phone calls and input in the hospital and thereafter. One caller said that a couple of weeks earlier on that lake some kids had been taking shots at a bear with a .22

just for fun, not to kill it but just to hit it. And the bear had run off.

I think black bears are the more dangerous bear. Grizzlies will maim you pretty good, but there's a chance you'll survive. But the black bear is the killer. He's going to eat your liver. The bite pattern on me is consistent with injuries to animals by bears— sever the spine or cut the hamstring. Bears are far stronger and more resilient than people give them credit.

I'm real impressed with black bear's strength and survivability. I think they're much underrated.

In the future I'll always be armed. If I'd had my pistol strapped to my side, I could have done more than I did with a twig. I would also carry a knife. Your adrenalin is going so high in that situation you become super human; and I think I could have killed that bear with a knife. I might be the world's biggest fool; but I think I could have sliced the bear's throat or even jammed a knife into his throat and pushed on the end of it so it went into his mouth and he swallowed it. It's real good practice to carry a knife.

I have no idea of what became of that bear. The fish and game people laughed when I asked them what they were going to do with the bear. They said they never go after a bear unless it kills someone.

Incidentally today that airplane still has the claw marks where the bear was on the back window trying to get through to my wife. But we haven't flown out to Cow Lake for any overnight tenting.

Source: *Some Bears Kill*

Student Comments

"I always enjoyed being in your class. You're one hell of a teacher. Sorry to see you retire but I can't wait until your book about teenagers comes out."

"Big K

"You're the best teacher my mom (Big Al) ever had. You're the best teacher I ever. I want my kids to have you. Thank you for seeing my mother before she passed. It was one of her wishes.

"It's been awesome having you as a teacher. You have taught me a lot, not just school work, but attitude, and how I should stand up for what I believe in! You have encouraged me to be a teacher, you're a perfect example of someone to look up to! (and I do) Stay cool and I'll come see you sometime!

Leon Dwiggins

Source: *The B.G.*

Sunny Day of Kayaking Becomes Brutal Fight for Life

HOMER: As Gabriel Kehn clung to cliff, his girlfriend, Bethany Lynn, slipped away. (Tom Kizzia, *Anchorage Daily News*, January 22, 2002)

I re-wrote Tom's article June 2021

Steve Ebbert of Anchor Point still isn't sure why he headed through Tutka on Saturday for a recreational run. He spotted an unfamiliar aid to navigation on Casey Island and turned. How was he to know his decision would label him a hero?

Tutka Bay was calm Wednesday morning, enticing the couple into their blue-and-white kayak for a rare winter's day trip. They were experienced, having kayaked as far as Homer, about nine miles away, the previous summer.

Bethany Lynn and Gabriel Kehn, both 26-years-old, were in the midst of their second winter caretaking the Tutka Bay Lodge on the south shore of Kachemak Bay. The couple from Idaho had been together five years and had come to Alaska in 1999. Kehn was writing a book about the lodge while Lynn was learning to paint. In an effort to escape the mundane, they had decided to kayak the waters.

Their voyage was interrupted when the wind came up suddenly Wednesday. They turned back hoping to cross the mouth of the bay to the lodge, several miles away. Strong wind gusts forced them to point instead toward the head of the bay. Tiring, they decided to turn around and let the wind push them ashore on Casey Island, which lay just behind them.

However as they turned broadside to the wind, a wave rolled their kayak upside down. They slid into 40-degree water. They kicked off their boots to keep from sinking. The 175-pound Kehn helped his 115-pound girlfriend into the half-submerged kayak, but it rolled over again. Holding onto the sides of the kayak, they drifted toward the rocky island.

Drifting pasted the island, they let go and swam for the rocks. The swim was tougher than he expected; Kehn gulped salt water, waves crashed over his head and Lynn splashed wildly, frightened. He yelled for her to keep moving.

At length they reached an exposed rock and with bodies still dangling in the water, they clung to the rocks with their fingers. Perhaps thirty minutes had passed when they finally pulled themselves up and passed out.

They spied a rib of jagged rocks sticking up from the receding tide, barely submerged. The rocks led to safety on the main island. They stumbled across, their socks ripped to shreds, and found a nook in the rocks at the base of a 20-foot cliff.

Confused by hypothermia, they slept, awakening in the dark. Kehn had a dry bag from which he pulled a headlamp and a lighter. Stumbling and falling several times, he managed to reach the top of the cliff where he collapsed. His numb fingers disallowed his fire building efforts with the wet grass and sticks.

He climbed back to Lynn and she stared blankly into the light of the headlamp. He wrestled with her, slipping and falling, pushing her up the cliff, until she grabbed onto a dead tree about halfway up. She clung to it, then let go. They both slipped to the bottom. After that, she was limp and couldn't be budged.

Kehn climbed up again, trying again to light a fire, thinking it would entice her up. Again he failed. When he came back down, his headlamp was growing dim and Lynn was asleep. He shook her and yelled at her but couldn't get a reaction. Finally he stopped. The light from his lamp faded out. He sat beside her in the darkness until the tide reached their perch. Then he climbed back up the cliff and gave up. He awoke in daylight and couldn't stand. He peered over the edge of the cliff. The rocks below were bare.

He stumbled, sometimes walking on his knees, toward a small cabin he'd seen on the island the previous summer. Once inside he found a little water and a plastic bottle of Ginger Ale. His feet were starting to bleed and burn with pain.

For three days, sometimes with frozen feet wrapped in towels and duct tape, he stumbled out to rocky points where he waved a red curtain from a cabin cupboard. Though several boats passed, no one saw him waving.

With changing weather and lowered temperatures, his situation turned desperate. Saturday he saw a speck on the horizon. Could rescue be at hand? He grabbed the curtain and hobbled out to the nearest rocky point.

When Kehn realized the skiff from Homer kept approaching, he said, "He kept coming...that was the first time I started bawling and my emotions came out, because I knew I was going to make it, and if Bethany had been with me, she'd have made it too. She kept asking me if we going to die?' I didn't think we were. I thought we were going to make it. The island was so close.

"She kept saying, 'Let's stick together.' I didn't want to let her down."

Kehn was rescued and taken to South Peninsula Hospital in Homer. He was listed in stable condition Monday. Doctors said he might have to remain a month because of frostbite.

On Monday, Kehn lay in his hospital bed with black swollen feet and wiped away tears as he described how his girlfriend fell irretrievably asleep on the rocks. He remained with her until the incoming tide lapped at their bare feet.

"There was a part of me that felt like she was dead. I kind of gave her a kiss. I knew that would be it. I didn't know what to do. I was so confused and disoriented myself...I keep going through it now in my brain, wondering what I could have done."

Alaska State Troopers called off a brief helicopter search for Lynn's body Saturday because three days had passed since the accident.

"Her family was OK with that," trooper Rick Roberts

said. "They understand that's the way it works up in Alaska sometimes."

Friends have searched since Saturday with skiffs and a diver, said Tom Hopkins, who runs the Jakolof Ferry Service. He said Lynn was well-loved, a "vivacious young gal in the prime of her life."

The trooper said Kehn's account of the accident checked out—both the physical details and the emotional timbre of his retelling.

Source: *Swallowed Alive*

A Tail and a Prayer

As told to the author by Pastor Paul Weimer

I swam and floundered back to the wing and got back up on the plane. I was soaked. My hands were beginning to get numb. What would it be like standing on a sinking aircraft in slushy lake ice during a cold April night in Alaska...in temperatures so cold that an inch of ice formed on the water around the sinking plane during the night? In 1986, Paul Weimer found out.

I heard about Pastor Paul Weimer from Dave Beeman of California. I was pursuing Dave's bear tale when he asked me if I'd heard Weimer's flying story. I told him no but that "I'd contact him." As it turned out, Paul is the father of Becky, a former student of mine. On Friday, November 27, 1998, I met Pastor Weimer at his Dimond Boulevard Baptist Church in Anchorage, Alaska.

The fifty-six-year-old preacher, a dark-haired, solidly built man with a smile in his heart, was flying his Piper Cub Super Cruiser light plane, constructed with aluminum tubing and cloth fabric. As Paul returned to Anchorage, he engaged in a long-standing practice. He shares his story and convictions below.

Slush ice sucked me into the lake. I fire-walled the plane and pulled my flaps. No response. One second I was in the air; moments later I struggled in watery slush.

That was the beginning of my adventure in Lake Tustumena, which proved to be a severe test of faith. Some people consider my experience the result of a foolish decision. My watery adventure began rather innocently but ended several hours later with some hard lessons learned.

As I approached Lake Tustumena on my way home from Homer on April 17, 1986, I looked carefully at the beach. I wanted to practice low-slow flight, which I've done hundreds of times on beaches in winter conditions.

During the winter of 1985-86 Mel Wick rebuilt a major part of my airplane, including the installation of flaps. Flaps are control devises that produce lift, allowing the plane to fly slower as well as to get off the ground quicker. Flaps slowed the landing speed about eight miles an hour. The addition of flaps meant that the plane would handle differently. It also meant that I would need to learn how to use them in order to fly my PA-12 more effectively. I was still trying to get used to the flap operation of my aircraft when this incident occurred.

To get accustomed to the modifications, I decided to practice a maneuver that has been very helpful to me through the years. If I'm approaching a long beach and I'm alone, I will sometimes come down and hold the power of the plane just above stall speed, say forty miles an hour, and fly just a couple of feet over the beach. The plane will stall once in a while, and the pilot acts accordingly, either touching down or adding power (applying gas). This procedure familiarizes you with flying in close proximity to things.

In my neck of the woods the top two to four feet of Alaskan lakes freeze solid in the winter. Tustumena appeared frozen from beach to beach with no open water anywhere. Since I was two-thirds of the way across the lake and had touched my main landing gear onto the lake several times, it appeared the ice was safe. It felt solid. The final time I touched down, approximately a mile from the north shore, I discovered a change in the ice. It was soft.

I immediately felt it. I knew I was in a stall and in trouble. I gave the plane full power and full flaps to counter the stall.

A stall involves the airflow over the wing. The attitude of the wing as the propeller pulls the wing through the air and the speed determine whether the plane will stay in the air. If you go too slowly through the air, the airflow will not support the wing anymore, and it falls. The engine can be running wide open and you still stall.

Power and flaps failed to pull the plane out of the slush. Combined with the stall, the slush simply pulled the airplane into the icy lake. The plane went up on its nose and began to sink.

Sitting at a unusual and precarious position in my shoulder harness and seat belt momentarily confused me. It lasted but a split second before I knew I had to get out of there because water was flowing into the cabin.

I unbuckled my belt and harness. Within the fraction of a second it took to open the door, water was almost to my knees. I grabbed the wing root and pulled myself up onto the right wing. By that time the plane had settled until the water was even with the wing.

The tail was two feet off the slush. I estimate the slush was three or four feet thick. Like a glass full of slush ice, it was completely rotted and there was no body to it.

My weight on the wing accelerated the plane's sinking, so I quickly scrambled back up the fuselage. The additional weight lowered the tail, placing more of the plane's surface on the slush and stabilizing it somewhat.

My problem was compounded because I was wet, and I had lost my hat exiting the plane. My down vest and Carhartt coveralls were in the cabin of the plane.

I've read a great deal about survival through the years. In thirty years in this country I have foolishly gotten myself into a few situations I wish I had not been in...some of them dangerous. I'd learned how to survive in cold weather a little bit, but never anything like this.

I believe the most important thing in survival is attitude. For me that involves knowing the Lord and knowing that I can look right into the probability of death and not worry about it because I know where I'm going.

Of course, I prayed immediately. The Lord gave me presence of mind to realize I had to get my emergency locator transmitter out of the airplane. Even though I didn't know if I could reach it, I took a jackknife out of my pocket, cut a hole in the top of the fuselage, and reached down into water nearly up to the ceiling.

I knew where the ELT was in the baggage compartment and pulled it out. It had been submerged. The activator light was not operating. I didn't know if my beacon was working.

Normally a 4-g impact activates an emergency locator beacon which transmits a signal on 121.5, the emergency frequency. Satellites overfly the position every ninety minutes. Once a satellite picks up a signal, no action is taken until a second signal is received. Your location can be pinpointed within five miles, though sometimes the reading is affected by terrain such as mountains.

When a pilot is reported missing in Alaska, a flight service station is called to determine his last location. If the response is negative, the Rescue Coordination Center at Fort Richardson Army Guard near Anchorage is informed. RCC then contacts the pilot's employer or other persons familiar with his flying habits before the officials decide on the urgency of the search. Normally the Civil Air Patrol, Alaska Air Guard, and private pilots take part.

I was sixty-five miles south of Anchorage on an isolated lake thirty-two miles long and seven wide. You might say, I was in a world of hurt. My only hope was that my locator beacon would transmit my location and that the Lord would bail me out of my misfortune.

My next thought was to attempt to walk the thousand yards across the ice to the shore where a small cabin sat near the beach. Gingerly I walked to the end of my right wing and tested the ice with my foot. It wouldn't hold three pounds. So I went back to the tail and tested the ice on either side. It was just as bad.

I went back up to the wing root and walked the left wing out to the end. I put my foot onto the ice, four inches below the wing. It was hard, so I walked a little bit farther...a little bit more, and a little bit more. With all my weight on that area it seemed stable. I thought I'd try walking.

I got five feet from the wingtip and down I went. It was just slush.

I swam and floundered back to the wing and got back up on the plane. I was soaked. My hands were beginning to get numb.

I looked down through the skylight over the cabin area and saw my down vest and Carhartt coveralls floating near the top. I decided to get those items out. I was unable to free the vest, so I cut it in half with my knife. At least I had half of a vest. I retrieved the Carhartts and wrung out the vest and coveralls as best I could. I sat down on the wing, took my shoe packs off, removed the liners, and wrung them out.

My hands were stiff and I couldn't do a very good job. I put the clothes and boots on and was immediately cold. I wondered, "What am I going to do?"

All of my nice survival gear was stashed neatly under the rear seat out of reach!

It was probably two-thirty in the afternoon. Water had not reached the top of the wing. An area two, two and a half feet wide at the center of the wing (at the fuselage) was not underwater.

I thought of taking the fuel caps off and lighting a match to see if the gasoline would burn. I reasoned that it would not explode since it was surrounded by water. I understand now it was not a good idea.

I had a bottle of matches I had removed from the water. The bottle was watertight, but enough moisture was in the bottle to prevent any of the matches from lighting.

By necessity I stayed on the tail, which became my perch. I made my way back to the tail surface where a wire comes off each side of the vertical stabilizer and connects to the horizontal stabilizer or elevator portion of the tail. The wire runs at a thirty-degree angle, and I hooked one leg over the wire to give myself more support and waited.

I was cold. Terribly cold. Frigid. My body and knees never quit shaking. Every hour I shouted as loud as I could. That relieved me some.

About five in the afternoon I heard the unmistakable and heartwarming sound of a Civil Air Patrol beaver approaching. He came up from the northwest end of the lake and worked a pattern back and forth. I knew then that my beacon had been working.

I watched him for over two hours as he worked a pattern from a thousand yards to a mile away. Apparently his direction finder was getting a wrong reading from my beacon because he had me placed over on the beach in the hills going up from the lake. He never came my way.

I prayed. I shouted. I did everything I knew how to do. Finally about seven o'clock the beaver made a ninety-degree turn and headed straight out across the ice toward me. I thought, "Oh, happy day, here he comes."

He crossed approximately two hundred yards to my right and seven hundred feet high, went out across the ice, did a 180-degree turn, and then came back on the same track. When he got to the beach, I heard his voice over the loudspeaker. It was a mile away, so I couldn't understand what he said. Since it was getting late in the evening, I assumed a helicopter would be there within an hour or so.

It turned out the pilot hadn't spotted me at all. He had misread the beacon's signal and assumed that someone was near the beach. The loudspeaker had instructed the person to shut off his transmitter when the pilot came over the top of him.

Nine o'clock came on and it began to get dark. I knew it was going to be a long night.

All the time the plane was settling a little more into the slush. The water was even with the top of the fuselage with very little clear space on the wings. An inch or so of water covered the tail surface I occupied.

I prayed some more. At nine-thirty or quarter to ten it began snowing. It snowed big flakes real hard. Then a little westerly wind came up, and it got colder. I have no way of knowing how cold it was, but before the night was over, the ice on top of the tail where I stood froze over an inch thick at my feet. I didn't jump up and down because that would jiggle the plane down into the slush. All night long I tried to convince myself that I could run fast like a deer and make it across the slush to the beach. But my feet felt like clubs and I couldn't do that. The constant shaking exhausted me. I was dehydrated. The time dragged. I looked at my watch and it was 10:05. Two hours passed, and I looked again. It was 10:15. All night long it went like that.

I shouted. I prayed. A lot of verses came to my mind. A verse in Deuteronomy says, "The everlasting God is our refuge and underneath are His everlasting arms." Psalms 91 says, "He will give His angels charge over you keeping all your ways...they shall bear you up in their hands." I shouted that one out.

Nobody can hear you, so you might as well act like a fool. I hollered as loud as I could. Every hour or so I yelled some more.

About eleven or so the clouds cleared away and it was a beautiful night. There was a half moon and stars, but who could enjoy it?

I watched a satellite pass over. Whenever I saw a satellite, heard or saw a high–flying jet, I switched on the ELT.

About two in the morning I fell asleep standing straight up. I had draped myself over the vertical stabilizer beacon light, which is about the size of a glass, and dozed off. I could sleep only about three or four seconds because the light was jammed into my side and hurt so bad. But it was good. I guess I did that twenty or thirty times during the night. I never did come close to falling off.

I took my jackknife and cut some fabric off the tail. I wrapped it around my body to use as a windbreak and held it on with my belt. I cut some more fabric for a hat and cut thin strips to tie it to my head. What a relief it was to have a hat.

I wondered why the Civil Air Patrol wasn't flying at night in the fog for someone as important as I was. I began to seriously question why the accident had happened. I said, "Lord, I'm an idiot to do what I did. I was stupid to do that. And I confess that.

Now, Lord, forgive me…and get me off of here."

I thought maybe the Lord had something for me to do and the devil wanted to stop me. Maybe he's trying to put doubt in my mind. I've preached to people for forty years about living by faith and trusting the Lord in hard times and trials. And here's my test. I prayed, "Lord, I don't know whether I've done something wrong or not, but if I have, I'm confessing to you."

Maybe my airplane's an idol to me. Maybe I love it too much, spend too much time with it. "Lord, if you want to take the airplane away from me, it's all right with me. If you want to rescue me, I'll never fly another hour in my life." Basically I surrendered totally to Him.

I learned some lessons that night about how the Lord works in a practical way with his children.

As the moon came up, I kept watching the angle of my shadow. I kept praying for daylight. I figured if I could survive until daylight, I had a chance. As I looked at the northeast sky, I knew it wouldn't be too long before sunrise. A light shade of blue was beginning to develop. It was clear.

I reached down with my left hand for some lake water to drink.

My back and legs hurt terribly from standing in the same upright position. I was bitter cold.

As daylight developed, I could see for a hundred yards across the ice. But the fog came in from both directions and closed off the sky. I said, "God, they can't even hunt for me in this fog. What are you trying to do now?"

It was around six o'clock in the morning, and I'd been standing there for sixteen hours. Then I heard an airplane. I never saw it, but I could tell by the sound that they were back flying the same pattern they'd flown the night before. I shouted to them, "Why don't you come out on the ice!"

Later several planes came out. I couldn't see them, but I heard them flying grids. About nine o'clock I heard a helicopter coming up from the west end of the lake. And that was the sweetest sound I ever heard...whop, whop, whop, whop.

He came over the beach directly in front of me and flew back and forth, back and forth. I could see his light reflecting through the clouds like a weird, clattering ghost. They were convinced I was somewhere near the beach.

I prayed that God would lift the fog. I talked to the fog, "Fog, get out of here!" Didn't do any good.

I prayed, "Lord, you know how long I can stand here. I don't. I'm sure I can't make it through another night; and the airplane won't stay on the surface that long anyway."

I said, "I'm ready to die, but this would be a terrible way to do it to my family and to my church. They'll never find me in this glacial lake full of silt." My plane top was white, the same color as the ice, and nearly impossible to see.

After about two hours of flying around, the helicopter set down on the beach and cut his engines. I heard music. I thought, "Maybe he will hear me if I yell."

The two state troopers in the chopper knew the beacon was right on the beach somewhere. They were frustrated. They thought somebody left a locator beacon in the cabin. The pilot said to his friend, "I won't be happy to leave here until we check that cabin out."

I hollered as loud as I could, "Heeeyyyy! Yeeeeoooowww!" I did that for ten minutes. It took three seconds for that sound to cross the ice and run a half mile up the beach. The men never heard me.

They went into the cabin and came back out and had some lunch. While they sat there, the sun burned the fog away. The pilot asked his friend, "What in the world is that out there on the ice?"

His friend replied, "I don't know. It looks like a moose."

They gazed with binoculars for five minutes but couldn't figure out what they were looking at. So they decided to check it out when they left.

The finest picture I've ever seen was that big mosquito coming straight across the ice toward me. They ran the shoe of the helicopter right beside the tail of the plane. I stepped onto it and fell into the helicopter. They took me over to the beach, stopped it, opened the door and asked, "Anyone with you?"

I said, "Yeah, the Lord was."

And the trooper said, "How are you?" He asked me a few questions, gave me some quick energy food and we headed for Soldotna. My feet were not frozen. When I took my boots off, my ten toes were as blue as any child's crayon I've ever seen. The troopers were concerned because the circulation was gone.

I was deeply moved when the helicopter landed at the Soldotna airport. There stood my friends Marvin Moser, Tim Cooper, Ed Renner, Lee Browning, and Jimmy Miller. Thom Hibpschman and Hope Anderson and Pam Lefel and ten or fifteen other people welcomed me. We went over to the restaurant to get some hot soup.

After that I got into Eddie Renner's airplane and flew to Kenai and asked the Lofstedt's at Kenai Air Service what the possibilities were of going out with a ranger helicopter to retrieve my airplane. They said they'd done that a lot of times and headed out right away.

Three hours from the time they took me off the plane, the mechanic stood on my plane's roof, took a couple of tools out of the helicopter, set them on my plane and immediately they were covered with water as my plane began sinking. He jumped back into the helicopter and the airplane made its final journey to the bottom of the lake.

I don't believe I would have survived another hour and a half on the plane.

I lost five pounds or more in twenty-one hours.

That night my feet swelled up so I couldn't get shoes on. For a couple of days I had to be a little careful of my feet. I couldn't close my left hand, but it's all right now. I don't think there are any ill effects at all from my accident, so I'm thankful for that.

I want to thank the Lord for keeping me.

EPILOGUE

A news reporter later said I must have been in pretty good shape to survive my situation. I told him, "My physical conditioning had nothing to do with it. Somebody else kept me, and I don't get any credit at all. I want it to be known that God answered my prayers, and I owe Him everything for my life. I was a dead man."

I start every day reading several chapters from the Bible and committing my day to the Lord, I prayed that day about the trip.

Jesus healed ten lepers who were at the extremity of life. One thanked him, and Jesus asked where the other nine were. He stated it was our duty to glorify God. If we fail to glorify God with our lives, we sin.

Source: *Danger Stalks the Land*

Radio Sportscaster...

Prize fight announcer around 2011

One night while babysitting three grandsons in 2011, Pam announced the big fight of the evening... "the Austin Wolverine fighting the Old Man from Alaska." The oldest grandson had his boxing gloves and shared them with his next younger brother. Each boy fought the Old Man from Alaska a few rounds, exchanging gloves. Between rounds Pam used a towel to fan the boxer who challenged the old guy. During each round she gave play by play as to how badly the kid was thrashing the geezer: "Hit him harder."

"That's a good blow to the jaw."

"Keep 'em coming."

"You're wearing him out."

Somewhere around the 8th round while the boys were trading gloves, the geezer felt a small fist landing on his jaw from the left. Number three grandson who was around 3-years-old sucker punched the geezer with a pretty good right to the jaw. We had a blast. The geezer was sitting with his back against the wall covering up with his arms protecting his face and trying not to laugh too hard. The boys punched away, having a good time beating up the geezer.

Source: *Heavenly Rose*

"What Happened?"

As told to the author by Don Frantz

A series of fortunate things happened after the unfortunate.

In March (or April) of 1996 I heard that my former coaching mentor and teaching colleague Don Frantz had been in an accident and was hanging on to life by the skin of his teeth. I was shocked and called Don to see if I could visit. Thinking stories of peoples' life-and-death struggles might inspire him, I took a him a copy of my book *Cheating Death*.

As Don lay in his recliner, ashen-faced, he told me his story. I told him that when he got well, I'd like to get his story on tape for a future book

Time flew by and suddenly it was the second week in February 1999. I sat in Don's office taping his experience. He was the same old Don, a little grayer, but he still had that twinkle in his eye and his sense of humor. When he told me he'd recovered from his physical injuries, he couldn't help poking fun at himself. "However, I've needed mental therapy all my life."

It is great to see Don up and about and in good spirits. Here's his story.

A tree-cutting project took me to my cabin in March 1996. I flew my Aeronca Sedan, single-engine plane fifty miles northwest of Anchorage to No Name Lake, an oblong body of water a mile long and half a mile wide. When I taxied to the cabin, it was really too late to get started, so I just goofed off that night. My good friend and neighbor Greg Gullickson volunteered to fly his plane out the next day to help me and to spend some time ice fishing and snowmachining. Although I didn't really need Greg's help, I went to bed anticipating his arrival.

I got up the next morning, March 23, and decided to put off work until Greg and his son Berndt arrived. I wanted to enhance the view out the front of our cabin 150 feet from the lake. I was cutting it all down and had previously thinned out a number of various-sized trees, including two or three spruce trees over a hundred feet tall. I had half a dozen trees to finish

Before long Greg landed the Aeronca Sedan, exactly like mine. I got the boy lined up with a snowmachine and some fishin' gear, then Greg and I went out to work, using my two twenty-five-year-old Homelite chain saws.

Greg started cutting up the trees I had cut the previous weekend while I went to cut down a big two-foot-diameter birch. The tree was on the edge of the clearing I'd cut and stood by itself, leaning toward the lake. It was about thirty degrees off vertical, so I didn't have to worry about which way it was going to fall.

I've been cutting trees most of my life and know about widow makers, trees hanging up and all that. This one was a giveaway because there was nothing around it. I had cut other trees close to it before and this was almost the last one that I had to do on the project. I cut it down.

I stood beside the stump and the next thing I knew I was beat down in the snow. If I was knocked unconscious, it was just momentary. All I knew was that something had hit me on the head. I have always read the cartoons that show stars when people get hit on the head. Now I know where that thought comes from because I saw flashes of light and stars in my eyes. The wind was knocked out of me.

I grabbed the stump and straightened myself up so I could breathe and sat there in the snow.

I knew immediately that something was wrong with my right leg. I figured my leg was broken because it didn't work, but it didn't hurt. I had absolutely no idea what in the heck had happened.

Even though I wore snow pants and boots and it was relatively warm (in the twenties), I was immediately cold. I didn't have a coat but wore a flannel shirt. My stocking cap and safety goggles were gone. I was thinkin', "What in the world happened?"

I got a breath. Greg was runnin' the chain saw, so I knew he couldn't hear anything. When the chain saw stopped a few minutes later, I hollered for him.

Greg came up and asked, "What happened?"

I said, "Man, I don't know. Somethin' hit me in the head. And I'm freezin' to death. Go up to the cabin and get the sled and get me into the cabin."

He knew what had happened, and he looked at me and said, "Ah, I think we better get you to town."

"I'll be all right. I'm soakin' wet." I was startin' to sweat.

"I'll get a sleeping bag and get you down on the lake.'

"All right."

"How do you want to go?"

"There's something wrong with my leg, so just grab me and pull me down the hill...get me down on the lake."

About that time his boy came back and Greg sent Berndt over to his plane to get a sleeping bag.

Greg grabbed my arm, pulled me down the hill, and got me on the sleepin' bag.

Berndt came over and Greg told him, "Stay here and help Don." Then Greg got his parka and put it over me.

Berndt was scared to death.

Twice I had a little trouble talkin' and I asked Greg, "Hey, are my eyes dilated? Is blood runnin' out of my ears or anything?"

He got down and said, "No, your earplugs are still in."

That explained why I was having trouble hearing.

He said, "There's no blood. You have a little tiny cut on your face."

That's the only cut I had. When I got knocked down, I hit the chain on the saw, which wasn't turnin'. A tooth took a chunk of skin and hide out. Fortunately it wasn't runnin' 'cause the facial cut could have taken my eye.

He said, "Your eyes and ears and everything look good."

Since it had been there less than an hour since he'd arrived, his plane was warmed up and ready to go. He said, "Look, I'll go over and get the plane and taxi over here and we'll get you to town."

Because I was having' more trouble breathin' and thinkin' maybe I had a brain injury, I said, "Yeah, I think that's a good idea." I was getting really concerned because it was getting harder to breathe. Then I became deathly afraid of passing out…if you pass out, you're out of here, you're history.

I was still cold and asked Berndt to go up and find my hat. He went and got my stocking cap, shook it off, and brought it back. It was about fifteen twenty feet away from where I felled the tree. He was tryin' to help me and put it on me.

Greg taxied over, turned his engine off, got out of his plane, came over to me, and asked, "How we gonna get you in?"

"I think if you stand me up, I'll hold on to the strut and you can get around and slide me in backwards."

So he did, and as soon as he turned me loose, I fell. He said, "That's not gonna work."

"Just pick me up and poke me in the back."

He had a sleeping bag, a little nest built in the back compartment. So he picked me up under the arms and laid me in over the doorsill headfirst on my chest and stomach. Then he went over to the other side and pulled me across, then came back around and stuffed me into the back, grabbed his son, and off we went. Within ten or fifteen minutes of the accident I was in Greg's plane.

It became more difficult to breathe. I started talkin' to myself and singin' anything I could do to maintain consciousness.

It's only a half-hour flight from my cabin to Anchorage. By the time we got to Lake Hood, I started to hurt. My back, chest, and especially my leg were tearin' me up. Even though

Greg had called ahead, we had a little trouble connecting with the ambulance when we landed. But when we finally met the ambulance, I was glad to see one of the drivers was Mark Nokelby, an EMT and a friend I've known for years.

When I told them I'd been hit on the head, they protected my head and neck. They got me out of the plane kind of the reverse of the way I got in except I was on my back. They transported me to Providence Hospital.

The doctor on call was a man I've known for years. He said, "Don, what happened?

I was restrained from head to neck. I'd been movin' my head and neck. By the time I got to the hospital, I was in serious pain. They don't like to give you anything for pain because they want to poke you: "Does it hurt here? Does it hurt there?"—this sort of thing.

They started X-raying, and of course my blood pressure was rapidly falling. My symptoms weren't congruent with what I was tellin' 'em.

I was really hurting. Finally one of the X-rays they shot from my neck across the top of my chest cavity showed my inside was black. Then they said, "Hey, you've got some problems." And they started checkin' farther down.

The worst thing they discovered was a ruptured aorta. After all was said and done, they figured I had had about a half hour to go until I would have died from lack of blood. I had two crushed vertebrae and every rib was either broken, cracked, or separated. My right leg was fractured in five places.

They got with it.

I was fortunate in that people were there, the plane was warm, I got to the hospital, and of the two people in the state who were capable of doing the kind of surgery that I needed, one was available. He was there within twenty minutes. They got all the medical stuff goin', dopin' me up, and I went on the operating table. I was in surgery a little over five hours, and they repaired my aorta. They gave me three units of blood.

That afternoon, Greg, two other friends—Walt Kephart and neighbor Don Hoshaw—and my son Dowell decided they'd fly out, close up the cabin, and bring back my plane, but fog prevented them.

If my accident had been a little later, I couldn't have flown out and no rescue helicopter would have had time to save me due to the fog.

The next morning they returned and spent two hours removing the three-hundred-pound stove from my airplane and taking it up to the cabin on a sled (I had help loadin' it and knew Greg was going to be there to unload). They put everything away and took a bunch of pictures. Walt and Dowell flew my plane back while Don and Greg flew their own.

The next day, Sunday afternoon, they came to the hospital after Kephart got the film developed and showed me some pictures. Apparently when I cut that tree down and it hit the ground, the vibrations caused a standing dead birch tree thirty feet away to fall. It was dead and rotten but wasn't tangled up and had nothing to do with the one I cut down.

It was about fourteen inches in diameter where it broke across my back. I got a glancing blow to the back of my head before it knocked my head over again to the stump that I had cut. I'm sure the blow on the head stung me and kept my attention from the hurt in my back, chest, and leg injuries.

A series of fortunate things happened after the unfortunate. One was that I didn't have to sit there for months and think that I did something stupid or careless. It was almost like being struck by lightning: if you're in the wrong place at the wrong time, it's going to happen.

It was the first time in my life since I was little that I've been totally dependent upon people. It makes you appreciate people being able to help you. My wife Georgette provided twenty-four-hour-a-day care for several weeks and made my fantastic recovery possible.

I've always tried to take reasonable care of myself, and the healing went miraculously. I'm happy I was in reasonable shape and good health. Now almost three years later, I have some aches and pains but I'm doing everything I ever did, and the only residual effect is that I'm exactly two inches shorter than I was because of the crushed vertebrae.

I had two primary MDs; one was the surgeon John Broda, and the other was a bone doctor Michael Eaton. My constant concern was nerve damage. The doctors conferred and decided that I had a bunch of potential problems but no nerve impairment. They decided that I wasn't going to go dancin' and hoppin' around anyway, so they didn't set a cast on anything. That leg caused me more grief than everything else combined. One of the breaks was in my fibula, and it's not a major weight bearing bone, so they didn't set it.'

I was up after surgery within three or four hours. I was up several times a day thereafter, and their attitude was, "If it hurts, don't do it." I was X-rayed every two or three days and the vertebrae were monitored. I was only in the hospital seven days.

The surgeon knew from experience that the most comfortable place a person can be is in a recliner. So he kept pushin' to get me home. He's correct. When I got home, I virtually lived in that recliner for three months—I wasn't able to lie down on a bed or anything until July.

The crushed vertebrae were healing well. About a month after the accident my doctors referred me to a spine specialist, who came in cold. He couldn't believe that I had walked into his office...very slowly. After he had assessed the X-rays and the damage to the worst vertebrae he said, "When those heal, it may fuse those vertebrae. If it does, that's the best thing that will happen because as badly crushed as it is, if it doesn't, you'll have to have surgery to fuse those vertebrae."

The ribs healed and fused the bad vertebrae to one on each side, so I've got three fused vertebrae in the thoracic region of my back. That's a pretty rigid part of your back, so I don't really suffer from inflexibility. It doesn't appear that I'll have to go back under the knife.

The other vertebra wasn't as badly crushed.

The spine doctor wanted to measure me, but at that time I couldn't stand up straight. I said, "Nah, I don't even want to know now. When I can stand up straight and stretch and do all that, I'll worry about it."

He said, "Get yourself ready because you're going to be considerably shorter than you were."

When I had a physical in February '95, I was five-ten, and when I went back in February '97, I was five-eight."

EPLILOGUE

I was fortunate. First, the tree was rotten or it would have crushed me like a bug, killing me instantly. I never thought about dead trees when I was cutting. That's changed now. When I hunt or walk through the woods, it seems that I see every dead tree. It's funny how your perception changes.

Second, my aorta had torn in a spiral shape a little over halfway around. The sheath around the artery also tore, but off the line of the vessel rupture. Instead of going spurt, spurt, spurt, which would have caused me to bleed to death in a minute, it was leaking. Every time my heart beat, the aorta leaked, but obviously not huge volumes. The surgeon explained later that many people who die of accidental injuries have ruptured aortas and bleed to death very quickly.

Then there was Greg. He was severely disturbed because he knew what had happened when he walked up to me. I'm sure I didn't look any too good. He was just petrified. Greg's a big man and very strong. It took a man like Greg to get me into the plane because there's no way I could have done it on my own. It may seem that he was a little hasty, dragging me off the hill and pulling me into his plane in my condition but if he hadn't, we wouldn't be conducting this interview. You gotta do what you've gotta do.

Source: *Danger Stalks the Land*

P.S. It was my privilege and honor to teach and coach with Don. He was on a return trip to Anchorage July 15, 1917, aboard his Aeronca Sedan, when he crashed into the trees along the Yentna River northwest of Anchorage, Alaska. Listed as a heart attack, it may be that the original tree falling injury affected his heart...and been unnoticed.

Larry Kaniut

S-turn, you Say?

My flight instructor Rick Ruess may have doubted I'd ever solo. He may have wondered if I'd ever acquire the flying skills necessary to keep from denting his bird. I never asked him. Regardless, I soloed November 7, 1994.

Six weeks later Rick and I descended, quite literally, upon Anchorage's Merrill Field in the name of Touch and Go's. I suspected the Rickster was evaluating my performance in order to again turn me loose upon his innocent and trusting Cessna 2467 Juliet.

After landing a few times in a closed right pattern on runway 6, I got my answer. Rick instructed me to "come to a full stop on the next landing, call ground and taxi to tower."

We landed, called and taxied to the tower base.

Rick informed me, "Do as many touch and go's as you want."

"Five, six or what?" I asked.

"Doesn't matter, just fly as much as you want. Build up your solo time."

While he stood and watched me from the safety of the lightly snow covered ground, I called ground control for permission to taxi. I indicated I had information Uniform, forgetting to tell them that I was a student pilot. The controller told me to taxi to runway 6 for takeoff. After taxiing I called the tower, letting them know that 67 Juliet was ready for takeoff. The lady controller gave permission and Juliet and I skipped down the runway.

As I lifted off the runway, I discovered at 12 o'clock a departing and slow waddling Super Cub upon which I was gaining rapidly. Rather than trim his tail feathers, I figured it best to divert around him, which meant overtaking him to his right. About that time the controller told him to turn short of normal crosswind. She instructed me to "extend your climb out to Boniface."

We both complied.

Before I knew it, though, I was bearing down on the Super Cub again in the downwind. There he was, about a hundred feet above me at 10 o'clock. The controller instructed him to drop and turn short base.

I continued on in the pattern. As I turned base, I observed the Cub dropping in on final. I had determined to try a full flap landing and went through the procedure, lowering flaps 10 degrees on downwind, 10 more on base turn and the final 20 degrees at the end of base—just before my normal turn on final.

Up until now the flying was pretty routine. But I was about to get a surprise in the form of a maneuver I knew but had difficulty applying to the situation at hand.

I was at 400 to 500 feet elevation above sea level, and about 300-400 feet above the ground...pushing forward on the yoke and dropping in at a steep angle. That's when the controller said, "67 Juliet, perform an S turn before final."

This young boy was momentarily confused. If she had said, "Extend your base" or "Perform an S turn on your base to final," I'd have been okay. My mind tried to compute the S turn lingo into the base to final transition. Therefore I continued my base, trying to figure out her jargon...all the while rapidly scanning the oil pressure and air speed indicator gauges.

Everything happened fast...as in nanoseconds!

Mind you, I was at approach-descent at 1500 RPM's with full flaps. Now, if you know anything about staying in the air with full flaps in a C-150, you know that staying aloft requires more than 1500 RPM's.

I was losing airspeed and altitude at an astonishing rate.

Needless to say, in my confusion about the S-turn and with the ship dropping like a rock, it became immediately apparent to me that in order to keep from denting Rick's aircraft, I had to do something FAST!

By this time I guessed I was 100 to 200 feet above the

ground. The air speed indicator had dropped (in what seemed like 5 mile per hour increments)...60, 55, 50, 45, 40.

Did I say forty!

This slow pilot immediately equated 40 with STALL. And through the cobwebs I heard the famous three most important things a pilot needs to know...FLY THE PLANE!

The light bulb popped on. The adrenaline erupted. My first impulse was to yank back on the yoke. You know that means s-t-a-l-l.

In one smooth movement I flipped the flap switch up, firewalled the throttle, pushed carb heat in and pushed the nose of 67 Juliet down to gain airspeed...wondering how many feet I had left before hitting terra firma.

The airspeed, RPM's and flaps rose; and so did 67 Juliet.

The adrenaline gave way to shakes and sweating palms.

The air traffic controller came on the radio and instructed me, "67 Juliet, do a go around." I had already begun an upwind leg and was only too shakily happy to comply. Then she told me to cross at midfield and hold right closed pattern...which I did. Was this what my instructor had meant when he talked about close calls and secrets between the pilot and his laundry lady!

Later I learned that the controller was a student controller... and I learned a lot more:

First, know the relationship and results of airspeed and flaps extended—when flying full flaps.

Second, maintain enough power to stay airborne, unless you're landing.

Third, Airspeed! Airspeed! Airspeed!

Fourth, know terminology...and if you're confused by ATC instructions, ask for clarification.

And fifth, you are the pilot in command...fly the plane!

Source: *Alaska Air Tales*

Beer and Boom

A group of men were drinking beer and discharging firearms from the rear deck of a home owned by Irving Michaels, age 27. The men were firing at a raccoon that was wandering by, but the beer apparently impaired their aim and, despite the estimated 35 shots the group fired, the animal escaped into a 3 foot diameter drainage pipe some 100 feet away from Mr. Michaels' deck. Determined to terminate the animal, Mr. Michaels retrieved a can of gasoline and poured some down the pipe, intending to smoke the animal out. After several unsuccessful attempts to ignite the fuel, Michaels emptied the entire 5 gallon fuel can down the pipe and tried to ignite it again, to no avail. Not one to admit defeat by wildlife, the determined Mr. Michaels proceeded to slide feet-first approximately 15 feet down the sloping pipe to toss the match. The subsequent rapidly expanding fireball propelled Mr. Michaels back the way he had come, though at a much higher rate of speed. He exited the angled pipe "like a Polaris missile leaves a submarine," according to witness Joseph McFadden, 31. Mr. Michaels was launched directly over his own home, right over the heads of his astonished friends, onto his front lawn. In all, he traveled over 200 feet through the air. "There was a Doppler Effect to his scream as he flew over us," McFadden reported, "Followed by a loud thud." Amazingly, he suffered only minor injuries. "It was actually pretty cool," Michaels said, "Like when they shoot someone out of a cannon at the circus. I'd do it again if I was sure I wouldn't get hurt." submitted by Peter Putrimas (direct quotation)

Source: *Swallowed Alive*

Danger Ignored

As told to the author by Chris Nolke

"We didn't have any ropes. We were all wearing running shoes. We weren't prepared."

Temptation, Flattop, The Ramp. Suicide, O'Malley. Wolverine, Williwaw, The Wedge. Mountain peaks towering above Anchorage, Alaska, in Chugach State Park only a few miles east of Alaska's largest city. Mountain peaks enticing hikers, runners, backpackers, mountain bikers, and skiers. On July 12, 1987, these peaks lured a trio of young Anchorage runners to challenge their flanks. The three were running partners on that day. On some days they were rivals.

Chris Nolke, a junior from Service High School, was the oldest at fifteen. Andrew Lekisch and Doug Spurr were fourteen-year-old freshmen from West Anchorage High. Lifelong best friends, Andrew and Doug had grown up competing since grade school in a variety of activities. On the other hand, Chris had known the two pals only a couple of years.

Their jumping-off point was the Glen Alps parking lot at the foot of Flattop Mountain. They would jog the Powerline Pass right-of-way road on a twenty-plus-kilometer run. As they left the trailhead, they good-naturedly bantered.

Scattered mountain junipers ten to twelve feet high welcomed them as they covered the half mile to the power-line road.

The young men wore cross-country running gear—long-sleeved running shirts and running shoes. Chris Nolke wore two long-sleeved cotton shirts under a rugby top. A pair of cotton Sport Hills pants, comfortably tight, covered his lower body. His footgear consisted of his favorite Asics Tiger running shoes. Doug and Andrew wore similar gear.

They left the timberline and pushed eastward up Powerline Pass toward the distant ridgeline that separates Anchorage from the Indian Creek and Ship Creek drainages. Five-thousand-foot peaks surrounded them. Their plan was to run the road to The Ramp, a high bowl that dissected Flattop and the twin Suicide Peaks from O'Malley Peak and Mt. Williwaw. At the upper end of the bowl they would ascend The Wedge on the left and return along its spiny ridgeline.

The three figures bounced along the trail in the comfortable fifty-degree weather. The shared the joy of their sport, the freedom of summer vacation, and the enchanting landscape.

The valley was nearly a mile wide. An inch-thick layer of vegetation called tundra covered the rocky ground. A narrow stream coursed the valley floor, with tall grass lining its banks and shortening in length as it stretched ridge-ward. Low willow bushes blended with the streamside grass, giving way up the slope to rock slides, ledges, and scattered snow patches in the shaded gullies. In a few short weeks the hillsides would be fired with changing ground cover dominated by reds and yellows. Whispering close behind, snow would blanket the landscape to a depth of six to eight feet. But today it was great running.

Bobbing rhythmically over the trail, they reminisced about former runs and competitions where they'd taxed their wills and spirits, each realizing this run was like many they'd learned to enjoy. That it bonded the body, mind, and spirit of each as well as bonding their friendship, while enhancing their physical stamina.

Chris Nolke remembered their run:

We ran back the pass that goes up The Ramp from Powerline Pass. We noted our destination, then headed off along the grassy and rocky spots, bypassing any dangerous areas. Sometimes the trail necessitated rock climbing up ten-or fifteen-foot high areas. That doesn't sound particularly bad, but if you stacked a bunch of those areas on top of each other, you see potentials that we didn't really consider. The inherent danger in those mountains was such areas.

We had run several miles when we started up into The Wedge for our return run. That was quite a perilous climb. When it came to safety, that was one of the most dangerous parts to climb.

The danger element never occurred to us as we continued. Looking down one of the chutes, we casually joked, "What would happen if you fell off here?"

Doug said, "I'm sure you'd pretty much break your neck."

"No," I said, "you're toast. If you fall off here, there's no way you're going to survive."

The fact that we had just climbed up that chute never gave us concern that we could fall. We didn't have any ropes.We were all wearing running shoes. We weren't prepared. What we were doing wasn't really a good idea. We were young teenagers with a sense of immortality about us. So we continued to climb.

We maneuvered along the knifelike ridge toward town, which wasn't too bad. The ridge was suddenly interrupted by a twenty-foot-square boulder. The ground supporting the boulder had eroded away with rocks having tumbled down either side of the ridgeline. It looked oddly balanced.

Since the boulder was obstructing our way, I started to climb around it to continue on the trail. The north side of the boulder stuck out over a ravine. To follow the trail, we would have to scale sideways around the boulder. Doug had determined to go down and around the other way.

Facing the boulder, I extended my hands to search for a handhold. I couldn't find one.

Even though none of us had ever done any rock climbing, I figured it wasn't that big of a deal. The terrain was steep on either side of the ridge, fifty to sixty degrees. Although you could walk on the slope, you'd slide or tumble quite a distance if you slipped. The grass-covered slope was riddled with boulders.

I said, "I'm not going to go this way. I'm going down where Doug went."

I followed Doug, I think I would have ventured out of the

slope if I hadn't looked down and realized it was quite a fall. Andrew decided to go along the boulder and find a way past it. I don't think he looked down.

While Doug and I skirted the boulder, we heard Andrew yell.

Not realizing what had happened, we quickly returned to where we'd left Andrew. I figured it was nothing too bad.

We crossed a grass area, running down below the boulder. We easily ascended the trail and returned without doing too much side-tracking.

Doug ran ahead down the mountain. I couldn't find Andrew and yelled, "Doug, where is he?"

Finally Doug found Andrew and ran to him.

When I reached Doug, he was standing by Andrew. Doug kept asking Andrew to talk to him. I was ten feet away from Andrew before I finally saw him and realized how far down the hill he had fallen. He fell straight down for quite a ways, free fall—it could have been twenty feet, it could have been three hundred. I really don't know.

For some reason I didn't even start worrying about it. Rationalism took over...what's going to happen now?

I said, "Okay, here we are. Out in the middle of nowhere. Probably ten kilometers from Glen Alps. One of us has to go back to alert the authorities. One of us needs to stay here with Andrew." Doug was going into shock. Having him go for help would keep his mind occupied and I could stay to assist Andrew.

So I said, "Doug, run back and call the authorities and tell them where we are. Tell them they'll need a helicopter."

Doug immediately took off.

I tried to evaluate the situation. I had never had any CPR training. I was going into a sort of mild shock, which may explain my rationalism.

Being alone with Andrew gave me a lot of time to think about our past few years. I had met Doug and Andrew when I was in the eighth grade and they were in the seventh grade. We were all part of the Junior Nordic Ski program, which allowed us to train together and provided us a tool to gain more training time than a normal school practice.

I like training with several people because it offered a better workout for me. Junior Nordic also granted me the opportunity to train with a different group, to use a different technique, and to have a different coach.

The Junior Nordic coaches, Lynn Spencer Galanes, Bill Spencer, and Jim Galanes, all Olympic athletes, were good coaches.

By the time we were in high school, we'd met numerous coaches and others involved in Junior Nordic, including a lot of really good skiers from early-college age down through late-junior-high-school age.

It wasn't an openly devouringly competitive environment. When you're around the people you compete against, you undoubtedly want to be the first one back to the parking lot. There's a little bit of competition there, making the group quite fast. That summer session we trained a lot in the mountains because it avails diverse training. Kincaid Park offers good training, but the same terrain twice a day depletes running possibilities. The monotony of the same course caused us to look for variety in training. The mountains behind us guaranteed a limitless number of places to train, so we capitalized on that.

Runs include Goldenview to Bald Peak. Mc Hugh Peak is a little farther, a great run. There's Flattop and Ptarmigan. Then Little Ptarmigan. All of those offer really good training opportunities because they're uphill. There's always the added incentive of an incredible view once you've reached the top of a peak.

The Saturday prior to our run we were training near The Ramp, to the left of The Wedge. Jim Galanes coached and ran with us. We went quite a ways up there and explored around.

The Wedge offered some neat-looking places to climb. Doug,

Andrew and I were ahead of the group and started toward The Wedge. We'd gone a short distance when Jim cautioned us, ""You guys, I don't want you up there. Stay with the group."

We responded that it looked like a lot of fun, implying we would continue toward The Wedge.

But he said, "If you want to do it on your own time, that's fine. I'm responsible for all of us. Stay with the group."

We said, "Okay." We filed away his comments in typical teenage fashion, knowing that we would probably do it sooner or later because he was an adult and had told us not to.

A couple of days later we were looking for some place to train. Traditionally someone calls up someone who calls someone else...we get a phone tree going. I called Doug and said, "Hey, let's go hit that peak." We thought it had great potential, and we knew how to get to it. At least this time we wouldn't' have any coaches telling us we couldn't do it.

One of the best ways to train on the mountains is to go up a valley like Powerline Pass or Rabbit Lake. If you follow the Anchorage mountain valleys to their heads, the ridges on either side intersect. By jogging up valleys to gain elevation, it's possible to return along rides without having to climb up steep faces. When the ridge terminates, you descend either side of the valley floor.

We had never come along The Wedge because it starts farther back, and it's sitting in the middle of the valley by itself. We'd never wanted to go far enough back to get on the Wedge.

But now we had. Here we were. Doug's gone for help. Andrew's injured. I'm trying to figure out how to help him.

He didn't look that bad. I've seen people badly beat up that looked much worse. I thought, "He's gonna make it."

His head was pointed downhill with his feet uphill. I turned him so his head and feet were reversed. I gently placed him on his side and tried to take his pulse. I was holding him sideways so that he could breathe. I held him to keep him from rolling down the mountain.

I took all my stuff off, right down to my little Lycra tights, and put them all on Andrew.

Weather conditions were deteriorating, and it began to rain. It was a typical dreary, drizzly Anchorage summer day with clouds packed back into The Wedge. The falling rain chilled me. Because it was raining, my clothes were on Andrew, and I was not moving, I was going into hypothermia.

Crouching down and holding Andrew was a grueling task. During the last twenty minutes I held Andrew, all of his vital signs gradually deteriorated. I tried mouth-to –mouth resuscitation. But it didn't work. His breathing slowed down, then went away.

I kept thinking, "He's still alive," perhaps willing him to be but knowing that he wasn't. There was absolutely no sign of consciousness. As I battled my thoughts and looked at Andrew, I prayed that he would live.

I was fearful of moving him, but at length I didn't think it would matter. Gradually I realized Andrew was more than likely gone, so I moved him fifteen feet to a spot where he wouldn't roll.

My legs were cramping up, and my strength was deteriorating. I knew I needed to warm my body. My condition dictated action. I started doing jumping jacks and aerobic exercises to warm up.

My thoughts demanded the helicopter's arrival. I was getting a little bit delirious. My mind played tricks on me, and I thought I heard 130 helicopters in half an hour.

I went into minor shock, getting upset. There was something about being alone and unable to help in a situation like that. No one was anywhere near. I'd been alone for over an hour.

I thought, "What in the world happened? Where's the helicopter?" It was about a 10K run to help, so it would take Doug about forty minutes to reach a phone. After his call it would take about ten minutes for a helicopter to reach our position.

An hour and forty minutes into the accident, while I was

exercising, I heard a helicopter. The pounding rotors drew closer, Then I saw the chopper coming directly at me. It hovered about a hundred feet away. I wondered if the pilot saw me. Then he flew away, which I thought was strange.

It was crucial to me that I not remain alone, and the chopper's leaving disturbed me for a moment. I needed someone with expertise to come to my aid and my comfort.

Within thirty seconds the pilot flew from behind the ridge and returned. I hadn't thought of it at the time, but obviously he was looking for a spot to land.

He landed the chopper on a little flat indentation halfway down the final ridge at the end of The Wedge. We were a hundred yards from the end of the ridge, close to having finished the run.

I hiked down to the helicopter and told them everything I could about what had happened.

A paramedic grabbed a life pack (for monitoring vital signs), a defibrillator, and a monitor and headed for the accident site. He tried everything to save Andrew. But there was nothing he could do.

The paramedics said there wasn't a pulse. Even though I had earlier thought Andrew would make it, he must have sustained internal injuries that were irreparable under the circumstances.

A lady with the crew, perhaps one of the paramedics, was to help see us through any psychological needs. She was very helpful.

Originally the authorities had planned for the helicopter to take Andrew to the hospital. A Chevrolet Blazer would transport Doug and me (Doug had shown the pilot to the scene). Realizing that there was nothing that could be done for Andrew and with Doug and me in shock, the helicopter crew changed plans and took us back.

We just hopped into the helicopter and rode to Glen Alps. Authorities prepared to bring Andrew out later.

Mr. Lekisch and Mr. Spurr had been notified by the officials and were at the Glen Alps parking lot.

Doug and I had to sit in the fire truck and go over things, explaining our experience. Quite a number of emergency vehicles were there. The new media were there. I became upset with their insistence on gathering information by hounding us as well as Mr. Lekisch. My attitude went from incredulity to pure anger. I wanted to unload on the TV cameraman, but I'm glad I didn't. My attitude was affected by my condition.

After things had finally quieted down, Mr. Spurr took me home. That's the first my father knew of the accident.

A few days later, services were held for Andrew. At a funeral I envision twenty people dressed in black standing around a hole in the ground. Not this time! There must have been two to three hundred people in attendance at the Anchorage ski center at Kincaid Park. Anchorage's mayor was there.

It was weird being involved in the memorial service since I didn't know Andrew as well as a lot of other people did.

Andrew was involved in so many activities that this life touched a lot of others' lives. Andrew was success in sneakers, a champion in cross-country togs. He had developed quite a reputation. A few years earlier he had come to the attention to older athletes, who predicted great things for this young competitor who excelled in cross-country running and skiing, bicycle-racing, triathlons, swimming, and tennis.

Doug took the accident much differently than I did because he was much better friends with Andrew. He saw him daily in school. Their friendship may best be symbolized by Doug's run for help. He covered ten kilometers in thirty minutes, an incredibly fast time. Nationally, racers cover that distance in twenty-seven or twenty-eight minutes.

Since the accident, I've learned to look more carefully at everyday situations. I recognized things in my everyday life that I'd never seen, potential disasters waiting to happen—driving down the highway, skiing, things like that. I became more aware of the number of situations in everyday life exposing one to danger. For some time after the accident I overreacted to danger.

I looked at Andrew and the fact that he had died when he was fourteen. Many people said, "He lived a full life. Even if he died at fourteen, he still had a wonderful life."

Andrew did have a positive effect on people.

Before the accident I felt I should live as fast as possible. It occurred to me after the tragedy that we only get a little time here. So, I've slowed down to a normal level of living...making every day count.

Source: *Danger Stalks the Land*

The Bottom Fell Out

"He lived life to the fullest and always had time for his friends."

It was around 4:30 PM Wednesday, April 8, 1992. Thirty miles northeast of Summit Lake 46-year-old Steve Keier and some friends rode their snowmachines across a glacier near Paxson. Cruising over the snow and ice they rode along the edge of a crevasse that spanned twenty feet of space.

Without warning the snow at the edge of the crevasse beneath Keiner collapsed, plunging both him and his machine into the gaping hole.

Keiner's friends stopped. They could not see him and called out to him. There was no response. Some of his friends travelled to Summit Lake to alert authorities and to instigate his rescue.

The Arctic Man Ski and Sno Classic Eight was in progress and eight people rode their machines to the crevasse. When they arrived, they attempted to lower a rope to Keiner.

It appeared the crevasse was at least eighty feet deep.

A team of rescuers worked until 8:30 PM and then a second team took over.

Wednesday night Alaska State Troopers from Glennallen and an Anchorage-based helicopter with the troopers Mountain Rescue Group responded. Alaska Air National Guard also took part.

Thursday rescuers descended 140 feet into the maw of the crevasse but melting snow and ice began falling on them. They were forced to give up the search, knowing that hope for Keiner's survival was futile.

"He lived life to the fullest and always had time for his friends. He loved helping others and will be dearly missed by all who knew and loved him." 3

Letter to the editor: "Rescuers showed true selves"

I would like to express my thanks to the many people who helped in the attempted rescue of my dear friend, Steve Keiner.

Steve died on April 8 when he fell into a crevasse on the Cantwell Glacier.

During the search, many people, almost all complete strangers, came to our aid with support and encouragement.

To the approximately 30 skiers and snowmobilers who came to help, thank you. Thanks, to the couple who snowmobiled out at midnight with hot coffee and sandwiches, your company and the food made a terrible situation easier. A special thanks to Jeff Babcock and pilot Bob Larson of the Alaska State Troopers, Capt. Ernest of the Rescue Coordination Center, The National Guard, and Doug Fesler, who headed the volunteer Alaska Mountain Rescue Group. The troopers, Mr. Fesler and rescue team Mark Williams, Kenich Kibe and Will Renden showed a lot of courage and professionalism. To all of you, my sincere thanks and admiration.

Steve's death is a tremendous loss to his family and his many friends. However, there is something positive I witnessed as a result of this tragedy. I saw that during a crisis, people show their true self. The courage and selfishness shown on the glacier that day proved to me the basic goodness and decency in people, the true spirit of Alaskans.

--George Branche

Source: *Swallowed Alive*

Yesteryear, the Youngster, and Yellow Eyes

"I went with the old galoot. It was my honor to be taken into his confidence. I chose to saddle up, to ride the trail and to be his sidekick…to watch and fly and shoot."

There was a time in Alaska when aerial wolf hunting was legal. The joke is that after some months or years before it was banned, the activity read like a baseball box score, Wolves 5, Hunters 0. So, what was it like in those days? How many men took to the skies to chase Old Yellow Eyes? And, what was the profit margin for the pilot versus the predator?

In past outings how many shooters hit the propeller or the struts…or the wing? What number of blasted struts resulted in failed wings and crashes; or how many pilots were too low and too slow and spun into the ground?

There's an oral tradition that captured some of the action, those who participated in failed efforts didn't want their story known because they'd be too embarrassed (if they survived the episode).

From what I've learned, the following scenario represents some of the action.

The Super Cub cruised along a few hundred feet above the deck. The pilot and shooter scanned ahead and from side to side looking for wolf tracks. The fresh late winter snow covering the tundra would help them spot tracks. The plan was to intercept a track then follow it until meeting its maker.

That's when the hunters saw wolf tracks 300 feet below. The pilot turned left to follow the tracks, and within a minute or two he barked, "There they are!" The animals stuck out plainly against the white background. They looked as large as caribou, standing sixty yards apart and half mile ahead, both looking up at the plane. They appeared out of the left window as the bird passed and swung around. The shooter wondered why the wolves were not hightailing it.

Then the pilot said, "Let's go get 'em," and dumped the nose of the Cub over and banked right. He spoke into his mike and his words came through the shooter's headset, "Rack a round."

The pilot reduced power and dropped his flaps, lowering toward the snow below.

The kid pulled back the loading mechanism and injected a round into the chamber as the pilot opened the door. The plane settled in over the frozen river, foot-wide skis kissing the snow, routine action for the pilot. The plane skittered across the ice and the wolf ran for its life at a 45-degree angle away from the plane a little over a hundred yards to the right.

The shooter shouldered the AR15, found the wolf in the scope, centered the cross hairs behind the near shoulder, thumbed the safety off and pressed the trigger. Pop.

Mr. Wolf kept running, neither it nor the plane gaining on the 100-plus yard gap that separated the two. Pop. The spent shell rattled off the Cub's metal interior. Pop...and another rattling round.

How'd I miss?

The pilot suggested, "Keep shooting."

"Pop. Pop."

The shooter was dumbfounded that the wolf kept running. He'd held behind the shoulder all but once (when the crosshairs moved ahead of the fleeing animal's nose; possibly the plane lurched). On the third or fourth shot, it looked like the wolf stumbled or missed a stride.

I'm sure I hit that wolf. Another "Pop" and the wolf hit the ice and slid to a stop, in a stone dead heap.

The pilot chopped the power, pulled the mixture control, waited for the engine to stop, and turned off the mags and ignition before climbing from the plane.

In seconds it was over. One second the pilot said, "Let's get 'em," and within 15 seconds the wolf was dead and the plane stopped. Five or six shots. One dead wolf. Standing in front of the struts, the pilot faced the shooter, thrust his right hand out and said, "Congratulations, partner."

The men walked over to the golden, brown-gray animal and looked at it. An ever-widening splotch of dark red blood from its head seeped into the snow and across the ice. Its teeth bared, the yellow-ivory canines looked to be an inch long. The canis lupus would go over a hundred pounds, possibly 140, was 4-5 years old and the hide measured nearly 8-feet in length.

The pilot told the shooter to hold the animal up and "I'll take a picture."

Grabbing the sides of the neck just below the head, the shooter said, "It smells like a big, wet dog."

Curious about his shooting, the shooter retraced the wolf's tracks. Did I miss it that many times? If I hit it early on, will there be any blood evidence? And, how many times did I hit it?

After taking only a few steps, the shooter noticed blood spatters off to the right of the tracks. For more than 80-plus yards blood spots proved without a doubt that the wolf had, in fact, been hit before the final bullet exited its skull and stopped its flight to freedom. The bullet entered behind the right front leg, fragmented with a fragment exiting the top of its skull. When the wolf crumpled to the ice at 40 miles per hour, it pushed the two inches of snow across the ice a dozen feet or more, piling up in a little hump.

The men bent over the wolf and the pilot drew a pen knife from his pocket and opened it. He sliced through the skin at the ankle of the dog's right hind leg. The shooter held back the skin or pulled on it a few minutes then withdrew his pocket knife, "I guess I can give you a hand." They worked together on the first leg, before the pilot cut around the anal opening and the tail then sliced into the left hind leg. The shooter pulled steadily on the skin with his left hand while slicing the connecting tissue of the left leg with his right.

On this day it was Hunters 1 and Wolf 0. The hunters did their civic duty. They hadn't shot a wolf, they'd increased the moose and caribou population.

Source: *Alaska Air Tales*

Compelled

Another hot one. Been that way for days. Not unusual in my neck of the woods. When it's hot, it's hot. Perfectly normal.

I routinely fill my ten gallon cooler with ice and water every day before hauling off to the construction site. Toss the trusty stainless steel water jug into the bed of Ol' Blue and rattle off for another day of blue collar livin'.

Kissed the missus good bye, gave the kids a hug and patted the hound dog for good measure. Runnin' later than usual, but I could make up time by fudgin' a bit on the speed limit. Hit the freeway with a song in my heart—tryin' to remember the words.

Wasn't long before I noticed a silver rig and people on the edge of the highway. Shoot. This will slow me down some.

Pulled over and discovered a tourist, his wife and five younguns. Looked under his hood and discovered his computer run vehicle was too much for me. I dialed 911 on my cell phone for a tow truck and suggested he get the kids into the shade of the car while I fetched some water. After a long drink by each kid and the parents, I poured water in a couple of containers they had. The tow truck arrived and I sped off for the job.

A few miles down the freeway I turned onto the off ramp, slowed for the yield and noticed a man sitting on the curb. He didn't look right so I swung over off the shoulder, got out and approached him. "You okay, mister?" No response. He looked dazed and finally told me he'd slipped and bumped his head. "Feeling groggy," he said.

I checked his pulse. Not wanting him to get dehydrated, I fetched my cooler and a cup. Gave him a little bit of water. I called 911 on my cell and waited for them to arrive.

That's when the cryin' kid showed up. He'd lost his dog and

was lookin' for it. Said he was pretty thirsty. I poured him a cup of water when an older gent said he'd flag down a patrol car to see if he could help the little shaver. I left the kid with the old timer, watching them in my rear view mirror as a black and white pulled up.

I'm still on time.

The song came back into my heart but not the words.

Turned a couple of blocks before the job site and saw a bunch of the local kids on a corner selling lemonade. Pretty cute. Always wanted to stop and give kids like that a crisp twenty or hundred dollar bill for a cup. But never had the dough. I recognized one of the kids from his visits to the job site. He kind of flagged me and I pulled over.

"What's up?" I asked.

"We're out of water for our lemonade. Think we could get some from your job?"

"I've got a better idea. How about I pour my cooler of water and ice into your container and you can mix your lemonade. Come by later if you need more."

I drove off with an empty cooler deciding to refill it first chance I got.

Pulled into the job, waved my way through the crew and parked in the dusty lot. Grabbed my nail apron, Skil saw and the cooler. I'll fill it right away and hope some of the cool from the ice is left in the cooler.

Set my nail apron and saw down and twisted off the cooler lid before grabbing the hose. I turned on the water and started to fill the cooler.

Holy smoke! What's this? The cooler was full of water with gobs of ice cubes floating on top. How in the world...?

Left work as usual still wondering about my cooler mystery. I'd promised the wife and kids to attend the Christmas eve service at church that night. I'm not much of a church goer but a promise is a promise.

Got to church and sang our way through several carols before the pastor spoke. I thought he chose a strange text …Matthew 10:42. He preached about giving water and doing good and concluded with the words, "Anyone who gives a drink of water in My name will be rewarded."

I gave away all my water today. But He gave it all back.

Big Britches

Some folks get a little too big for their britches. They might be common folk or they might be elites. It doesn't matter. Somewhere along the line they outgrew their undies.

Common folk include those who grew up in poverty or in a working class environment. The elites include celebrities in every field but we see mostly sports greats, movie "stars," music icons or financial wizards. Both groups have outgrown their peers, neighborhoods or financial standing. They have paid too much attention to their press clippings or social media comments. They imagine themselves as superior.

Many of these elites have obtained millions of dollars over multiple year contracts. Some of them have lost it all. Others married and divorced several times. A common denominator that many share is the raging hormones they failed to tame-- they turned their backs on their spouses and morals and "slept" with a host of others. Some of these celebs brag about their "conquests" as if it were a badge of honor.

As their popularity, fame and pocket books expanded, so did their wants and britches.

Some early folks who outgrew their undies in a huge way were the Pharisees. They strutted their traditional rules, toyed with their beards and prayer beads while playing the "we're better than you" card, condemning Jesus Christ and questioning His authority...the Pharisees were "duty bound" to destroy the King of Kings.

When Jesus told the thief on the cross that "today you will be with me in paradise," one must wonder...would it be better to be with Jesus for eternity...or to be too big for your britches?

Dirt and Dolls

*Mmmmmuurrrrr…mmmmuuurrrrr…..mmmmmuurrrrr…*the car trudged along the makeshift road until it came to the end. Then Johnny climbed onto his Caterpillar tractor and punched a road from there forward, avoiding rocks and sundry windfalls until he'd built more roadway for his toy car. Then he hopped from the Cat, back to his car and mmmmuurrred to the Cat… where he repeated the process for hours.

Johnny loved playing in the dirt with his car, his Cat and other trucks and cars. He played all the time in his yard…he didn't know it but he was laying the foundation for his future.

He built the road and travelled onward, avoiding or adjusting to adversity. He may have wondered "who am I ?" or "where am I going?" or "what will I do with my life?"

"There you are, Little Girl. I've changed your diaper; I've fed and burped you; now it's time for your nap. When you wake up, we'll see if I need to do it again. Then we'll go for a walk down by the creek. But on the way we'll say 'hi' to Bossy our cow, see if Kitty Cat is in the barn and, of course, invite Bowser to go with us. He enjoys the walk and playing in the water."

As Dolly grew up and played with her little baby doll, she often wondered who she was and where she was going. Instead of playing with toy cars, trucks and heavy equipment as Johnny did, she resorted to her dolls and doll furniture and such. But both Dolly and Johnny shared the same thoughts about who they'd become and what they'd do with their lives when they got older. Dirt and dolls helped them along the way.

Twenty or Thirty and Stupid

When you are twenty or thirty and stupid, you're twenty or thirty and stupid. You're young, virile, full of bravado. You can do more without a cape than Superman can do with one. You may not know it all, but you plunge ahead as if you do.

"Coming to Alaska. To hunt? Sheep? In the Wrangell-St. Elias Mountians. Yeh, I can take you."

After speaking with a former college dorm mate Norm Carrell of Casper, Wyoming, in 1972, I had a rude awakening. I would NOT take him. I was not related by blood nor was I a guide. *Hmmmmmm.*

Plan B. A big game guide friend agreed to let me be his assistant, get that license and guide Norm's party which included his father, older brother Dean and younger brother Cliff. No problem. They were accomplished hunters. All I had to do was tag along. That's all.

Arrangements for the foray included letting Norm know about proper Alaskan hunting attire, boxed and sealed cardboard boxes of food for two weeks, Carrell's travelling to Alaska via pickup and camper from Wyoming, meeting at the Chitina airstrip and flying east up the Chitina River to Hawkins Glacier, near Canada.

The pilot would fly from Anchorage while I drove roughly 200 iles from Anchorage with my brother-in-law Les Smothers and Tony James, a former student. Tony planned to take a full curl Dall ram. So we headed for the wild and wooly Wrangells. We drove Ralph's pickup with av gas aboard

We met at the dirt airstrip. Transferring cargo into Ralph's PA 12 aircraft would require multiple trips with ensuing passengers. Dean and I were the first to depart. Ralph flew up the glacier to show us sheep and our camping spot. It looked pretty easy… from the air. Ralph continued flying all passengers and gear to the foot of Hawkins Glacier. We met part way up the glacier and spent the night.

The next day we reached our campsite and Ralph, with the assistance of his son Ralph, flew over us about 20 feet off the deck and dropped visqueen and the sealed boxes. The boxes came unsealed and we witnessed a myriad of flying food—split liquid margarine container pin-wheeled, spraying margarine everywhere; individually wrapped butterscotch hard candies turned to powder and large Hershey candy bars were reduced to bite-sized morsels. The visqueen was 1) to provide shelter in the form of a cook area and 2) a clothes drying rack area.

The following day was the opener and our group split up with Norm and his dad taking the valley behind camp. Dean and Cliff chose the next valley, up-glacier. Les, Tony and I ascended the face of the mountain west of camp, targeting the ridge between the two valleys.

Although the mountain was somewhat steep, we enjoyed good going for a while. Part way up a mist fell, creating an element of slipperiness and contributing to the difficulty of the climb. What we didn't know was how to access the ridge and that the face grew steeper with only hand and foot holds to provide us upward mobility. AND we did not realize that we could not see the foot and hand holds once we moved beyond them, thus we could not go down the mountain.

At length we reached an area that seemed impassable. There was a horizontal ledge about six to eight yards long and eighteen inches wide, angling about ten to fifteen degrees downward. Did I mention that looking over our route up the mountain, we noticed a 3-foot ledge about three hundred feet below? Another three hundred feet down was another ledge about 6-foot wide. The next 6-foot ledge was six hundred feet below that. So, we looked down about 1200 feet at nothing but air. In other words, a slip meant a serious bruising at best. Probably resulting in one less hunter.

Tony was an athletic 21-year-old and we decided he should cross the shale covered ledge to see if we could reach safety on the ridge. He shuffled across the ledge, returned and told us the ridge was just beyond.

Our plan was for Tony to anchor the far end of my doubled parachute cord. I would anchor the near end. Tony and I held the cord tightly against Les who faced the mountain with arms outstretched over his head. Without raising his feet, Les carefully slid them across the ledge until he reached Tony. Then I faced the mountain and slid my feet across the ledge to join them. Safety at last.

Just after that, Tony dropped a ram. After gutting and placing it into our packs, we headed down the mountain in mixed rain and snow. Dean and Cliff joined our group later that afternoon.

That day our group took four full curl Dall rams. The next day Cliff shot his. Five full curls in only 28 hours. Not bad for our team.

Les (32-years-old) and Tony and I (31-years-old) learned that a boxcar full of bravado was outdone by a thimble full of common sense. No more twenty or thirty and stupid stuff.

Larry Kaniut

Mud Pie

While waiting to be seated at Red Robin, he observed two ladies yucking it up and having a good time. He told them, "You're having too much fun." Then as he passed their table, he pulled out his wallet, stopped, pointed them toward a plastic carousel horse by the window and said, "I'll give you ten dollars if you'll ride that horse."

Laughter embraced the three.

He and his group sat a table away from the ladies and when his order of monster mud pie arrived, he caught the ladies' attention, pointed to the slab of ice cream covered in whipped cream, chocolate and caramel glaze, and hooted to them, "Eat your hearts out! It's non-caloric, gluten free and I'm on a see food diet."

His wife suggested he whack off and eat a portion and give the remainder to the ladies…so he did.

He enjoyed his "meal" and observed them eating his offering.

When they left, the ladies said, "Have a good day. Be sure to share your future meals."

Larry, his wife and daughter Jill leisurely visited and enjoyed the next half hour. Jill tried to pay for the meal with the table screen but failed. When the server came, she told him that the screen didn't work. He said, "It's locked. The ladies you shared your mud pie with paid for your meal."

My Valentine

She wore a red and white skirt. Her long, auburn hair hung below her waist in a single pony tail. She was petite and floated as if on a golden stairway to heaven, like a goddess in her regalia. She captured his eyes and his heart.

She was an 18-year-old tomboy and a flirt. Come to college to get her man. She had decided she didn't care if she learned anything—she was going to flirt and have fun. She did.

For 62 years I loved that girl. The sun rose and set upon her... and the moon overshadowed her sleep. She was my compass in brightness and in storm. She was my anchor and my guide. She was my companion who blessed my life—even before she was my valentine.

Pamela Diane Timmons. My GOAT...Girl Of All Time.

Because her health was so poor, I thought I could compile comments from family, friends and neighbors...so that she could read them when she was down. I never knew the project would continue for a couple of decades. But then what I thought would be inspirational to her, I decided would be inspirational for others to learn about her. So I turned the compilation into *Heavenly Rose*.

Source: *Heavenly Rose*

Larry Kaniut

Dirty Jeans *

She meant well. Maybe she just didn't know about little boys and bugs and worms and rusty nails and fish.

Maybe it's because she grew up with no brothers.

Maybe it's because she wasn't a boy.

Maybe it's because she was used to a clean house.

Maybe it's because she didn't like the smell of fish.

She was startled when she saw the boy's pants on the floor—they were moving. When she finally got nerve to approach them, she jiggled the jeans and a frog fell to the floor and hopped across the room.

When the mother came home, the babysitter explained the mystery of the moving pants, asking the lady about the bugs, worms and rusty nails she'd shaken from the holey and dirty jeans.

"Oh, you had a normal day. He's always coming home with critters and odds and ends in his pockets. When he plays outside, he usually goes through at least two pair of pants a day. What with his trips to the fields, the woods and the pond, he's a one man expedition.

"In the beginning I didn't know how to deal with him. He was always dirty, full of energy, bringing home stuff. He was often cut or bruised. And did I mention...hungry? He's a boy. That's what boys do. Dismantle stuff. Bring home things you don't want in the house. They grime their bodies.

"At first I didn't understand.   I complained to my neighbor Cy. Told him my little boy was a mess. That he was always dirty, bedraggled or bleeding. He didn't like baths. He preferred dirt to soap.

"My Little Guy brought home fish and asked me how to 'fix' them. I didn't want them in my kitchen. I didn't know how to 'fix' them. But I learned. I asked Cy. He showed me how to clean and cook fish. Then I taught my son.

"Cy told me my son was experiencing the blessings of boyhood.

"I didn't want to deny my son those boyhood blessings. I learned that it wasn't MY kitchen. Even more important, in his wise, old way, my neighbor showed me that there was something more valuable than my kitchen. And I told my boy to bring those smelly fish into the kitchen whenever he wanted. And he did, along with the rusty nails, bugs and worms."

*Sub title: The Kitchen or the Boy

How often do we marginalize those we love...perhaps assuming we'll have them forever? Or how often do we place more value on stuff than we do on people? While contemplating these ideas, I thought it would be nice to take a closer look...at a boy, a babysitter, a parent and a gentleman whose decisions were based on their experiences. I wanted to portray the benefits of knowledge... and to show that personal relationships are more valuable than things—in Alaska and beyond.

Pathway

Having participated in a myriad of activities and graduated high school, I was college bound. My first year I had pastoral ministry or missionary thoughts in mind. My passion was youth. Should I work with kids before they go bad or after? My college was not certified so I chose to go elsewhere in Oregon. I could be a walk on at the University of Oregon. Just because I'd played some high school football, I thought I could play college? But Coach Len Cassonova was having none of that. Plus I was told I was a non-resident. So I considered and committed to Linfield, where I could graduate sooner anyway.

Figuring I could get a degree then be a truck driver or some such, I changed majors from Bible to English and grunted through classes while working my way along. I spent a year in Mac Hall, got married the summer of 1964 and obtained my English degree in 1965, while student teaching in Newberg, Oregon. In my youthful naiveté I was pretty clueless when my supervising teacher J.B. Conoway suggested I enter the master's degree program. I concurred, applied and was accepted. On to Renne Junior High in Newberg, where another intern and I joined two mentor teachers and were responsible for teaching English and social studies to the entire 7th grade.

As the time approached for finalizing that year, I had applied at sixteen Oregon schools to teach English when Pam read an article about Alaska and suggested I apply in Alaska. So, I did.

Next thing we knew, Anchorage offered me a job. What do we do now?

We prayed if the Lord wanted us in Alaska, that we wouldn't hear from any Oregon schools. We didn't. Looks like we're going to Alaska.

While at Renne, I had coached football, wrestling and

track...but I wasn't quite ready to accept any coaching jobs in Anchorage...especially cross-country running. I told the athletic director that I didn't know what the runners did in the woods. He gave me a whistle. The runners knew more about running that did their coach.

When wrestling started later, I asked the coach if I could watch a practice. Next day the principal asked me if I'd like to be the assistant wrestling coach. Dare I tell him I know what a whistle is? Again, the wrestlers knew more about the sport than I did. Poor kids.

While teaching literature of the North, it was obvious that there were very few high interest books. Hoping one could produce an anthology of adventures which my English department could purchase for a classroom set, I wrote publishers for some years before one suggested I could do a book on bears. I wrote that I was not qualified and gave the info to our friend Al Johnson who had been chewed on by a mama grizzly in Mt. McKinley Park. He had changed his mind and I alerted the publisher that I'd give it the old college try.

After the highly successful *Alaska Bear Tales*, other publishers wanted more titles.

At age fifty I told Pam I wasn't' going to sign the teaching contract for the following year, that I was going to give the Lord a chance to re-direct my life if He so chose. He did.

My sabbatical proposal to get kids published went down in flames. I very reluctantly retired. But completed *Cheating Death*.

Five years after retirement, I spoke to the Lord about my need for money. I told Him I'd do three things every day for six months—read the Bible and pray, mow the lawn or do a push up and write. And if I didn't get a concrete answer, I'd get a job.

Within a couple of days of my imposed deadline, a voice contacted me saying, "I believe you're the man to write my biography." *Hmmmm.* That's pretty concrete. Icing on the cake came a day or two later when a lady suggested she be my literary agent. *Hmmmm.* Okay.

I told the Lord, "Looks like I'm supposed to be writing, even if I don't make any money."

So I helped Eddie Feigner organize his book *From an Orphan to a KING* and Stephany Evans became my literary agent.

Since those days, I have completed or compiled a dozen and a half titles. The bottom line of this tale is that God's fingerprint is all over a person...that to live a life of wonder—without wondering—is possible if one lets God define and direct the pathway.

I attended public school and college, changed majors because I felt comfortable doing so. Events occurred and I prayed for guidance. The Creator of the universe intervened. I see His finger directing me to English, teaching, Alaska and writing. It was never my plan to teach, to go to Alaska, nor to write. But He had other ideas. He actually had a plan for me (Jeremiah 29.11)

APPENDIX I

Kaniut books (chronologically)

Alaska Bear Tales: Man-bear encounters from false charges to fatalities

More Alaska Bear Tales: More humor and bear tales from Alaska

Cheating Death: Eighteen misadventures with Mistress Alaska

Some Bears Kill: Thirty-seven tales of man and bears in Alaska

Danger Stalks the Land: Misadventures involving danger and death

Bear Tales for the Ages: 22 of 28 selected and re-written from out of print books

Instant Sourdough: Humorous definitions of Alaska (geography, transportation, people, recreation, wildlife, pests)

Alaska's Fun Bears: 94 pages of Alaskan bears dressed-engaged in people activities

Trapped: New York photo-journalist falls in love with Alaska

Alaska Air Tales: Pilots share stories of their flying in Alaska

Brachan: Roman soldier follows John the Baptist as possible threat to Rome; then Jesus

SAFE with Bears: 464 page, 1.5 pound volume telling how to stay out of a bear's mouth

The B.G.: Novel about life in high school...where every kid matters

Heavenly Rose: family, friend, neighbor comments about Mrs. Pamela Kaniut

Larry Kaniut

What's Bruin? Mostly non-violent stories about bears

Charlie's Tails: Cartoons based on the author's experiences

Swallowed Alive (2 volumes): Sequel to Danger Stalks the Land—drama, general interest, bizarre

Snatched from Death Bible characters who were "rescued"

ALASKA...comin' atcha: Anthology of multiple stories from our previous books

Kaniut books (by subject)

Bear

Alaska Bear Tales

More Alaska Bear Tales

Some Bears Kill

Bear Alaska Bear Tales

SAFE with Bears

What's Bruin?

Alaska's Fun Bears

Cartoon

Charlie's Tails

Misadventure

Cheating Death

Danger Stalks the Land

Alaska Air Tales

Swallowed Alive

Snatched from Death

ALASKA...comin' atcha

Non-fiction/Personal biography

Heavenly Rose

Novel

Trapped

Brachan

The B.G.

Terminology

Instant Sourdough

www.ingramcontent.com/pod-product-compliance
Lightning Source LLC
Chambersburg PA
CBHW022042020426
42335CB00012B/510